A–Z OF DOG DISEASES & HEALTH PROBLEMS

Signs • Diagnoses • Causes
Treatment

Dick Lane
BSc FRAgS FRCVS
& Neil Ewart

Howell Book House

New York

HOWELL BOOK HOUSE
A Simon & Schuster / Macmillan Company
1633 Broadway
New York, NY 10019

MACMILLAN is a registered trademark of
Macmillan, Inc.

Library of Congress Cataloging-in-Publication data
available on request.

ISBN 0–87605–042–9

Printed in Hong Kong

10 9 8 7 6 5 4 3 2 1

CONTENTS

This book is dedicated to all
guide dog owners, and to
those people who have
provided ideas and
stimulated the writing
of this book.

ACKNOWLEDGEMENTS

Grateful thanks to all those who have supplied photographs
to illustrate this book. We acknowledge the contributions
of: Dr K. Barnett, J. Simpson, the late Charles McKenzie,
Helen Haighton, Sue Kent V.N., Dr S. Guthrie, Steve Nash,
Carol Ann Johnson, and Sarah Richards for her artwork.

PREFACE

There are many reasons why the total number of dogs has declined in recent years but, with more selective ownership, there is now a much higher standard of dog care as the worth of each dog is increased to its owner. With the greater appreciation of each dog's value, there is a need to achieve a better understanding of the dog so as to avoid many of the disorders that dogs used to suffer from. Responsible dog owners want to know more about the health of their dogs, and there is a particular interest in socialisation and training of the well-mannered dog.

The role of the dog in society has greatly increased in the second half of this century: the so-called human companion-animal bond has become a major factor in dog ownership. At one time there were 'house dogs' that would be turned out in the daytime and allowed to forage for themselves, but this was at a time when road traffic was much less threatening to a free-running dog's existence than today. There were also the shepherd and cattle dogs used to working on farms with the minimum of care and feeding. Gundogs were better looked after but, again, they received much less human contact than today's prized working dogs. Those dogs or hounds that were used for hunting were kept in packs. They were fed on the carcasses of diseased animals, and one of the more extreme methods of training was to use an iron shackle to couple a young dog's neck to an older hound. The house pet-dog may have suffered equally badly from a lack of knowledge of nutritional and exercise requirements, resulting in obesity, bad teeth, and a number of other problems which led to an average life expectancy of just over seven years.

The Guide Dogs for the Blind Association was founded in the UK in the early 1930s, and similar organisations, such as the Seeing Eye in the USA, were developed at around the same time. These organisations have played a leading part in establishing the trained dog as a valued working partner for the visually disabled. Their training methods have been used in the obedience work that many domestic dogs now participate in, and similar methods are used by other service dogs including those worked by the defence organisations and the police forces. Agility work has also developed from these methods, which helps in the overall control of all dogs. There are many examples where working dogs have been studied and the information has then been passed on at instruction classes and lectures, in books and video for the better care of the pet dog.

New information on canine diseases and health problems is regularly reported in professional journals and in books using technical terms that are not understandable to the average dog owner. In trying to understand what may be wrong with a dog, well-informed friends may not always give the right advice, and some reference books may only confuse the person who is looking for something beyond simple first aid for dogs. It should be remembered that recognising health problems or diseases at their earliest stages may bring about quicker cures – or prevent a small lump becoming an incurable cancer. Yet the average dog owner often meets too many obstacles when trying to seek this knowledge.

To overcome this situation, the *A-Z of Dog Diseases and Health Problems* has been written in order to explain dog illnesses in simple language, with an emphasis on good health care and good breeding as a way of preventing disorders. This

A healthy dog, well-groomed and in excellent condition.

expertise is based on my experience as a veterinary surgeon, first working with army guard dogs in the UK and overseas, and then over 35 years working with guide dogs in training and with guide dog owners. The valued assistance of Neil Ewart, who also has spent a lifetime in guide dog training and, more recently, as Breeding Centre Manager for the GDBA, contributes to the book's authenticity. His help in preparing and collecting material is sincerely acknowledged. Many other peope have given advice on particular aspects of the book, especially Helen Haighton, who read the A-Z section and made many improvements to the scientific content.

The A-Z of Dog Diseases and Health Problems can be used as a handy pocketbook for quick reference by the novice or the more experienced dog owner, without the need for technical knowledge. It will also be of value to students of canine studies, animal care and dog breeding courses. The lavish use of illustrations should also be a major point of interest as well as being of great practical help.

Dick Lane

HOW TO USE
THIS BOOK

This book begins with nine short chapters focusing on the health care required to keep a dog at peak fitness and avoid disease. The basic structure or anatomy of the dog is described to enable the reader to understand the importance of conditions such as hip dysplasia and elbow diseases. The signs of a healthy dog are listed to provide a standard to compare your own dog with. This is followed by advice on general care, feeding, and grooming of the healthy dog. The in-whelp bitch, preparations for whelping and problems that may be encountered, dealt with in the next chapter, is largely based on the Guide Dogs for the Blind Association Breeding Centre's routines and gives information on practical dog breeding for health. The following chapter on the care of the young dog, rearing puppies and litter socialisation, gives a good introduction to the breeding of dogs. The saying 'It all begins with the breeding' should be remembered in many dog health situations. This section concludes with guidance on when to call the veterinary surgeon, practical tips for first aid for injuries, and how to administer treatments.

The second section of the book, Signs of Diseases and Health Problems, helps the owner to recognise signs of disease and illness and to diagnose what is wrong with his or her dog. Further information can then be found in Section III, an alphabetic listing of the Treatment of Diseases and Health Problems. The selection of subject matter is a personal one based on the common conditions dog owners meet, and some less common conditions that have confused dog owners in the past. Obviously, not all the treatments can be given by a dog owner, and whenever it is considered that a condition is better treated by a veterinary surgeon, this is pointed out.

SECTION I

HEALTH AND HUSBANDRY

The responsible owner must learn to spot signs of ill health in order to keep their dog in top condition.

POINTS OF THE DOG

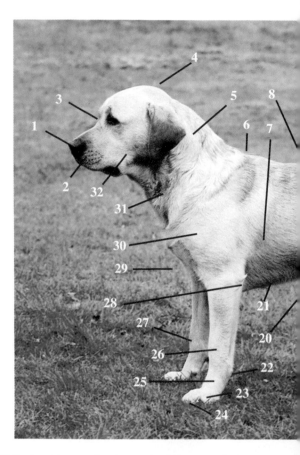

1. NOSTRILS: A wide opening is required for a good airway to the lungs. The Breed Standards will specify the preferred shape of the nose.

2. MUZZLE: Refers to the end of the nose and the shape of the upper jaw; may be self-coloured or carry white or pink markings.

3. STOP: The depression on the bridge of the nose in front of the eyes. Breed Standards may specify a moderate stop or 'no stop' if the face is to be smooth in contour. It probably has little effect on the dog's ability to breathe freely since the overlying bone structure of the maxilla and the frontal sinus controls the final shape.

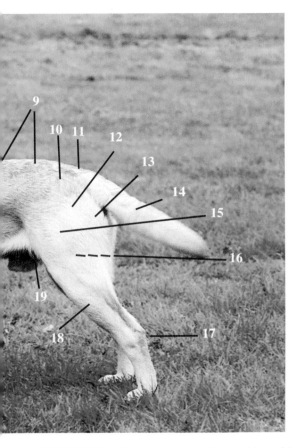

4. OCCIPITAL: The occipital crest is a ridge of bone at the back of the skull to which the strong neck ligaments are attached. The occipital region is an area above the exit of the spinal cord from the hind brain and therefore it is vital for it to be adequately protected.

5. NECK: The neck is the area between the head and the chest carrying strong muscles and ligaments as well as the important main nerve tracks, the airway to the lungs and the major arteries and veins supplying the head and the brains. The length varies with the breed. Unflattering shapes of neck may be described as 'goose', 'swan' or 'ewe-shaped', although animals with such necks have a perfectly a functional neck.

6. WITHERS: The area at the base of the neck between the shoulder blades is a prominent ridge where the neck and back join; traditionally it is used to measure a dog's height. Dogs have the ability to lower their spine between the prominent shoulder blades and this reflex is used during propulsion forwards in sporting dogs.

7. CHEST: The chest or thorax encompasses the vital organs of heart, lungs and, in the puppy, the thymus of the lymphatic system. There are 13 thoracic vertebrae each with a pair of ribs, the curvature of which decides the dog's chest shape. The 13th rib is called a floating rib, as unlike the others it is not attached by cartilage to the sternum; sometimes it will stick out as a prominent bulge. 'Slab chests', 'well ribbed up' and a 'good spring of ribs' may be seen in written descriptions of a dog's conformation.

8. FLANK: This area of the body below the loin is supported by fairly thin muscle stretching between the last ribs and the massive muscles of the thighs. 'Flat-sidedness' is generally considered to be a fault, but is more the effect of the arch of the ribs on the abdominal wall behind it.

9. LOINS: The loin or 'coupling' is the short area of the back from the last rib to the strong muscles attached to the pelvis. The strong muscles on either side of the seven lumbar vertebrae in the spine help to protect the nerve structures supplying the back legs, and the lumbar muscles are also used for jumping and rearing up.

10. RUMP: The area between the loin and the tail head is the highest part of the hindquarters; the part closest to the tail head is called the 'croup' which may be rounded or slope down at an angle to the tail. The position of the pelvis and the degree of muscle development present, will control the shape of this end of the dog.

11. CROUP: The point at which the tail joins on to the body.

12. HIP: The point of the hip is a bony prominence that can be felt just forward and below the croup. The bone is in the head of the femur and can be rocked to assess the attachment of the hip joint to the thigh. Muscle development varies greatly in this area, making for greater or lesser stability of the hip-joint structure.

13. BUTTOCK: The fleshiest part of the hind leg below the tail head. Strong muscles attached to the ischium in the pelvis will affect the shape of the area. The ischium, as the hindmost rigid bone of the dog, can be felt on either side of the anal region.

14. TAIL: It is composed of many coccygeal vertebrae. The length and tail carriage vary from individual dog to dog. 'Pump handle' tails are one extreme of low carriage whilst the vertical tail of the terrier is described as a 'flagpole'.

15. THIGH: The area between the hip and stifle may have little hair on its inner surface and is a valuable area for examining a dog's skin or take the dog's pulse.

16. SCROTUM: The skin covering the two testes may be covered in long hair or almost hairless depending on the breed. It may be pendulous or neat and held close to the body. The contents of the scrotum are usually examined during any judging as a mark of entireness. Castrated males have a flat scrotum.

17. HOCK: The hock is the joint at the back of the leg made up of many tarsal bones. The hamstring tendon attached to the point of the hock is important as it connects the strong muscles to the point of the hock.

18. STIFLE: The stifle is the joint at the end of the thigh bone corresponding to the human's knee. It has several joint surfaces and numerous ligaments and may be a weak point where injuries can happen.

19. PREPUCE: Also known as the 'sheath', it is prominent in the male as it protects and usually covers the penis except when the dog becomes sexually aroused.

20. ABDOMEN: Described as the lower part of the body between the rib cage and pelvis, it contains within its muscle walls all the vital organs known as the viscera.

21. NIPPLES (vestigial in male): The prominences on which the openings of the mammary glands can be found will vary in size depending on the dog's breeding history.

22. CARPAL (STOPPER) PAD: A small pad just below the carpal joint is usually covered in black leathery skin. The metacarpal pad is larger but situated behind the toe pads.

23. DIGIT: The toes of the dog are each composed of three separate bones, the last of which is covered by the nail. The foot pads protect the bones as a 'digital cushion' and are unusual in that they carry sweat glands. The dewclaw if present is known as digit one, the others are numbered from two to five as the outside toe.

24. NAIL: The claws of the feet have an inner quick and a hard, outer keratinised structure.

25. PASTERN: The area of the foot between the carpal pad and the toes. It is a term borrowed from the points of the horse where any tendon and bone injury is far more damaging.

26. FOREARM: The length of the front leg extending from the elbow to the carpus.

27. KNEE (CARPUS): The carpal joint of the fore leg should not be confused with the human knee as it has a totally different structure being made up of many carpal bones (equivalent to the human wrist).

28. ELBOW: The elbow is a complex three-bone joint with coronoid and anconeal processes that can become damaged during growth. The point of the elbow is a bony prominence, often poorly protected, and it can develop calloused skin especially in the larger breeds.

29. BRISKET: The lower line of the chest between the forelegs is shaped by the sternum and the muscles of the chest that cover it. A prominent sternum is known as a 'pigeon chest' in the dog.

30. SHOULDER: The joint formed between the shoulder blade (scapula) and the humerus is well supported by muscles and very difficult to dislocate. A 'straight shoulder' is an upright shoulder where there is little angle between the humerus and scapula. A 'well laid back shoulder' is one where the scapula is at 90 degrees to the humerus, but there is no anatomical reason to suggest this is any healthier. The head of the humerus is subject to injury during the rapid growth stage of a puppy's development.

31. THROAT: The lower surfaces of the neck usually have some loose skin which may help to protect the essential structures of trachea, jugular veins and carotid arteries that run

below the skin. 'Throatiness' is the term used where there is excess skin folding, and the 'dewlap' is where the skin fold hangs down in front of the chest.

32. CHEEK: The side of the face, the muscle and skin are suspended from the zygomatic arch below the eye. Sometimes the masseter muscles are very well developed and will bulge out the cheeks below the eye.

THE SKELETAL SYSTEM

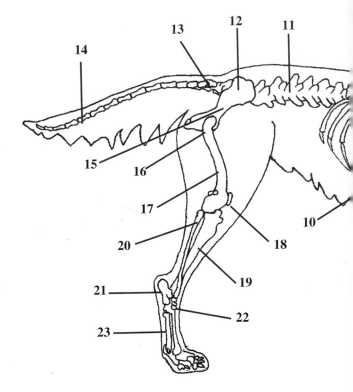

1. CRANIUM: The skull of the dog protects the brain as an important centre of the whole nervous system; the cranium encloses the brain. Terrier breeds have a prominent nuchal crest to attach the ligaments of the neck to, and this bony ridge further protects the brain at the arched vault of the skull bone.

2. MAXILLA BONE: In front of the cranium, this bone forms the upper jaw. The left and right bones together contain most of the nose cavity and the sinuses.

3. MANDIBLE BONE: The two mandibles, left and right, are

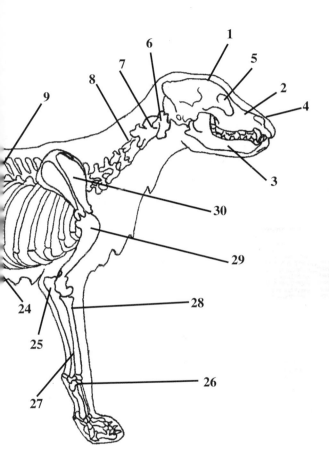

joined together at the chin, making up the lower jaw of the dog. The jaw bone carries the lower set of teeth, and the angle of the jaw has strong muscles to help in closing the mouth and chewing. The hinge with the cranium is called the temporo-mandibular (TM) joint.

4. NASAL BONES: The inside of the nose is divided by the nasal septum. There are two scroll-like bones called the nasal turbinates that are covered with mucous epithelium and carry the scent receptors of the nose.

5. ORBIT: The bony recess constructed to protect the delicate structures of the eye has its weakest point in the zygomatic arch that runs across the face, immediately below the eye. Most of the bony protection for the eye is provided from above, so a blow to the side of the face may fracture the bone, and the eye may prolapse with disastrous results.

6. ATLAS: Traditionally the strongest bone of the spine as it has to join the spine to the skull, and allow for all the neck movements and posture changes controlled by the brain.

7. AXIS: The second neck bone is often described as the weakest – it has to allow a wide range of head turning movements. As an elongated vertebra with a projecting process, it is most likely to snap if the head receives a major injury and this will lead to paralysis.

8. CERVICAL VERTEBRAE: There are five more of these to make up the seven neck bones. They are relatively weak bones and rely on the surrounding muscles and nuchal ligament to take most of the weight of the head. Intervertebral disc protrusions of the cervical vertebrae can cause severe pain, and any narrowing of the nerve channel in the vertebrae may lead to the condition known as 'canine wobbler disease'.

9. THORACIC VERTEBRAE: The 13 bones have an important function to allow for arching of the back and provide a base for the pairs of ribs. Each bone has bony spikes to provide attachment for the muscles. The nuchal ligament runs from the spine of the first bone up to the axis and skull.

10. THE RIBS (13): These are part bone, part cartilage that curve round to provide protection to the organs inside the chest. The first eight pairs are attached below to the sternum. The cartilage of the next four ribs joins to the costal arch, but the last one rib of the pairs may be described as 'floating' since they do not join to the cartilage part of the arch. Occasionally these ribs may stick out, causing a noticeable bulge on the flank of the dog.

11. LUMBAR VERTEBRAE: These strong vertebrae provide attachment for the back muscles that are important in propulsion, especially when dogs jump as well as run. There is a point of weakness in the joints between each of the lumbar vertebrae. Protrusion of disc material in any joint may be a cause of pain or paralysis, especially in the long-backed breeds such as Dachshunds.

12. WING OF ILIUM: This structure is part of the pelvic 'girdle' and provides a point of attachment of the spine to the back leg through the sacro-iliac junction. The ilium is also an important point of attachment of powerful leg muscles.

13. SACRUM: A triangular-shaped bone formed by the fusion of several vertebrae, the bone plate make up the top of the protective ring of the pelvis. This can be a point of weakness after accidents. In young dogs the sacrum may be raised during the birth process to allow for the expulsion of puppies.

14. COCCYGEAL VERTEBRAE: Numerous small bones make up the tail. They get smaller in size until, at the tip of the tail, they become like a jointed rod of bone.

15. PELVIC BONES: Three in number on each side, they are joined together to make up a bony ring around the rectum, vagina or urethra. The pubis on the floor of the pelvis is probably the weakest bone – sometimes it carries a prominent knob that can cause difficulties in giving birth. The ilium may be damaged in road accidents and the bones fracture quite readily.

16. ACETABULUM: The socket for the head of the femur makes the hip joint – it is composed of parts from all the pelvic bones. A small, round ligament runs across the acetabulum to connect the head of the femur to the deepest part of the acetabulum. The muscles over the acetabulum have the strongest effect in preventing dislocations – the attaching ligaments are fairly weak. The acetabulum, as a ball and socket joint, has to allow for a wide range of movement and, for this reason, seems especially likely to suffer during a puppy's growth or by dislocation at any time of life.

17. FEMUR: The main bone in the hind leg, it joins with the acetabulum by the femoral articular head. Known also as the thigh bone, the lower end forms part of the stifle joint.

18. PATELLA: Commonly known as the knee cap, it provides support to the front of the stifle joint and allows the important flexor tendons to run over the joint. Its attachments are not strong, and it relies on a groove in the femur – known as the trochlea – to stay in place. Dislocation of the knee cap takes place in road accidents, or sometimes there is a congenital weakness of the joint as found in many small and toy breeds of dog.

19. TIBIA: A long bone that has a flat articular surface to carry

the knee cartilages that help to make up the stifle joint.

20. FIBULA: Smaller in width than the tibia, it is a parallel long bone that runs from the stifle to the hock joint.

21. HOCK: The point of the hock is made up of the single tarsal bone which acts as a lever for the hamstring (Achilles) tendon to attach or run over. It is an important structure for working dogs and Greyhounds that have to extend their back legs rapidly.

22. TARSAL BONES: Numerous bones contribute to the hock joint and they are arranged in two rows. Ligaments hold all the tarsal bones together and these may become torn causing displacement of some of the bones in the hock.

23. METATARSAL BONES: Four slender bones that connect the hock to the toe bones. Some dogs have a vestigial hind dewclaw that makes a fifth metatarsal bone.

24. STERNUM: A flat cartilagenous bone that forms the lower part of the rib cage structure. Being soft, it is seldom injured even when ribs are broken, and it helps to preserve the shape of the chest after injury.

25. OLECRANON: The point at the back of the elbow joint acts as a muscle attachment point. The olecranon has in front the anconeal process that often shows changes in osteochondrosis, so it is frequently examined when X-raying for this disease.

26. CARPAL BONES: A row of small bones that make up the dog's wrist.

27. ULNA: As an important part of the elbow joint, the head prevents dislocation except in the most severe twisting injuries. It has a coronoid process in the elbow joint that may be subject to osteochondrosis changes as well.

28. RADIUS: A long bone that is rod-shaped. It carries most of the weight, lying close to the ulna. It also has its own coronoid process in the elbow-joint structure.

29. HUMERUS: A strong bone that connects the shoulder to the elbow joint. It is well covered with the muscles of the forearm and not as liable to injury as often as some of the other leg bones.

30. SCAPULA: A flat bone that lies over the rib cage and provides the attachment of the spine to the fore leg.

SIGNS OF A HEALTHY DOG

It is very important that you really get to know your dog, as you will easily identify when the dog is not right or is 'off colour'. You should then be able to decide whether the dog needs rest, or to take the dog to the veterinary surgery or, in some cases, to request a visit from the vet to the home or kennels. It is also important to know the signs of a healthy dog when you go to buy a puppy or an adult.

APPETITE
A healthy dog should always have a reasonably good appetite. However, some individuals can be quite 'picky' with their food, while others will eat anything put in front of them, regardless of the quantity or quality. Do not pander to the reluctant eater too much, but any sudden and persistent loss of appetite can indicate a problem. The regular weighing of a dog allows you to see if the poor or shy feeder is taking in enough food to maintain body weight. Sometimes dogs on their own will eat smaller quantities of food through the day, though

A young, healthy dog should have a shiny coat, carry no excess weight and be full of energy.

Dogs vary in the amount of feed they require, depending on size, age and the amount of work they are doing. A sudden and persistent loss of appetite could indicate a problem.

when fed in a group, they will race to eat all the food in the bowl as quickly as possible. When fed in a group the animal lowest in the 'pecking order' has the least chance of obtaining its full ration, but the same animal fed on its own can obtain its share of food by free choice feeding, i.e. when fresh food and water are available most of the day.

BODY TEMPERATURE

The practised owner can detect a feverish dog by the feel to the hand, and by the dog's rapid breathing. A more accurate estimate can be obtained by taking the temperature in the dog's rectum with a clinical thermometer. Some dogs will sit down during this process and it is always best to have a second person present during temperature taking to stop a dog turning and accidentally snapping a glass thermometer. The normal temperature is or 100.9 to 101.7 degrees Fahrenheit (38.3 to 38.7 degrees Centigrade).

Temperature abnormalities should be viewed in the same light as with humans. Watch for a rising temperature when measured at two-hour intervals or a persistently low temperature, both of which may be serious for the dog.

COAT AND SKIN

A really healthy dog should have a nice shiny coat with no signs of white dust, black flea dirt, bare patches or any other skin blemishes. The check for parasites should be very thorough, as often fleas will not be discovered until the coat is inspected under a bright light. Lice may only be seen after a very close inspection of ear fringes or the angle of the elbows.

It is considered normal for a dog to lose (moult) hair from its coat twice a year. However, with many dogs being kept indoors now, the room temperatures do not change from season to season, so that many house dogs will shed their coat throughout the year. The most common reason for a perpetual moult is living in a centrally-heated home where each winter the temperature is raised slightly higher so that there is then very little change in a winter indoor temperature to the summer outdoor temperature. A dog left in an unheated but dry kennel will grow a very thick coat for the winter months which is then shed in the spring, in the space of two or three weeks as a heavy moult, to allow the thinner summer coat to come through.

It is advisable to spend ten minutes a day grooming your dog. This way the owner is disciplined to give the dog a daily check-over, and there is a better chance of observing things before they become serious. The skin of the dog should be free of unusual patches, sores, lumps, bumps, inflammation or foreign bodies.

CONDITION (WEIGHT)

Dogs that are overweight can suffer unnecessary health problems. Obesity is invariably caused through over-feeding coupled with under-exercising. It is quite rare for there to be any reason that is not linked to the amount of food the dog takes in.

Neutering is often put forward as an excuse for a dog or bitch being overweight. This is a myth. Any tendency to be overweight from reduced activity and greed for food can be controlled by lowering the energy content of the food given. Some dogs seek out food from alternative sources. Scavenging is not uncommon in dogs on a restricted food intake, or there may be well-intentioned friends or children in a family who are feeding a dog unknown to its owner. There is the dog that is kept on a strict diet in the daytime but is "always given four biscuits" when it comes in from its evening walk. It is not unknown for neighbours to provide extra nourishment, either over or under the garden fence!

An underweight dog may appear thin due to insufficient food of the right type being given. If the dog suddenly, or gradually over a period of time, noticeably loses weight, then there may well be a health problem. An increase in the quantity of feed will often have been tried, but a veterinary health check is necessary if there is no improvement.

Some dogs are naturally lean and, although they look as though they are underweight, they are perfectly fit – even though they appear to have no body fat. It is a good idea to weigh all dogs on a regular basis. The dog that appears thin but is still actively fit has fewer reserves to fall back on, and weighing on a weekly basis can detect further weight loss before a disastrous change can occur. Each dog should have an ideal weight and, within a narrow range, the correct weight for the dog will act as a guide.

Keep records of the dog's weight:

    a) Normal weight of dog.

    b) Weight loss/gain (since last weighing).

    c) Diet fed. Quantity consumed. Extras.

    d) Any changes in faecal output: diarrhoea.

The dates of the last worming should be noted as well.

EARS

Some dogs' ears stand erect and others show a natural droop. In the case of pedigree dogs, this will usually be mentioned in the Breed Standard as a particular characteristic of the breed. An erect ear may be pressed down if there is pain in the ear, or the dog with pendulous ears may droop them more than usual. In both situations the ear tube becomes moister and warmer than normal, and this will predispose to certain bacteria and yeast-like organisms multiplying in the outer ear canal. The thickness of the ear flap or 'pinna' should be checked, as bleeding can occur between the cartilage and the skin,

The English Springer Spaniel: A problem may be indicated if the ear droops more than usual.

The German Shepherd Dog: An erect ear may be pressed down if the dog is experiencing pain.

producing the condition of an aural haematoma. In most breeds, routine ear cleaning is unnecessary unless it is advised after veterinary treatment. The problem of the very hairy ear canal, as was found in some Poodles, Sealyham Terriers etc., can be bred out to some extent and it now seems less of a problem than was formerly found. Ear plucking is generally discouraged as it may cause irritation to the delicate skin lining the ear.

When grooming the dog, always make a point of checking the ears both inside and out. There may often be a not unpleasant sweet smell, but when problems occur the aroma becomes very pungent. The start of ear trouble can be detected by observation of the way the dog holds its head, and the use of your nose to smell out trouble!

EYES

The eyes should be wide open with a clear and moist surface. Occasionally a dried-on black discharge in the corners of the eye represents the overflow of a grey mucoid material that gathers at the corner. There should not be excessive watering. In pale-faced dogs there should not be the continuous overflow

Normal eye: Note the dark pupil at the centre of the tan-coloured iris, with dark-pigmented edge next to the white sclera. The eyelids fit perfectly the globe of the eye, and there is no discharge.

of tears, seen as a stained orange colour stripe down the face.

The colour of the eyes is controlled by the amount of pigment in the iris. In some eye conditions the pupil opening will be very small and more of the iris pigment is visible, showing as a darker eye. The white of the eye, or sclera, is not normally visible except in breeds with very prominent eyes. If the blood vessels of the sclera increase in size or number, then a red eye would be seen. The cornea or window at the front of the eye is normally clear but it also takes the colour of the iris behind it. In some ageing processes the cornea becomes more hazy and blue-coloured due to reflective crystals in the fluids behind the cornea. This is not a disease, although it is frequently confused with a cataract that causes opaqueness in the lens and a white glow is reflected back out of the eye. There are other facto that affect eye colour. Jaundice will be seen as a yellowness of the sclera, corneal lipidosis will be seen as white clouds on the cornea, and ulceration of the cornea will produce a variety of yellow to greenish defects on the eye surface. All need veterinary attention.

FEET

The pads of the feet should be soft to touch and not leathery or horny (hyperkeratinised). The pigment of the foot pads is often similar to the nose colour. Between the toes is an area of skin that is hairy and contains sebaceous glands used for scent marking. Sometimes cysts and swellings develop if the glands become blocked. The skin between the toes is very sensitive to chemical burns, or some alkaline clay soils will provoke inflammation with lameness known as 'pedal eczema'. Warts are sometimes found on the feet of young dogs, especially those kept in kennels where the washing of concrete leads to excessive wetting of the dog's feet.

The nails should be of even length and not split at the ends after being allowed to grow too long. If the nails are too long, they will have to be clipped, being especially careful to avoid hurting the dog by cutting into the quick. Exercise on hard, concrete surfaces and slabstone pavements is normally sufficient to keep nails at reasonable length. Tarmac roads and tarred pavements often do not provide enough friction to wear down nails. Dewclaws, if present, are not a disadvantage to the dog unless, as in some Terrier breeds, they grow in full circle and penetrate the flesh causing an infected wound.

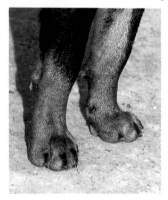

The pads of the feet should be soft to the touch, and the nails should be of even length.

MOUTH

The lips should be dry and not soaked in saliva, nor should strings of saliva hang from the mouth. The normal healthy dog has 42 teeth, but there are seldom opportunities to count these.

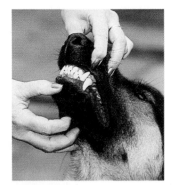

A dog has 42 teeth, and in most breeds the bite is similar to the blades of a pair of scissors.

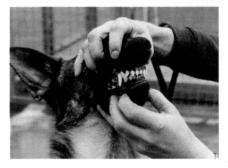

An undershot jaw.

Some dogs are born without premolar teeth, which reduces the total count. The bite of the front teeth is normally similar to the blades of a pair of scissors, but jaw abnormality may produce the conditions known as undershot and overshot. Incisor teeth sometimes cross over so that the row of front teeth is not straight. All these are defects to the show dog's disadvantage but, in practice, they do not seem to cause much of a problem regarding the dog's ability to feed itself.

Excessive salivation or smell from the folds in the lower lips are often the result of tartar building up on the teeth and, either by pressing into the gum or by forming a ledge where food lodges at the margin of the tooth with the gum, it causes gum inflammation. Dogs will salivate excessively when fed aromatic foods. There is nothing you can do about this and it should be regarded as part of the normal digestive process. Saliva lubricates and moistens food so that it can slide down the oesophagus quicker to reach the stomach. It may help, by coating the food, to prevent air-swallowing as the dog feeds.

NOSE
The two nostrils should be open and not obstructed by any discharge or crusts. The nosepad or 'rhinarium' should be

thick-skinned and hairless, and it contains sweat glands. Most dogs lick their noses repeatedly, and this has led to the belief that a cold wet nose is a sign of health. Common sense will suggest this is not the case, particularly if the dog has come back in from strenuous exercise. Each nose pad has a distinctive print that has been used as a method of identification. The colour of the nose may be pale in some breeds, particularly in the winter months when there is a lack of sunshine. Older dogs sometimes have cracks and fissures in the nose pad that are difficult to heal. The young dog with a scaly dry nose may have suffered from a previous virus infection.

FAECES
A dog will pass several motions at times in the day. The normal motion should be firm but, as with any other living creatures, there are bound to be variations in the consistency and quantity of the faeces from time to time. Faeces are normally passed one to three hours after feeding and exercise will also stimulate emptying.

Soft or loose consistency faeces may be described as diarrhoea. If diarrhoea only lasts 48 hours and clears after supervised feeding, this may be a sign of a digestive overload. Diarrhoea is defined as the passage of soft unformed faeces with an increased fluid or bulk content. It does not relate to the number of times the intestines are emptied but to the appearance of the faeces. The colour and consistency may vary with the type of food eaten. Black faeces may be due to the diet, or, if tarry, it is known as melaena, which is when digested blood originating from the stomach or small intestine is passed in the faeces.

URINE
Urine is produced by the two kidneys as a continuous process through the 24 hours, but the healthy dog will be able to store fairly concentrated urine in its bladder. The dog has conscious control of bladder emptying, so will void urine as a free-flowing stream three or four times in the day at an appropriate place when out of the home, or sometimes after a word of command. A male dog after puberty will use urine for the purpose of territory marking as a powerful scent deposit. In the course of a walk a male dog may squeeze out many drops at every available marking point. Pheromones or 'scent hormones' are used to mark out the territory covered by a dog away from its home or 'den' where it lives. Similarly, the bitch about to come on heat will deposit urine, at various strategic

points, more frequently than she normally would when taken for a walk. Any delay in passing urine or frequent urination other than in the two situations described should be cause for concern.

MOVEMENT

Abnormality in gait is always difficult to describe in words. Dogs can show unusual leg actions, and, when checking the dog, always look for a cause of a limp. Lameness may be due to injury, or to the presence of a foreign body in the foot, or, in some cases, an hereditary joint or bone condition will be the cause. Detailed observations should be made of how the dog moves: whether a lameness gets less after exercise or, more often, gets worse after the first few paces are taken. Making a dog sit to command and making a dog walk up a flight of stairs may also be used to study a dog's 'action' when moving.

In some hip conditions an audible click can be heard when the dog is walked in a quiet place, although often the nails will cause more noise than any joint. Some dogs on recovery from an injury or an orthopaedic operation will limp through habit. Small terriers seem to be able to progress faster on three legs than four, once they have got used to saving a joint in the hind leg.

Making a dog sit to command is an effective way of studying movement.

POSTURE

The dog should sit easily and, when standing, should look bright and alert. Some dogs are so phlegmatic that they can be quite deceptive. An unhappy dog may carry its head low, appear hunched up in its back, with its tail between its legs. This may be a temperamental problem, but more likely it is a sign the dog is unwell.

RESPIRATION

When resting, the dog should have almost imperceptible breathing, except on a warm day when panting should be expected. The control of the respiratory rate is by a centre in the hind brain, which will be influenced by any increase in body temperature or an increase of carbon dioxide in the blood. The normal resting rate is between 10 and 30 breaths a minute, although faster rates may be a sign of excitement as much as of disease. Exercise is the most common reason for panting, as the excess waste gases have to be washed out of the lungs, and oxygen brought into the body for circulation by the blood.

Some poisons will cause rapid respirations if they upset the normal control mechanisms of breathing. An increased respiration rate may be seen with anaemia or any disease affecting the heart or lungs. Severe pain may also cause a rise in respiration rate. All changes should be reported to the veterinary surgeon.

TEMPERAMENT

An unexpected change in temperament in a dog may be a sign that all is not well. A dog in pain or just under the weather may not be happy about being touched. Dogs naturally have a sense to tolerate many of the things that children do to them, but when a dog is in pain it may be quicker to growl or even bite. A normally placid dog may show signs of protective aggression which, if out of character, may be its way of communicating that there is a problem. Dogs that have brain tumours can show an altered behaviour and staring eyes as if trying to recognise something in a haze. Such dogs get progressively worse usually in weeks rather than months.

FEEDING, GROOMING AND EXERCISING

DIET AND NUTRITION
It can be said that good nutrition and good teeth will see a dog through most of the problems that it will meet during its life. Feeding standards have greatly improved, and the realisation that dogs will have different nutritional requirements at different stages of their lives has gone a long way to extending the useful life of the domestic dog. Pictures of starved and stunted puppies belong only in history books, but the spectre of the grossly overweight dog, short of breath and long in its toe-nails from lack of exercise is still to be seen.

A 'balanced' diet has become a slogan for many dog feed companies producing a great variety of foods suitable for dogs. In order to understand what constitutes a balanced diet the dog owner should be aware of the major nutrients in the food groups. These are: proteins, carbohydrates, fats, minerals and vitamins, and the essential component, water, which is required in larger amounts than any of the other five groups.

ENERGY FOODS: These are needed in large quantities by working dogs and, to a lesser extent, by pet dogs that are regularly walked, and by those dogs that are active in the home, rarely sleeping, and spending their day going from room to room showing zeal to guard the home and police the garden as well. Energy is required to keep the dog warm in cold weather, and energy is required for all metabolic reactions taking place inside a dog, as well as the more obvious burning-up of energy during muscular activity. This means the requirements can vary from breed to breed, and between individual dogs in a breed depending on what they are asked to do.

The guide dog walking five miles to work, not resting entirely in the work place, then walking five miles home again will have a much higher energy requirement than the Labrador in the home that is 'exercised' by two ten-minute excursions with its owner at either end of the day, spending the rest of the day sleeping in a warm house. Energy requirements largely control the dog's appetite for food, and one of the best guides to the energy balance is the dog's weight. Regular weighing and charting the weights is of great value in avoiding obesity or helping to build up a thin dog that tires easily on walks.

PROTEIN: This food source has become of greater interest than anything else in recent years, partly due to the focus on growth in the young, and partly stemming from the suggestion that intake of excess protein over the years may lead to kidney damage and premature ageing. There is also an awareness that protein foods are not as fattening as starchy foods for humans, so dogs will also benefit from eating the more expensive protein foods, and that this will ensure an active long life. There is now a veterinary opinion that many dogs now receive excessive protein in their diet. As a result some has to be used as an energy source, as the body is unable to store the

A diet with 16-20 per cent protein is sufficient for the average adult dog.

component amino acids. A diet with 16 to 20 per cent protein is quite adequate for the adult dog as a maintenance ration; only in young or pregnant and lactating dogs is the protein requirement increased to as high as 28 per cent. It is also thought that if too much protein is given for growth in some breeds, it may contribute to bone disorders such as osteochondrosis and 'wobblers' (canine cervical spondylo-pathy). In the earliest days of studying the inheritance of hip dysplasia, it was found it was possible to mask the development of abnormal hips by underfeeding puppies and severely restricting their exercise in cages. A high protein intake encourages rapid bone growth and orthopaedic problems may result later.

FATS AND FIBRES: Fats and fibre should not really be grouped together as they have totally different functions, even though they are used as appetite suppressants in many weight reduction diets. Fats have an important function and must be included in a ration: the EFAs (essential fatty acids) have become well known in recent years as a requirement for coat condition and as part of the body's immune mechanism. EFAs are used for treatments in inhalant allergies, arthritis and skin keratin disorders. In veterinary medicine we do not have to worry about the risk of saturated fats in the diet, as such fats in the dog do not predispose to atherosclerosis as they do in human diet. Fibre is a way of filling a dog up and, by binding water in the large intestine, producing a firmer stool that is easier to pick up than sloppy faeces. The adverse effects of feeding a high-fibre diet are more gas formation and a bulkier faecal output. Soluble fibre as found in some vegetables and in oatmeal, has a special value in the diabetic dog in slowing the digestion of carbohydrate with the release of sugar into the blood stream.

VITAMINS AND MINERALS: These are both groups of substances that are needed in very small quantities and may be essential for the dog's health. The dog can provide its own supply of vitamin C and vitamin K from its gut bacteria, and these may only need to be given as a supplement in specific disease situations. The elderly dog on a diet restricted in choice of foods can benefit from a vitamin supplement. In true rickets, and in some other bone diseases, Vitamin C and D supplementation is called for. The vitamin B group, K and E will be needed if there is liver damage due to hepatitis, for instance. However, the adult dog will get most of its requirements for the other vitamins and minerals from its balanced diet. Over-supplementation of vitamins and minerals in the growing dog should be avoided as it may result in bone and joint disease.

PALATABILITY AND PETFOODS

There are a bewildering number of dog feeds now available and it is difficult to recommend any particular brand from this wide choice. Palatability is the reason why most dog feeds are selected by owners. The commercial breeder will be more influenced by the economy of feeding. In a kennel situation, with large numbers of hungry dogs, palatability becomes less of a driving force to make sure a dog consumes its bowl of food. A balanced diet need be only of low palatability for it to be acceptable to the dog, which will then obtain all the nutriments it requires. Some individuals are known as shy feeders: even with the competition of other dogs waiting to steal their food they will only eat slowly and, in this situation, a large number of flavours and textures of foods may have to be tried before the dog will eat enough to maintain its own weight.

PRACTICAL DOG FEEDING

Petfoods may be commercial or home-made. When a puppy

Weighing out rations will ensure your dog is fed the correct amount. This is particularly important with complete feeds.

Teething puppies will benefit from being given marrow bones.

arrives in the home for the first time it is best to keep the food the same as before, since most of the other things that happened at feeding time will change with the new home. The buyer of a puppy should ask for the diet sheet used by the breeder to feed the puppies so as to make as few changes at first as possible. Any reputable breeder will tell you what the puppies were previously fed on just before they leave. The diet sheet does not have to be followed totally, but it will be based on that breeder's experience of what works in the rearing of that size and shape of dog. It is a general rule that all changes in feeding should then take place slowly.

If you opt for a 'complete feed', remember that is exactly what it is. Read the instructions closely, and follow them strictly. 'Good enough' will not do when feeding the growing dog; any additional ingredients introduced by yourself can create an imbalance and problems can occur. Calcium and vitamin D supplements were often given whether the puppy needed it or not – and now even the bone meal supplement has fallen under suspicion, even though the calcium and phosphorus ratio is exactly right for puppy bone growth.

A guide for constructing your own diet for a Labrador-size puppy might be:

Breakfast: Half a pint of milk with some cereal, or a milk-pudding like rice or semolina, provide variety and are well-liked.

Lunch: Quarter of a kilo (half a pound) of cooked meat (or less for smaller dogs) minced or cut up fine. This meat should be mixed with about 70g (2-3 oz) of puppy meal or brown bread soaked in a gravy. Beef, lamb, chicken, rabbit, and cooked fish (bones removed) can all be given. Lean cooked pork is an alternative, but it was once discouraged because of the risk of tapeworm cysts and other parasites. Alternatively canned dog meat can be used, but the content should be checked to see if it already contains cereals.

Afternoon: The same as breakfast or a more crunchy rusk food can be given with less milk than in the morning, as too much lactose will cause diarrhoea in some puppies.

Supper: The same combination as the lunch meal.

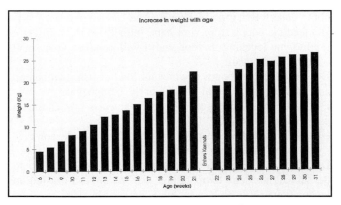

A Labrador puppy's growth chart

The aim when feeding growing puppies is to have a weight gain of 2 to 4g per day per kg of the adult weight, i.e. for a Labrador puppy 60 to 120 grammes each day or half a kilo in a week. A 58 1/2lb Golden Retriever about one year old might be seen to be getting fat on 13 ounces a day of a proprietary complete diet, but when cut down to 10 ounces a day becomes a slimmer dog at 57lbs.

Supplements should be given in moderation; there are many powders, tablets and fish oils that find favour with various breeders. If bone meal is used, one teaspoon a day is quite adequate. A large marrow bone can be given and the chewing will exercise the jaw and perhaps help teething.

Frequency of meals – A rough guide for puppy feeding:
Four meals a day should be given from six weeks to four months.

Three meals a day from four to six months, cutting out the breakfast.

Two meals a day from six months to maturity (often by 10 months).

All the above amounts are approximate and should be adjusted for the particular breed you have and the condition of the individual. A large German Shepherd puppy may need as much as 800g of meat a day (1 1/2 lbs).

Fresh water should be available at all times and some drier feeds do require puppies to drink more than the normal amounts consumed.

SOME DO'S AND DON'TS

DO remove any uneaten food, but offer it again later, or dispose of it.

DO not overfeed a very young puppy, but be even more careful not to underfeed a rapidly growing one.

DO feed the puppy from your hand initially, as this will get it used to you touching its food and it will associate your smell with the food reward.

DO NOT feed the bones of chicken, fowl or fish. Lamb chop and neck bones are lethal if stuck in the oesophagus.

DO NOT feed large portions of potatoes – raw starch in potatoes is indigestible.

DO NOT feed titbits from the meal table, and do not give snacks between the dog's set feeding times.

DO NOT feed foods straight from the refrigerator. Milk should be served at room temperature. Ice cream can be fed in moderation as it is high in fat but is enjoyed by dogs.

DO NOT feed the pup immediately before or after exercise. Excited or tired, hungry dogs are more likely to bolt their food and swallow quantities of air in the process, sometimes with unfortunate results.

ADULT NUTRITION

These guidelines on practical feeding when applied to the adult dog should follow the same principles as for the youngster. Although a mixed diet is good for humans it is not necessarily the case for dogs. A common trap is to assume that the dog will need to have its diet changed several times a week to avoid it getting bored with its food. Once a suitable ration is found, stick to it. There is no need to alter the flavour, or purchase the most expensive dog food in the supermarket as a special treat meal.

When choosing a feed, remember the time it will take to prepare and also the need to be able to exercise the dog 3-4 hours after eating, to allow for defaecation before the dog settles down for the night. In some situations, specially formulated, high-energy foods will be needed to maintain body condition. Feeding one meal a day is usually sufficient for health. With regular weighing, if a dog is found to be putting on too much fat then a low calorie commercial diet is best, as the dog can eat this without feeling underfed in quantity.

As dogs get older usually the energy requirement decreases, the dog walks less both in the home and when out on the lead, it goes slower so less distance is covered. The aim should be to maintain the body weight of the dog at the level of when it was younger. At the first weight increase in excess of 2kg, introduce a restricted-calorie diet. It is much easier to make this adjustment at the first sign of a dog being overweight than to try dieting when a lot of 'fixed fat' has been deposited under the skin and it is then more difficult to get it burned up by the dog.

The protein content of the food is often associated with increasing palatability; the advised percentage of 14-18 per cent is slightly lower for dogs in old age. Any suggestion of reduced kidney function should be confirmed by blood-testing the dog, and diet adjustments made based on the blood and urine test results. The protein then provided should be of high biological value and, as muscle meats contain a lot of phosphorus, these should be restricted, as the phosphates cause as much or more damage as the waste products of protein digestion, to the old dog. An increase in the fibre content of the food may guard against a tendency to constipation, and when there is heart disease, a lower sodium and phosphorus intake will be required. In the circumstances of heart, kidney or liver disease, feeding is made much easier if one of the special veterinary prescription diets is used.

GROOMING

Grooming is a very important but often neglected aspect of looking after the dog. It has positive health benefits and is of value too in establishing a closer contact with the dog than any other activity.

Grooming requirements vary with the breed: long-coated dogs need combing as well as brushing, Poodles need regular clipping to keep them tidy. The example of the Labrador Retriever, with a relatively easy coat to maintain, will be used. They do require daily grooming, especially at times when they are moulting.

Grooming your dog is an ideal time to inspect the body closely, to look for any unexpected abnormalities and assess the general condition. The sooner a health problem is noticed, the quicker the veterinary adviser can be asked for an opinion, and the better the chance of a full recovery in a progressive disease or a tumour. The puppy should be groomed from the earliest age in order to learn that handling is a pleasurable experience, and the procedures will be easier to carry out if commenced early in life. If a dog is used to being handled in this way, it will be far easier for an examination to be made by a veterinary surgeon, and a visit to the surgery becomes less stressful for the owner as well as the dog. Before you start to groom the dog, carry out a thorough physical examination to check for any abnormalities. Always start at the head end (as the hands are cleaner), looking at the orifices on the head before handling the feet and the anal region.

INSPECTION BEFORE GROOMING

EYES: Inspect the eyes first for matter or discharges in the corner. There should be no excessive watering, and the white of the eye should be checked to see that it is not red or discoloured. The surface of the eye should be clear and bright, and the expression should be one of alertness. There are specific diseases that affect the eyes, so any abnormal signs should be noted and reported to the veterinary surgeon if needed *(See Eye problems, page 101)*.

EARS: A painful ear can be a very irritating complaint for your dog, so preventing ear problems is important. If there is a noticeable build-up of wax in the ear canal, this can be easily removed by first softening the wax with an ear-cleaning fluid and then wiping gently with cotton-wool. The use of cotton-wool buds in the ear is discouraged, and all cleaning should be the most gentle possible.

MOUTH: The dog has 42 permanent teeth, present from about six to seven months of age. The number and condition can be used to estimate the age a dog, show if the dog regularly chews stones, if the dog has had distemper as a puppy, or if it has had some other nutritional setback.

Each day the gums should be checked for redness or inflammation. This can develop as the tartar builds up on the teeth, and food particles from the last meal get caught at the gum margin. The food will produce breath odour if not removed, and mouth bacteria can produce even worse halitosis. The conditions of caries (decay), dental calculus (tartar) and periodontal (gum) disease will be seen when the teeth are

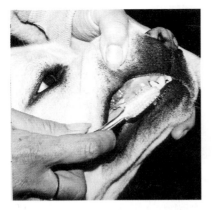

Regular tooth-brushing will help to keep to keep the teeth clean and the gums healthy.

inspected. Regular tooth-brushing and the provision of things for a dog to chew will help to keep the dog's teeth clean and the gums healthy. Puppies lose their milk teeth between four and six months, and sore gums should be noted at that age. Massaging the skin just below the eye will help when the molar teeth are about to erupt. While grooming the older dog, mouth warts, excess saliva or white froth at the back of the mouth should be looked for as signs of abnormality.

NOSE: Any discharges should be removed, and cracking or fissuring should be looked for. There is little point in worrying about a 'cold wet nose' as a health indicator.

SKIN & COAT: Examine all of the body when grooming. Tell-tale black dirt or white scurf may indicate a parasite infection. Patches with hair loss, redness of skin and abnormal lumps may first be found during grooming. The healthy dog's coat will normally have a slight shine, and oil from the sebaceous glands will give it a waterproofing grease that gives the smooth feel as the hand is run over the hair.

NAILS & FEET: Nails should be worn short, as over-long nails may splinter painfully, especially in cold weather when the nail is brittle. If the dog is regularly walked on hard surfaces such as concrete, paving stones or rocks, the nails will wear down naturally. Once the nails become too long they are difficult for the dog to wear down, as the heel takes more of the weight of the leg and the nails may then split with painful consequences. Clipping nails is a delicate task as if cut too short, blood will flow and the dog will show that it is painful to cut into the quick. Filing may be safer for the beginner than cutting across the nail with new sharp clippers. The area

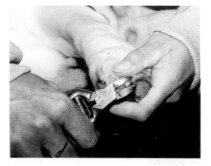

Extreme care should be taken when clipping nails so as not to cut into the quick.

between the toes should be felt, tufts of hair attract sticky substances, clay soils ball up between the toes and tar or chewing gum can be picked up on a walk. Cuts and pad injuries should be noticed when handling the feet for grooming.

A GROOMING ROUTINE

After the first physical examination has been carried out, the grooming routine as used for the Labradors at the guide dog centres in the UK should be followed:

1. Using your finger-tips massage the coat against the normal backward lay of the hairs. This will loosen up the dead hairs and encourage the skin to secrete the sebum oil that gives the healthy shine.

2. Use a bristle brush, again working against the lay of the coat to pick up the hair you have loosened. Brush vigorously against the coat, then brush in line with it.

3. Using a metal-toothed comb, you can now work your way in a methodical order over the dog's body. For longer-coated dogs, combing with the lay of the coat is advised, paying particular attention to the feathering down the hind legs, tail and around the neck and ears. If a dog is very tangled up it may be necessary to cut the knots away. Try to use a thinning action, working away from the dog's skin until the knot can be lifted off.

4. Finally, to finish and bring a shine to the coat, use a bristle brush down the back and limbs, and brush the neck and head, praising the dog or offering a small food reward.

A rough guideline is to set aside ten minutes a day to groom your dog, and apart from the odd occasion, this should alleviate the necessity to bath the dog. Specialised breeds will require professional grooming and the owner of a Poodle puppy will have to consider the lifelong cost of keeping a dog in tiptop condition with grooming every four to six weeks throughout life. It is worth checking with the breeder what the grooming requirements are likely to be before taking delivery of a puppy.

Regular tooth-brushing is another form of grooming with positive health benefits for those dogs that do not have regular jaw exercise with foods that help to keep the teeth naturally clean.

BATHING

Unless it is imperative for reasons of hygiene or to remove an obnoxious smell, do not bath your dog very often. Frequent immersion in detergent solutions can damage the coat and the skin underneath, natural orifices may also become sensitive to repeated applications of some shampoo substances. If a dog has rolled in some 'anti-social substance' or any other unpleasant activity has occurred, it may be possible to hose the dog down with tap water, then take the dog for a vigorous run to dry it off.

If you do decide to use a shampoo this may be an all-purpose dog shampoo or it may be one supplied by the veterinary surgeon to moisten and soothe the coat or, alternatively, to remove excess scale – a keratolytic dressing. Anti-parasitic shampoos are the best way of applying a liquid dressing directly to the skin, but read the instructions on the bottle very carefully as there are many restrictions and specific advice with the more potent shampoos.

If your dog has a skin problem, seek veterinary advice regarding the most appropriate shampoo to use. A small bare patch may be the first sign of demodectic mange, it may be 'stud tail' needing a seborrhoeic shampoo. Beware of the unrecognised ringworm patch on a dog. Always wear rubber gloves and a plastic macintosh where health hazards appear on the label of the selected shampoo. Wear glasses too to avoid getting splashed.

Use old towels to dry the dog; paper towels are seldom absorbent enough to dry any but the smallest dog. An ordinary hair-dryer can be used. It should not be hot enough to scorch the back of the hand and it should be applied gently, as some dogs can be upset at the noise and the heat.

Once dry, give the dog a good groom again. Try to make grooming and bathing good fun for your dog. Do not allow growling or any other signs of aggression. Some people bathe their dogs in their own bathrooms. In the bath, use a rubber mat to give the dog confidence. If you may be called away to the phone, the dog can have a lead left on – tie it to the bath tap, but make sure the tap is firmly fixed and could not be wrenched off if the dog tries to jump out.

Dry shampoos can be purchased but they are little better than brushing talcum powder through the dog's coat and hoping some of the dirt will come away too. Chalk whiteners for dogs are discouraged, but until quite recently it was not uncommon to see clouds of white dust coming off dogs before they went into the show ring. This did little for the handler's respiratory tract and less for the dog's natural white coat colour.

EXERCISE

It Might Be Said: The More You Take The Better.
Most dogs are under-exercised. Owners have limited time (except at weekends), there are fewer and fewer places where dogs can be let off the lead, and the vociferous anti-dog lobby wants dogs banned from all those open spaces used by children. In the USA a 1995 study of diet and exercise in dogs less than three years old, found that only 65 per cent of owners regularly exercised their dogs, and more than 70 per cent of dogs were confined in some type of fenced-in area. A total of 40 per cent of the dogs were exercised with others, but 20 per cent were exercised on their own, probably reducing the amount of energy expended.

Consideration should be given as to where and when the dog can obtain the necessary exercise. Collar and lead training comes first. Later the voice recall will be established as a method of control and, provided there is a safe exercise area for free running, this will greatly assist you in providing adequate exercise. The sit, lying down in one place, and the stay to voice command are all things your dog can be taught. Being able to walk a dog though a field of sheep without the animals being disturbed is a hallmark of good control, but very few sheep farmers will want to provide you with the opportunity to put this to test. Long 'flexileads' may be the best way of giving the dog more freedom without losing total control.

With your dog under control, agility work is now the best way to obtain the exercise that the dog needs in an urban or semi-urban situation. Jumping obstacles, tunnels, scent discrimination and searching for people all provide opportunities for the handler to develop their skills in dog command and at the same time give the dog useful exercise.

'Fun and games' is the other sort of exercise. Making the dog give you its paw may not exercise much more than the

ABOVE: Agility is a good way of keeping a dog physically fit.

RIGHT: Dogs benefit from free-running exercise, but the number of places where this is permitted is severely limited.

prescapular muscle, but rolling over gives opportunities for many body muscles to stretch and flex. Compare the actions of a horse let out into a field after a long period of stabling: it gets down on the ground and has a good roll with all four legs in the air, then it gets up and shakes itself. Other activities such as opening or closing doors, searching for hidden objects all provide exercise and stretch the dog's natural instincts. Ball games are generally encouraged, but try to avoid the wooden stick games. If wood becomes impaled in the dog's pharynx expensive and often repeated surgery may be needed before all the wood can be removed from the throat. In the USA exercise study, more than half the dogs played retrieving games, which included games with balls and flying discs.

BREEDING
AND HEALTH

BREEDING FOR HEALTHY PUPPIES

"It all begins with the breeding." The health of the new dog begins from the moment of conception when the sperm fertilises the egg. To be more accurate, the genetics for good health occurred long before the mating took place. However, in the confines of this chapter, the complexities of genetics will be summarised, then we will consider what can be done to make the whelping as successful as possible, concluding with the puppy's earliest upbringing which has a major influence on the adult dog's health programme.

The successful breeding of dogs is as much of an art as a science, and a large measure of luck may enter into achieving the final result, whether it be the perfect show dog or the purpose-bred guide dog. No serious breeder can ignore the laws of genetics and the inescapable effects that genes have on the eventual make-up of the puppies. The environmental factors and the feeding may be equally important in the successful rearing of some litters. When a particular dog is to be used to mate with a bitch, remember the influence of the choice of a sire is actually less than 50 per cent of the composition of the final puppy reared.

WHY DO YOU WISH TO BREED DOGS?

Many people fondly imagine there are large profits to be made from dog breeding. As with gambling, only a few lucky people

A litter of puppies is an appealing prospect, but there are many important decisions to make before planning to breed with your bitch.

make money from dog breeding. Consider the probable costs you may be involved in:
* The cost of rearing and keeping your bitch, as it will possibly be two years before there are puppies to sell
* The stud fee of a popular dog
* Travel costs once or twice to visit the stud
* The cost of rearing puppies to six weeks
* Veterinary costs
* Registration (and insurance) before the sale of the puppies.

DO'S AND DONT'S
DO decide why you want your bitch to have puppies.

DO make sure she is old enough to be mated.

DO NOT mate a bitch that is past her best – i.e. seven and half years or more.

DO NOT allow a bitch to have a litter of puppies more than once a year.

DO make sure she is in the correct time of her season for the stud dog visit.

DO choose the stud with care.

DO NOT use a stud because it is cheap or it is the 'dog round the corner'.

DO NOT allow the bitch to mate just because you thought it would be 'nice for her to have some puppies'.

DO NOT expect to make money easily.

DO expect to spend time with your bitch and spend money on whatever is needed.

DO check first that your bitch has a full pedigree and is registered.

Do check that the stud has a full pedigree, is registered and screened for inherited defects.

DO enquire about hereditary disorders in your breed and find out if your bitch is clear for mating.

DO breed the best with the best.

DO NOT be disappointed when, in spite of all this advice, the litter is not as perfect as you might have wished.

GENETICS MADE SIMPLE
The inheritance of factors, both good and bad, is a complex subject. An in-depth study requires extensive reading combined with a good mathematical skill.

For the new dog owner or breeder, it is sufficient to say that the dog, like any other living thing, is made up of countless cells. Each cell (except the red blood cells) carries a **nucleus** in which are found strand-like structures called **chromosomes**. The number of chromosomes present in each cell of a dog is 78

The prospective brood bitch must be free from all hereditary disorders.

The stud dog should be chosen to complement the bitch, also ensuring he is free from hereditary disorders.

(made up of 39 pairs) – this fact was established as long ago as 1954.

The male dog's sperm and the bitch's ova do not contain the 39 pairs but only half the number of all other cells. This arrangement is such that on fertilisation of each egg, the full number of chromosomes for the new puppy is then correct. Canine chromosomes are smaller and more numerous than human chromosomes.

Genes, which are made of the chemical deoxyribonucleic acid (**DNA**), are the units of inheritance and will pass unchanged from one generation to the next. There are about two miles of DNA in each somatic cell and between 50 and 100 thousand genes carried, each of which represents one, or part of, a genetic message. The messenger system works well; the only risk is that radiation or toxic chemicals may increase the risk of **mutations,** so that sometimes harmful changes can appear in the next generation if the DNA is damaged.

Much research is currently taking place in both the UK and the USA on gene mapping. The aim is to develop a simple blood test that could be collected from dogs before breeding. The test would be to diagnose the presence of any genes causing hereditary diseases in dogs. One example of the information that will come out of this study is already of benefit to Bedlington Terrier breeders. In the University of Michigan, a DNA marker close to the gene for copper toxicity in the Bedlington Terrier breed has been found. Copper toxicosis is known to be an autosomal **recessive disorder** and can be widespread in the breed; copper from the food accumulates in the liver reaching toxic levels and sometimes early death. Already breeders can have liver tests done that help to avoid producing more puppies with this condition. It is hoped that progressive retinal atrophy (PRA) blindness in Labradors will be the next to benefit from a genetic study at the Animal Health Trust in the UK.

The popular idea was that each characteristic of the dog is produced by a gene that influences only one thing in the dog. Similarly it was thought that all genes were either dominant or recessive. It is probably true that 75 per cent of all inherited disorders in dogs are due to recessive genes. In its simplest form, the dominant genes overruled the recessives, so you could then easily breed out a disease such as PRA of the Irish Setter, once it was known to be caused by a single dominant gene. Unfortunately when recessive genes are involved, whenever two carriers of a disorder are mated only 25 per cent of the progeny will inherit the disease. It should still be possible to breed out some diseases if test matings of very closely related animals can be used. However, even simple genetics is complex!

Many characteristics or **traits** will be influenced by environmental factors, such as feeding, exercise and housing. For this reason it has been impossible to breed out a condition such as hip dysplasia (HD), even with all the breeding advice of the last twenty years. The best progress so far is to make HD less of a problem in some breeding lines within a breed.

The proportion by which a character has been produced by genetic influence is known as the **hereditability**. The hereditability can vary from 1 per cent to 100 per cent, depending on the particular character that is studied. The following table has been compiled from various sources based on the experience in large-scale breeding kennels.

CHARACTER	HEREDITABILITY
Litter size	**10 to 20%**
Fertility	**10 to 20%**
Temperament	**30 to 50%**
Fear	**46%**
Hip Dysplasia	**25 to 45%**
Panosteitis	**13%**
Other features	**40%**

Figures show that certain characteristics are clearly more hereditable than others. For the study of characteristics, it can be seen that the strong influence of a standard kennel environment and diet cannot be ignored, and some diseases such as panosteitis have little genetic basis in a closed kennels.

To expect to breed large numbers of puppies who are completely free of any inherited disorder would be impossible using the present methods of sire and dam selection. If the perfect puppy was eventually bred, and eggs from the same dam were stored and cloned, then in theory this perfect puppy could be reproduced endlessly – but it would it would be a dull world if every puppy trained had an identical shape, size, temperament and life span.

DEFECT	TYPE OF DISORDER	MODE OF INHERITANCE (IF KNOWN)
Atopy	Skin disease tendency	Unclear inherited basis
Epilepsy	Fits or convulsions	Complex inheritance or non-hereditary
Elbow disease	Osteochondrosis	Polygenic, part nutritional
Hip disease	Hip dysplasia	Polygenic, part environmental
Panosteitis	Lameness fore or back legs	Unclear if inherited
PRA Blindness	Loss of vision	Autosomal recessive (Autosomal dominant in Irish Setter)
Cataract	Lens of eye opacity	Varies in breeds as autosomal dominant or recessive

A CHECKLIST FOR STUD AND BROOD SELECTION

- Pedigrees to study.
- Kennel club registered.
- Find out any hereditary problems already produced in

close relations: the hip scores of the parents and grandparents if available, eye examination certificates (if applicable). The temperaments of both parents should be good.

• Find out if the chosen stud dog will be available at the time you plan for mating.

Make a final decision based on the above information, weighing up the chances of producing the type of puppies you really want.

The checklist can be extended to researching earlier litters produced from matings of one or both parents.

The art of assessing a dog is important. It generally requires a lot of experience and a willingness to seek advice and the opinions of other people in the breed.

GETTING READY TO BREED WITH YOUR BITCH

It is important to understand the bitch's breeding cycle, as the reproductive system works on a puppy production pattern of one litter a year, but, with domestication, either of two breeding times a year can be chosen for the mating. The seasons of an un-neutered bitch are most likely to come in the spring and the autumn. There are many variations of this oestrus cycle pattern – some bitches come in season every eight months, some will have one almost imperceptible heat and then show a stronger heat on a once-a-year basis.

As an approximate guide, in the larger breeds:

* A bitch will come on heat first at 8 to 10 months.
* The heats should return every six months.
* The heat or 'season' should last 21 days.
• The common term 'heat' only relates to the swelling of the vulva and the increased activity at the beginning of the breeding time; there is no increase in body temperature.

At the commencement of the heat the vulva will swell and there will be a blood-coloured discharge. This may be first seen as spots of blood left on the floor, although some bitches are careful in licking and removing all signs of such discharge. Some bitches will try to roam more just before they come on heat and may pass small quantities of urine at strategic points when out on a walk. The pheromones in the urine are signals for dogs in the area to smell. Generally, the bitch will not stand still for the male dog that sniffs round inquisitively during proestrus stage and she may even 'see the dog off'. If a mating does take place at this stage it is unlikely to result in puppies being born.

After ten days the blood colour of the vulva discharge will

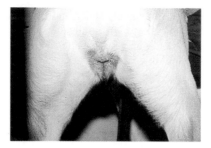

The proestrus stage of the bitch's cycle.

clear, and become pale straw colour and scanty. The vulva swelling changes from a stiff swelling to a softer wider-spread swelling, and the bitch may stand with her tail held to one side if approached by a dog. As a test, rub the back of the spine and the same response may be seen of the tail raised enticingly to display the vulva shape. At this stage the bitch is most likely to conceive if mating occurs. After a several more days she will go off heat, the discharge may again show some blood staining, and the bitch's attitude to males will be one of indifference or hostility. After 21 days the heat should be finished.

Male dogs in the area will be well aware of a bitch on heat and even three miles away, down wind, dogs can pick up a distinctive scent. Confine your bitch to the house or garden at this time, and remember attempts to escape may be made which would never occur when a bitch is not on heat. If you know or think a bitch has been accidentally mated (a disappearance of at least 20 minutes) then take steps to avoid the unwanted pregnancy. Contact the veterinary surgeon: an injection within 24 hours of mismating will stop any fertilised eggs implanting and developing – but this will put paid to a planned mating for at least another six months.

PLANNED MATINGS
The breeding of dogs is a perfectly natural process. In packs of wild dogs the males will compete with each other for the attention of any one female about to come on heat. The top or 'alpha' dog will then run with the bitch until her most fertile time when she allows that dog to mate. However, other males will keep nearby in case there is an opportunity for them to give an additional mating in the alpha dog's absence. Genetic selection of the 'best' male to produce puppies then takes place.

Normally the domesticated bitch meets only the one stud dog and matings are planned for the middle of the season, at sometime between the eleventh and the fourteenth day. Mating a bitch is not recommended until she has completed her growth, which may be by the time she is two years old. In the UK the Kennel Club discourages the mating of bitches more than eight years old by declining to register puppies unless there are special reasons for breeding later in life.

Timing the day of the planned mating is critical. It may be a waste of time travelling a distance to have a bitch mated, then finding she is not ready to accept the male. Any 'assisted' mating will distress the bitch, or the stud dog may be harmed if the visiting bitch turns to reject the dogs advances by snarling or snapping. There are two ways that the veterinary laboratory tests can help predict the best day.

1. The Pre-mate blood test: A small specimen of blood is collected from a vein by the veterinary surgeon to measure the hormone progesterone. A quick Elisa test is then used on the blood to predict when ovulation may occur, and advice will then be given on the best day for mating based on a sudden rise in plasma progesterone. It may be necessary to repeat this blood test every 48 hours until the bitch is ready. Inform your veterinary surgeon in advance, as the stock held of this test kit may be insufficient if a number of bitches are to be repeatedly tested.

2. Vaginal cytology: A smear is taken from the upper vagina with a swab or small syringe. It can then be stained with special stains and examined under the microscope to look for the signs that mating is possible. When 80 per cent of the stained cells have no nuclei, the bitch is considered ready for mating. Again, ask your veterinary surgeon in advance if the test is routinely done in the practice laboratory.

When a mating takes place, the stud dog will mount the bitch confidently and with co-operation by the bitch, a few thrusts cause the penetration of the penis when sperm will start to be ejected. The thrusting may draw fluids from the bitch down into the vagina. Then, unlike the mating of other animals, a 'tie' of male to female takes place. The muscles in the outer vagina contract around the swollen bulb of the penis and although some thrusting still takes place, the dog cannot withdraw the penis as it is locked in. The dog may then step over the bitch's back so that the penis rotates and the two face away from each other, back to back. This position may be held for twenty minutes or more. Novice bitches appear puzzled but not unduly distressed by the process. In this time, the dog is expelling a variety of fluid mixes into the bitch's vagina. Do not attempt to encourage the two animals to part, even though the 'tie' may last anything from a few seconds to a whole hour.

The semen has three fractions. The first, which comes mainly from the prostate gland acts as a liquid flush to get rid of urine and cell debris in the dog's urethra that runs through the centre of the penis. The fluid prepares the vagina for the second sperm-rich fraction of the ejaculate that soon follows. The third fraction, produced later in the tie, is thicker and acts as a lubricant to help the sperm pass through the cervix into the uterus. Eventually the sperm will reach the ovarian tubes where fertilisation of the waiting ova should result. Contractions of the uterus and the vagina during the tie probably help to propel the sperm up the fine channel at the centre of the long uterus in the bitch.

To help increase the chances of conception, most breeders try a second mating 48 hours later, but this is only of benefit if the bitch ovulates later in her heat.

THE PREGNANT BITCH

During pregnancy the bitch should be exercised and fed as normal. In the second half of the pregnancy, the bitch will be more careful for herself, and the feeds can be divided into two, ensuring that there is an adequate protein intake. The bitch must be kept as fit and healthy as possible. Medicines, unless they are prescribed by the veterinary surgeon, should be avoided. Worming courses in late pregnancy may be advised by the veterinary surgeon. Watch for any unusual discharges, but do not panic if a little blood should appear. However, a green or black-coloured discharge from the vulva suggests problems, and the veterinary surgeon should be contacted immediately.

It is not advisable to give any booster vaccinations after a bitch has been mated. Time the necessary boosters to coincide with the departure of puppies, or before the actual mating takes

The in-whelp bitch.

place. Unless there is a very specific reason, your bitch should not have X-rays taken once she has been mated. Pregnancy diagnosis is most reliable if performed at 24 to 28 days, either by palpation or scanning the uterus. If you wish to confirm pregnancy, it is now possible to use an ultrasound machine at about 28 days into the pregnancy, and the size of the litter can usually be predicted too. There is no evidence to suggest that, with experienced operators, this procedure can harm the foetuses, or the bitch. The time of scanning is important. Excessive application of ultrasound to a bitch's abdomen during pregnancy in unskilled hands, might cause damage to the brain of the foetus, and could be responsible for problems later in the puppy's life. Near the end of the nine-week pregnancy, the most demanding stages of dog breeding will be approaching fast, although the bitch herself will be unaware or, more likely, unconcerned at what is about to happen.

There are three stages of whelping. In the first stage, that commences at the very end of pregnancy, the bitch prepares herself for whelping by having internal contractions to dilate and make ready the birth canal. The second stage is the appearance of the puppies, and the third stage is the expulsion of the afterbirths.

PREPARATIONS FOR THE WHELPING

Well in advance of your bitch's whelping date, you should prepare the whelping area so she can get used to the place where birth is to take place. Make sure that you have carefully calculated the length of her gestation period. The normal length is nine weeks, or sixty-three days. However, the day she actually whelps will largely depend on the day of the season that the eggs were actually fertilised. If your bitch ovulates early in the season, she will have mature eggs waiting to be fertilised when she is mated. However, if she ovulated later in the season, the eggs may be fertilised several days after the actual mating. Thus it is quite common for a bitch to whelp five days either side of the expected whelping date.

Decide where you will want your bitch to have the puppies. Some bitches are best left entirely on their own, and peeping through a crack in the kennel door to watch that the bitch is not distressed may be the best form of supervision. There are not many bitches who wish to have an audience, which is not unlike humans in a similar situation, so plan to attend her on a one-to-one basis. No bitch should be left completely alone when whelping. It is worth remembering that bitches can delay the onset of birth, and they often prefer the quietest time of the day to have their pups – this is quite likely to be in the evening or after midnight! The bitch must have a chance to get used to the whelping area. About two weeks before the birth-date, show her the planned whelping area and change her sleeping arrangements. This will give her a fair chance to settle in her new environment. When she wishes to go outside, discourage her from digging holes in the garden. A uterus full of puppies will put increased pressure on the bladder, and the bitch may need to relieve herself away from the bed more often. Do not be surprised if her house training breaks down a little and, obviously, you must not chastise her if accidents occur.

In the final few hours, if you are not sure when the birth is due, always follow her in the garden – and watch her like a hawk! A pup born under the hedge or a under a bush may not be found until later when it is too cold to be revived. It is not unknown for the first puppy to be dropped out of doors, so look carefully if the bitch has gone out to strain then is seen coming back into the home again, apparently satisfied with her efforts.

THE BIRTH: THE PLACE AND THE EQUIPMENT
Before your bitch is due to whelp, it is sensible to have everything in place to avoid last-minute problems.

1. Make sure that the place where the bitch is going to whelp is actually the most suitable. It must be warm, dry and free from any draughts. She will enjoy a sense a privacy and security, so try to locate the whelping bed or box where she can attain this. Ideally, a quiet part of your house should be identified, where the whelping box can back on to a wall or is surrounded on three sides, if possible. Remember the need for access to the hind end of the whelping bitch. The veterinary surgeon may need to examine the whelping bitch, and remember that you will be required to steady her head at the front end. The whelping area should not be in so confined a space that an examination cannot be done without dragging the bitch away from her bed (and the puppies) to allow a proper inspection. If the whelping box is to be positioned under a table, for example, then the height should be sufficient to allow her to be able to stand up.

Remember that you may need space to attend to her and the newborn without injuring yourself – some bitches can become very protective over their puppies once born. There should be enough space to coax her out of the nest area for an examination.

2. There should be an electric point handy, because part of the recommended equipment is a heat lamp which should be hung

It is essential to position the heat-lamp at the correct height so the puppies receive sufficient warmth, but do not get over-heated.

above the bed. It is very important to note that, although this method of providing warmth can be a life-saver, it can also cause severe problems if it is hung too low and the temperature on the puppies' bodies exceeds 75-80 degrees Fahrenheit. You are recommended to hang the lamp up before your bitch is introduced to her bed, and, using a thermometer, adjust the height of the lamp until the correct temperature is attained. A height of about 4 feet (1.3 metres) should be about the right height to suspend the lamp. Then fix it in a way that it cannot be lowered any further. If it is too low it may lead to scorched puppies with skin damage, or early death. Your veterinary supplier should be able to advise you where to obtain a heat lamp.

You are strongly advised to have a spare bulb. If water is splashed on a hot bulb it may burst, showering the nest with glass. Care is also needed with utensils, brushes etc. when working near the lamp. Faulty wiring may lead to overheating and the risk of fires, so great care is needed, especially in wooden premises.

3. The bed should be suitable for the purpose. The size should be large enough to allow your bitch to be able to lie on her side and to fully stretch out her head and legs. Some breeders advise that a rail is positioned around the perimeter of the box to help prevent the bitch accidentally flattening a puppy by lying on it.

The bed should be made from a warm material such as wood,

and the sides should be about half a metre high. The front should be hinged so that you can lower it down as the pups grow bigger and want to explore. This avoids leg injuries with puppies jumping up or trying to scramble out.

4. Before the actual birth, use the following as a checklist.

* Note the 24 hour phone number of your veterinary surgeon in case you need to phone in an emergency – often this call will have to be made outside the normal working hours. Most veterinary surgeons prefer to have one or two days notice of a whelping due, especially if there have been problems with the birth of a previous litter.
* Assemble a large collection of newspapers for bedding. This bedding is very absorbent, almost sterile and can be disposed of easily. Because it is very cheap, it can be thrown away! Hygiene is improved, as there is a tendency not to have enough washable material at such a time. The bitch should be able to be clean when she wants to lie down and rest.
* Other bedding will eventually be needed and absorbent material (vetbed – a synthetic fabric) is recommended. This bedding can be machine-washed and tumble-dried quickly.
* Scales that are suitable for weighing tiny puppies accurately.
* Antiseptic lotion and sponge for cleaning the bitch before and after the whelping.
* Plenty of clean towels for drying the puppies.
* A clock for noting the time of each birth.
* Two thermometers. One for checking the ambient room temperature. The second one, a clinical thermometer, should be placed with the base in a jar of mild antiseptic liquid.
* A suitable small box where you could place puppies out of harm's way, if needed. This can be used as a temporary bed for some of the puppies when whelping is in full swing, particularly if your bitch tends to be a bit clumsy. A clean blanket should fill the base, and it is a good tip to keep a hot-water bottle handy to help retain the very necessary warmth for the pups. The hot-water bottle used should be warm (blood heat) only.
* Milk and glucose to offer the bitch as a drink during the whelping.
* A notebook to keep a check on each puppy as it is born, i.e. sex, weight, time of birth and other useful details which are easily forgotten in the excitement.
* A jar of Vaseline or other lubricant.
* A baby feeder and milk substitute (your vet can advise on a suitable product).

* Containers suitable for disposing of soiled newspapers, waste and towels.
* Strong sterilised silk or cotton thread in case a puppy's cord requires tying.
* Round-nosed surgical scissors.
* Spare bulb for the heat-lamp.

Organise suitable seating arrangements for yourself, and have some means of obtaining refreshment which does not require you to leave the bitch for more than a couple of minutes.

Finally, it is worth considering the fate of the rest of your household while your bitch is whelping. It is not a good idea to have people constantly butting in, although you may consider having someone on standby for emergencies, or to give you a short break. Remember, other pets need to be kept away. Your bitch will not relish an audience and, of course, sensible hygiene precautions must be considered.

CONCLUDING THOUGHTS ON BREEDING DOGS

1. Think very deeply: do you really wish to breed from your dog?
2. Are you willing to give up the time, and probably the cash, to do the job well?
3. Have you the facilities to rear the litter?
4. What type of puppies do you wish to produce: show, working or pet?
5. Only mate to the best: this will increase your chances of getting good pups.
6. Will you be able to find the right sort of homes for the puppies you do not intend to keep?
7. Remember there is a strong element of luck and you must be prepared for problems.
8. Listen to good advice. You do not have to heed it all, but you can always learn. In the end you must take your own decisions, then have the courage to stick with them. But we can all learn by our mistakes as long as we correct them the next time.
9. Approach dog breeding with a positive attitude; accept that it may be hard work but enjoy the involvement. There can be an educational value in dog breeding for children in the home too! There will always be someone quick to criticise your decisions, but if you have prepared thoroughly, there is nothing to be ashamed of if not everything is perfect.

THE BIRTH OF PUPPIES AND AFTERCARE

THE FIRST STAGE OF LABOUR

Experience will tell you when the bitch is showing signs of impending birth. For the beginner, it can be a worrying time and it is easy to get into a panic – and undue anxiety by the attendant will unnecessarily upset the bitch. There are various things that may happen and you only have to apply common sense and a little logic! The bitch is likely to behave in a restless manner and to be unwilling to remain relaxed for more than short periods. Coupled with this behaviour will be a lot of panting, and she may even shiver. Sleep periods will become shorter and she could start to refuse food. Some bitches are even known to actually vomit some food as they go into labour. A very good sign is a desire to prepare the bed by tearing up any newspaper you have placed in it, or roughing up any other form of bedding.

The bitch's temperature should drop from the normal 101.3 degrees Fahrenheit to 98 degrees F (38.5 degrees Centigrade to 37.0 degrees C) within 12 to 24 hours of birth taking place. The temperature drop is a very good guide and should give a clear indication that she is likely to give birth soon. The refusal of a meal is another sign of imminent birth. If the bitch is still eating well, she is unlikely to start whelping in the next eight hours. A good tip is to take her temperature twice a day for about a week before the expected date of the birth. This allows you to study any normal variations in body temperature through the day. Finally, there can be an increase in volume of a mucous discharge from the vulva. The vulva may also become more swollen and then softer in shape. The mammary glands will fill, but in the maiden bitch milk may not form until after all the puppies are born. You should remain calm, as your bitch may be upset enough without an additional source of worry. Dogs are very receptive to human emotions and our 'body language'. Someone constantly fussing around will make the bitch more agitated. It may be best to sit with the bitch as the first contractions occur, speaking in a reassuring manner, although this is when the puppies are about to be pushed through the birth canal and be born.

Always remember: most whelpings take place quite normally. with few if no problems requiring human interference.

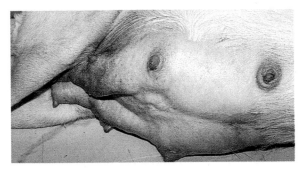

The mammary glands just prior to whelping.

THE SECOND STAGE

At the start of this, the most exciting stage, your bitch should become much calmer. The panting and the contractions to expel the foetus should become less frantic, and the foetal fluids or 'waters' will appear at the vulva as the membranes around each puppy usually break immediately prior to the puppy being born.

1. Observe the contractions: The bitch will appear tense, then she will relax her body. This will look as though she is squeezing from the ribs all the way down her body. Panting should, more or less, cease and contractions lasting just a few seconds, will now occur. Make an entry in the notebook of the time of this first contraction.

IMPORTANT: If she continues to have these strong abdominal contractions without producing a pup for 1-2 hours after 'the waters' have broken, there may be a problem, and you should contact the veterinary practice immediately when the two-hour point has passed. You will then be advised as to whether it is necessary for the bitch to be seen immediately (within the next hour usually) or if more time should be allowed. Be prepared to answer any questions the receptionist asks you over the phone with accurate answers. Your notebook should be handy, and you may need to speak directly to the veterinary surgeon.

The period of time between the births of puppies can vary in breeds and from bitch to bitch. A gap of a few minutes is common, but up to a couple of hours is not unusual. Provided the bitch is generally calm and quite relaxed, there is no need for worry. However, if your bitch has been straining hard for a couple of hours, without success, you should assume there is a birth problem.

2. Observe how the puppy arrives: The appearance of a discharge, particularly blood-coloured or a darkish green, before the birth of the *first* puppy can indicate that the placenta has started to separate from the wall of the uterus. This pup will need to be delivered quite fast as he/she is likely to be deprived of oxygen. If you see a similar discharge before the birth of the next puppies, then it is probably nothing to worry about and is more normal. You may see a blackish glistening ball at the vulva, which is the foetal fluid in the unbroken sac surrounding the puppy. Often the outer sac has burst as it comes through the pelvic canal, and the fluid released is called 'the waters'. The inner amniotic sac has darker fluid and can be burst as the puppy comes out of the vulva or will be broken by the bitch's tongue as she licks her newborn puppy.

All puppies, before birth, are enclosed in a double layer of membranes with fluid in between each skin-like layer. This fluid actually protects the pup while it is being pushed and squeezed by the uterine muscles. The membranes around the pups are known as the foetal sac, which holds the fluid. However, a yellow slimy fluid discharge can tell you that the outer membrane sac has broken before the puppy emerges.

Before appearing outside, the pup has to be propelled over a 'hump' at the brim of the pubis bone before entering the pelvis. Once over this hump, and as the pup is pushed through the pelvis birth canal, a bulge or swelling can next be seen in the skin just above the vulva. Soon after this, the head or rump of the puppy can be seen emerging through the vulva. During this process of straining, the water bag which surrounds the pup will usually burst, which causes a gush of fluid to appear from the vulva. This is a good sign that the pup is not far behind.

If the water bag does not burst, you may see the water sac emerge and retract several times in the mouth of the vulva. The sac usually has a dark colour and is shiny on the surface. These bulging movements coincide with the propulsive contractions of the bitch's uterus and her abdominal contractions. The water bag exerts a hydraulic force, stretching and dilating the birth canal, to allow the puppy to come through afterwards more easily. In the novice or tired bitch, the amniotic sac may smother the puppy's face. The attendant will have to tear the sac open for the puppy to have air to inflate its lungs if it is to have a chance of survival.

The next puppy really needs to be born within 20-40 minutes but may arrive much sooner once the birth canal is dilated and lubricated by the previous puppy. If you have had your bitch's pregnancy checked by the use of ultrasound scanning at about 28 days and the number of foetuses was counted, then you should have a good idea of how many puppies she is expecting. The number of foetuses counted would then be the minimum to expect – there could be one or two more extra not found in the scanning. Remember, it is not unusual for a bitch to give birth to only one pup or even numbers of pups, up into double figures. There are some distinct variations between different breeds of dogs; some German Shepherds will be able to rear 18 puppies with only a little help with their feeding.

THE THIRD STAGE

Expelling the afterbirth is known as or is sometimes termed 'the third stage' of labour. When the pup is born, it should be attached by the umbilical cord to the placenta, which usually follows immediately after the puppy emerges from the vulva, as a reddish-black mass. Unlike the human birth process that usually only requires the delivery of a single placenta, the bitch, as an animal with the birth of many puppies, does not have a distinct third stage of labour. Often the afterbirth will come out immediately before the bitch expels the next puppy from the vagina, so stages two and three are combined

Sometimes the afterbirth will not be expelled until much later and occasionally it may be retained. Therefore, it is a good tip to count the afterbirths and make keep a note for reference before you start clearing up.

CARE OF THE NEWBORN PUPPIES

At this time, the care of the puppies becomes important. Try to encourage the bitch to clean the pups herself. It is natural for some bitches, especially maidens, to appear a little frantic at this stage. They may be rather clumsy in their actions and might require gentle assistance. Help can be given by tearing the sac, and making sure that the pup's head is free from membranes over the nostrils and it is able to breathe. This is especially important for the first-born puppy as the bitch may not have become accustomed to washing the puppy with her tongue, after the effort she put into expelling the puppy.

Hand the pup to the bitch's face and encourage her, if she wishes, to eat the afterbirth. This is totally natural. She should actually chew the umbilical cord through, but watch that she does not continue to chew the cord too close to the puppy. The back molar teeth of the mother are specially adapted to crush and sever the umbilical cord so that any bleeding stops. If she does not separate the puppy, you will need to tear the cord yourself. Do not cut the cord with sharp scissors very close to the puppy's abdomen. Hold the cord a couple of inches from the pup's tummy with one hand. Pull the cord with the other

ABOVE: The mother will care for all the puppies' needs, cleaning them and feeding them.

RIGHT: The puppies are born blind – their eyes will open when they are around ten days old.

hand, stretching it across the thumb nail before it tears then breaks.

You should give the bitch a chance to fuss, clean and lick the pup herself before taking it from her. If you think the bitch is tired or slow to lick, give the pup a vigorous rub with a towel, holding it firmly close to a suitable work surface in case the pup slips from your hold. Hold the pup so that the head is lower than the rear as this will help any fluid to flow and will thereby clear the airways. An indication that it has fluid in its airways is that you will hear 'snuffling' noises.

When you are happy that the puppies have all arrived and are well, then check that you have noted the following:

• The time of each pup's birth, weight, colour.
• Male or female.
• The presence of front or hind feet dewclaws.
• Any obvious abnormalities.

PROBLEMS IN WHELPING

It is worthwhile knowing of some of the more common whelping problems which may occur. Such complications are fortunately rare but if you are well prepared, some puppies that might not otherwise survive can be born alive and reared successfully.

UTERINE INERTIA

If the bitch stops straining there are three probable reasons:

a) She has finished giving birth: In this case she is likely to show signs of relaxing with her new family by lying down contentedly with them, cleaning each puppy and generally acting like any protective mother.

b) She is merely having a break: Unless you are absolutely sure she has finished, then assume she has more pups on their way and be vigilant.

c) Your bitch is suffering from uterine inertia: There are two distinct types of inertia and she may be incapable of further effort.

1. PRIMARY INERTIA: This term applies to the bitch who is obviously in whelp but is reluctant to get the birth process started. She shows little or no sign of contractions. This is often seen in the older bitch, but it can stem from a bitch which is not relaxed in the environment in which she is expected to whelp. Fright can delay the release of hormones that start the bitch's whelping. Inertia can also happen when the bitch is overweight or unfit. Other causes are an over-stretched uterus following a previous large litter where the uterus has become so over-stretched that the paper-thin muscle is unable to exert any contractions.

When there are only a couple of pups present at the end of the pregnancy, the muscles are strong but these one or two puppies may fail to stimulate the hormone mechanism that commences the birth process; this is known as the single puppy syndrome. Normally the size and weight of the puppies decide when birth is due, and hormone signals are sent to the mother's pituitary gland in the brain to start the whelping. A bitch can go ten days beyond the birth time carrying a single puppy without distress but, often, a very large puppy is eventually born dead.

2) SECONDARY INERTIA: This occurs after the bitch has had at least one puppy successfully – often most of the litter will already have been born. She then loses the impulse to continue the contractions. Two possible causes are exhaustion or an obstruction from an oversized or malformed puppy.

An experienced breeder should have a good idea when to call the vet. However, if this is your first experience of breeding, or you are worried, then a birth delay of a couple of hours is long enough to wait before taking appropriate action. When the cervix is fully dilated an oxytocin (pituitrin) injection should stimulate contractions. If the cervix has not fully opened, then there is the risk that the uterus may rupture when such a hormone is given unwisely. The veterinary surgeon can give an injection such as calcium and often oxytocin, and a puppy may be born within ten minutes. However, this may be less successful if there are even more puppies waiting to be born in an already tired bitch.

If a puppy is not born within this time, or there are still many puppies left inside then a caesarean operation may considered by the veterinary surgeon as the best course to avoid further stress to the mother and to allow as many live puppies to be produced as possible.

CAESAREAN BIRTH

The operation of caesarean section or hysterotomy, will need to be carried out at the well-equipped veterinary surgery. If your bitch requires a caesarean following the birth of some of her pups, you should leave them in a warm box with a hot-water bottle under a blanket, while the bitch is taken away for the operation. Someone should accompany the bitch to the surgery. With luck, there will be some more live pups produced, so take another suitable box or container to bring them back home in.

Puppies born through caesarean birth will normally thrive in the same way as those born naturally. Watch that the anaesthetic used on the mother has not made the puppies unduly sleepy. If this is the case, keep them warm at incubator temperature and stimulate them to wake up by rubbing them and moving them round. Most veterinary surgeons will have developed their own technique for the operation, so that puppies are not too drowsy when they are born. If you are not certain of the date of the conception, some puppies delivered by caesarean may be premature – even though the signs of a full-term birth seemed certain. In this situation the puppies may have more breathing difficulties, as the lungs do not inflate fully after the birth. The use of an incubator to keep the puppies warm and oxygenated is even more necessary for maximum survival rates. The bitch should be able to feed the puppies normally after the operation, but maiden bitches may not be aware of what has taken place when they wake to find newborn puppies around them. The bitch may ignore the puppies, especially if they do not carry her smell – having been dried and cleaned for her – and she may want to go back to a familiar human for comfort. You will need to keep a very strict eye on the situation.

Try to get the puppies feeding by holding the mother down, and smear her milk on the puppies' heads. Sometimes the operation wound, which will be between the teats, is sore and the bitch will not want the puppies too close to her. If the amount of milk present is scanty then perseverance is needed with the feeding. Keep the operated area clean and dry. Use only the mildest of antiseptics – chemical smells may confuse the mother and delay the 'bonding' that occurs during suckling. If you are concerned in any way then do not hesitate to phone your veterinary surgeon after such an operation, particularly if the puppies are not feeding.

A bitch that has had one caesarean can normally be considered for breeding again, in consultation with your vet. The advice given will be based on a knowledge of the state of the uterus after the operation. Only the surgeon who operated will know exactly what things were like inside, so follow the advice given. If a bitch has uterine inertia at a subsequent whelping, a second need for a caesarean after inertia would indicate that she should then be retired.

A BREECH BIRTH

The normal presentation of a puppy is head first with the front legs appearing under its chin and the hind legs stretched out behind. About two-thirds of puppies are born this way. The other third are born with the hind legs and the tail coming out first, followed by the abdomen of the pup, then the shoulders and finally the head.

A breech birth is where a puppy is born with its rump presented first, with its hind legs tucked under the body. Often only the tail can be seen or felt, followed by the rounded mass of the puppy's buttocks. Problems are more likely to occur if this is the first born puppy as there is no natural wedge action to help dilate the birth canal. If your bitch is actually straining for over an hour with such a puppy, then contact your vet. A number of puppies can be born easily with their rump appearing first, but the 'true' breech birth may be a cause of trouble (known as dystocia). This should not apply with the puppy born with tail and hind legs stretched behind them.

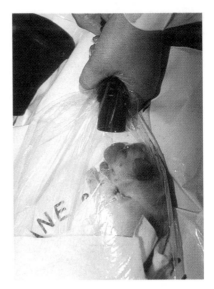

In cases of emergency, an oxygen tent can be used to revive a puppy.

STILLBORN PUPPY

If a puppy appears but shows no signs of life, do not immediately despair. Make every attempt to promote breathing by rubbing and drying it vigorously with a towel. Do not be too gentle, and keep trying for at least thirty minutes. Stand over a table or kneel close to the floor when doing this, as it is quite easy to drop the slippery puppy.

If the pup starts to show signs of life, continue the rubbing. Hold its neck and head downwards as this will help clear the airways of excessive fluid. If you find that a stillborn pup is actually deformed, then keep it for later examination by the vet.

EXCESS FLUID IN A PUPPY

If the pup still fails to breathe, or is having great difficulty because of liquid in the lungs and throat, it may be worth trying to "swing" the pup. Excess force should be avoided as there is the risk of damage when the centrifugal force of swinging sends fluids into the newborn's brain. First try swabbing out the back of the throat to help clear the airway of fluids or sticky mucus. Suction can be used if available, or a drinking straw can be improvised as a mouth-to-throat suction.

In order to swing the puppy, clasp both hands around the body and ensure its front legs are enclosed within your hands, and that its face points down towards the floor. Now place both of your thumbs on the nape of the neck to give it support. Wrap your index finger under the chin. This will stop the head swinging at neck level, which is a point of weakness. Position yourself well clear of any obstructions, walls, furniture, etc. Place your legs slightly apart, then in a downward action, swing the puppy down towards your legs in a vigorous manner. Throughout this procedure, keep your arms stiff.

Repeat the swinging about six times until the pup ceases to emit fluid from its nose or mouth. The centrifugal force produced by swinging is strong enough to force fluids out, but continual swinging might cause brain damage. Now, rub vigorously with a towel and place the puppy back with the mother. Gentle prodding at the puppy's chest, putting something stiff (like a straw) in the nostrils, to stimulate the breathing once the airway is clear may all help the lungs to inflate. The acupuncture point at the centre (philtrum) of the nose may be pricked gently as another way to start breathing.

RETAINED AFTERBIRTH

If the uterus does not contract down at the end of the whelping, the bitch will not settle down to feed her puppies. If it is the afterbirth or placenta that is retained then the symptoms can be a rise in the bitch's temperature to 103 degrees Fahrenheit (39.5 degrees Centigrade) plus very rapid panting, an unpleasant discharge from the vulva, shivering or a loss of appetite.

As these symptoms are also those of a retained puppy, the aid of the veterinary surgeon is imperative. An after-whelping (post-natal) veterinary examination within 12 hours of the last puppy's birth will detect problems before they develop into an illness.

FADING PUPPIES

At birth, if a puppy seems to be too small, weak, lacking in body movements or uttering mewing noises, then a very close watch needs to be kept on it. Warmth is vitally important and you may decide that the heat-lamp should be supplemented. In a breeding centre an incubator may be used, but in the home a little imagination is required to provide some similar device for a puppy to survive. Try to maintain it, if possible, at an even temperature of 80-90 degrees Fahrenheit (35 degrees Centigrade). Fluctuations in temperature may cause the pup to chill.

If the pup will not, or cannot, feed from the bitch every two hours, then you will need to feed with a suitable supplement which you should already have in case of emergency (see checklist). Use a suitable feeder similar to a 2cc syringe. Although hand-feeding may need to be continued for some time, keep trying to encourage the weak pup to suck from the bitch. Check that it is suckling normally by wetting your little finger with the bitch's milk and encourage the pup to suck from that.

Place the pup on a teat and hold its mouth there, supporting it from the rear. At the same time, push its face intermittently into the mammary glands to stimulate milk flow. Pressure with the other hand on the gland may help to squeeze milk from the teat into the mouth, and the warm milk may initiate a sucking movement. It is not always necessary for the teat to fully enter the mouth to get a puppy sucking enough to take in the milk. If the bitch shows little interest in the weak pups, it may be necessary for you to consider tube feeding. A veterinary nurse may be the best person to help with this. You then need to stimulate the pup to defecate and urinate. Gently massage the genitalia and rectum with moist cotton-wool, and with a little patience, there will be a response.

In many cases, despite all you do, these pups may be seen to weaken and die within a short time after the birth. Sometimes they can linger for several days, and this can be quite distressing for you and the bitch. Consider having a post mortem examination, as there could be a virus or bacterial infection causing the 'fading'.

FAILURE TO CLEAN THE PUPPIES
Sometimes a bitch will not show an immediate interest in her new pups. She may not clean them or stimulate them to defecate or urinate. Smear the genital areas with a little honey or sunflower oil. This should encourage the bitch to do the right thing and start to lick them.

There are not often 'careless' mothers in the canine world. Watch for ill health in the bitch if she is not caring for her puppies adequately.

NOTE: While your bitch has puppies, you should not allow her to be exercised anywhere but on your own premises. There is a high risk of her bringing infection into the nest and passing it on to the puppies – often with fatal results.

POST-WHELPING PROBLEMS

RETAINED PLACENTA (AFTERBIRTH)
See page 67

ECLAMPSIA
Symptoms of this very serious condition are quite dramatic and, once seen, will not be forgotten. Usually the body

temperature is very high, muscle contractions may send it as high as 106 degrees Fahrenheit (42 degrees Centigrade). This is quite unlike the equivalent condition 'milk fever' in farm animals where the temperature is subnormal. Fluctuating temperature may be accompanied by very rapid panting, shivering, unsteady gait, glazed eyes and convulsions.

These signs are caused by a large and sudden calcium deficiency. Calcium is withdrawn from the body through the milk at a faster rate than it can be replaced from the mother's bones. There may be poor availability of dietary calcium, as when cereal-rich diets are fed. Eclampsia normally occurs during the second or third week of lactation as the peak milk demand is reached. A milder form of eclampsia occurs just after birth and the bitch will usually respond well to calcium injections. It can occur irrespective of the size of the litter.

Immediate veterinary attention is needed. A bitch in convulsions will die unless intravenous calcium can be given.

The calcium cannot be replaced by tablet or medicine, but has to be given by injection or drip. Cooling the bitch may be necessary, and sometimes glucose also will have to be given. If the condition is left unattended, death will follow the onset of symptoms very swiftly.

MASTITIS

Watch for the bitch that does not like the puppies near her, and appears to still have full, well-distended mammary glands. Symptoms of one or more glands hotter and firmer than the rest should make you suspect mastitis. Hardening of one or more of the mammary glands may be accompanied by a rise in temperature. The gland(s) will become fiery hot and extremely painful. There will be, naturally, a reluctance on the bitch's part to feed her puppies, so alternative feeding arrangements may be needed until the mastitis is cured. In extreme cases a breast abscess develops, and one gland bursts leaving a large cavity. Fortunately, healing takes place quickly after the gland has discharged.

If a large swelling develops in one of the mammary glands when the bitch is suckling puppies, close observation will probably show that the puppies are not taking milk from the gland at all. If the retained milk causes the swelling, it can often be drawn off through the teat by thumb and forefinger pressure. If this milk is brown or shows other signs of infection, then mastitis has already developed. Often the swollen gland will become shiny and tense. This may be the time to apply warm cloth compresses, no hotter than blood heat, to the gland surface. The abscess will then ripen and burst, discharging the infected material. Antibiotics should be given. The cavity edges should be washed with saline, and the hole should fill up in three or four days.

METRITIS
Inflammation of the uterus can occur after whelping. This condition is said to be caused by dead puppies, retention of an afterbirth, injury or infection introduced during the whelping. It is avoided by good hygiene and monitoring of a bitch during and after the birth. Generally, there is no need to give a bitch antibiotics after whelping, but strict cleanliness, including the hands of the attendant, will avoid a great many problems.

DEATH OF THE BITCH
This is very rare, but is not impossible, so it is best to consider all possibilities.

1. If you know someone who has a bitch with a small litter of a similar age, it is quite possible to get some puppies adopted by a new mum. Introduce puppies gently and watch the bitch's reaction. If she is a little reticent, smear her own milk or a very little honey or sunflower oil on the fostered puppy. She will then almost certainly start to clean the puppy and will then treat it as one of her own.
2. Warmth and comfort for the orphan puppies are paramount. Supplementary feed can be given to the pups, but you will have to be prepared to present yourself, with a feeding bottle, every four hours throughout the day and night for at least three weeks. Puppies of three weeks of age and over stand a better chance of feeding themselves. Use a proprietary milk substitute powder, and follow the maker's dilution and quantity rates closely.
3. You may still have to encourage some pups to urinate and defecate. (See above.)
4. Early weaning at three weeks is possible, especially in the larger breeds of dog.

It will not matter if different breeds are used as foster mothers. Often, it is a kindness to let a bitch who has got a couple of pups of her own and plenty of milk feed a few more that are not her own. Cross-suckling is not harmful.

SWIMMER PUPPIES
This is a condition seen in puppies once their eyes have opened, where they fail to get up on their front legs to crawl or walk. It is characterised by a swimming motion of the legs as

the puppy tries to pull itself along. These puppies are often large for their age, and it is suggested that their shoulders are too weak to carry the weight of a large puppy. The sternum of the chest is often flatter than usual, and the muscular development of the forelegs is poor. There is little effective treatment, other than trying to stop suspected puppies from over-feeding and becoming overweight. In some breeds a large proportion of a litter may be affected to various degrees, and it is probable that there is a hereditary factor that occurs as strains in a breed. In other litters only a single puppy is affected. If there is no improvement by five weeks, euthanasia of the puppy may be advised.

WEANING

Weaning the puppies from the bitch should take place progressively between four and seven weeks to reduce the disturbance to the bitch. Treatment can also be given to dry up the milk production. Although your bitch can be upset, normally they are very relieved to see the puppies go and they can then return to their former lifestyle.

Restriction of water and a reduced protein content of the food are natural ways of stopping the milk forming in a situation where abrupt weaning is required. The fuller the glands are with milk, the more temperamental the bitch may become. It is best not to squeeze out the milk, as this will encourage further milk to form in its place.

PUPPY CARE

SOCIALISATION OF THE LITTER

The need to handle and play with puppies while they are still with their mother must be emphasised. Socialisation of the litter is very important in the puppy's development. Training begins at the earliest age and, at first, it will be given entirely by the mother of the puppies. Most trusting bitches will allow someone known to them to pick up and stroke the puppies, but, in the early stages, always keep the puppies close to the bitch so she does not feel you may be removing them for good.

As part of the puppies' development to become acceptable pets, they must be handled a lot by humans. This can start immediately after the birth. As their eyes and ears begin to open, the puppy becomes more responsive to outside stimuli. Each puppy will be growing fast, both physically and temperamentally. All the stimuli they experience in your home in these first few weeks of life will have a definite effect on their characters and temperament, which will then remain with them for the remainder of their lives.

Spend plenty of time playing with the young, particularly during the third to sixth week after birth – the period around the sixth week is the most critical for the human-animal bond effect to become firmly established. Encourage each puppy to play, not only with other members of the litter, but also with yourself and other members of the family, especially children. By providing suitable play objects, pups will be encouraged to be more outgoing and adventurous. If the weather is fine, take them into the garden to explore, ensuring it is secure and they are under constant supervision. Puppies like exploring, so beware of pools and other hazards in the garden. Flights of steps and low walls can be a source of injury to puppies with young bones that tumble over these objects in an impetuous manner.

It is very good for the pups to be exposed to normal domestic sounds like the doorbell, telephones, the vacuum cleaner or radio and television noises. This helps to develop their hearing sensitivities and will, therefore, lessen the chance of them exhibiting noise anxiety later in life. It is advantageous to handle each pup to weigh them at least once a week. In this way, you can accurately monitor their progress and inspect them at the same time. While it is away from the mother, use a very soft brush on each puppy and try giving a quick groom to each one after it is weighed. As your puppies develop, the bitch will gradually lose her obsessive attachment to them. She will want to spend less time with them, until approximately six weeks, when she may only want to visit them for additional feeding and cleaning. If your bitch does not follow this pattern, it may be necessary to encourage her to leave the pups for

As the puppies mature, they learn to interact with each other.

periods. By doing this you will lessen the impact of the puppies leaving her, which one can certainly consider at six weeks when they are fully weaned.

In most cases, it is the owner who is most upset about the departure of the puppies – not the bitch!

Although your litter of puppies will be of great interest to others, try to keep outside visitors to a minimum, apart from family members who live in the house. A queue of strangers coming to see the pups can upset your bitch, especially in the first few weeks – and the risk of infection is much higher. Prospective purchasers may have visited other kennels before coming to see your litter and their footwear could possibly carry parvo virus infection from walking in infected kennels on a previous day.

Throughout her time with the pups, discourage the bitch from showing any signals of protectiveness by barking, or growling at the approach of humans. Try to nip in the bud any tendency to behave in this way by gently, but firmly, telling her "no", and then praising, and reassure her when she stops. Her attitude to humans will be passed on to the puppies and a confident and friendly demeanour will give the puppies confidence.

CARE OF THE NEW PUPPY IN THE HOME

The need for the puppy to be handled while still with its mother has been emphasised. If you are intending to choose a puppy it is good advice to avoid buying a puppy from a breeder whose bitch shows any signs of severe worry or aggression when the puppies are examined by the potential purchaser. Puppies should be fully weaned at six weeks of age, and are then ready to leave their mother for a new home unless there has been some check in their growth for any reason.

Once you acquire a new puppy it is recognised that the sooner it is introduced to the sights and sounds of the outside world the better it will be for development. Experience in the Guide Dog for the Blind Association kennels for nearly thirty years has shown that puppies will respond to vaccinations at six weeks of age. This allows the puppy to have enough protection to take it out of the strict isolation of the home that was at one time thought essential. Most veterinary surgeons are willing to use a vaccine at six weeks, but it is best to discuss the practice's vaccination policies before you first visit the surgery with the new puppy – this may save embarrassment to owner and vet! Some breeders and veterinary surgeons emphasise the risk if the puppy leaves the home before it is fully protected, but as this may be as late as 15 weeks of age, it is not considered best for socialisation.

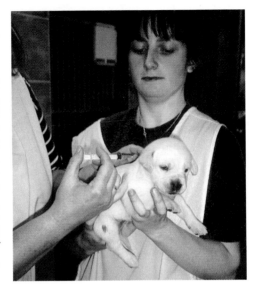

In the UK the Guide Dogs for the Blind Association vaccinate all their puppies at six weeks. Most vets have their own policy, depending on the local incidence of disease.

The veterinary surgeon will know the disease risk in the area you live, and there may be times when strict isolation is essential. Sometimes the mother may have been recently infected with a disease and she then passes a very high level of protection to her newborn puppies so that the six-week vaccine could be obliterated by the maternally derived immunity (MDI). Obviously with such a young puppy there are places still to avoid even though a six week vaccine has been given. Heavily-used public parks, grass verges and lamp-posts all should be avoided until the 15 week stage. There is no reason why you should not pick up and carry a puppy in places you think may be contaminated with dog disease. Usually rain-washed pavements and quiet roads are suitable for putting a puppy down to walk on, at seven weeks, if it has a light collar and lead for restraint.

The puppy should get used to wearing a suitable collar round the neck for half an hour at a time. In most cases, the puppy will not like to be pulled along by a lead attached to its collar for the first time. Try carrying the puppy out of the house for the first time in your arms, then after a short distance turn round and walk the puppy in a homeward direction with a loose lead attached to its collar. Always use words of praise when the right things are done. Do not punish or drag the puppy along by its neck while its four legs are dug in, in protest. You must be prepared to be very patient and give the pup plenty of encouragement so as not to damage its confidence in this frightening new outside world it is experiencing.

TRAVEL

Travel by car may be frightening at first for the young puppy. The first car journey made by many puppies is the one where it is removed from the security of its caring mother and the reassurance of the presence of its litter mates, to travel to an empty home with strange smells, new foods and a whole new range of activities ahead of it. The next journey may be the one to the veterinary surgery, with all that that implies to the fearful puppy. Take the puppy for very short journeys again. Try to provide a happier ending – a romp and play, a morsel of food or a new piece of grass to walk on. The puppy will quickly accept this, and it will minimise the chances of car sickness ruining all journeys later in life.

Do not worry if a puppy should be car sick. Sometimes they only salivate. If this is the case, try to stop the journey before large quantities of saliva are swallowed, only to be returned again during the journey. Only use travel sickness tablets as a last resort or for a particularly long holiday trip or other unavoidable long period in a car. Take a towel, mop the puppy up and praise it in a confident way. A lot of car sickness is brought on by anxiety; seeing many objects race by causes distress. Some dogs are best caged so they can only look out of a front window or the rear window of a hatchback or van. The presence of another family pet during travel may have a calming influence – a mature dog put into a large cage in the car with a puppy can give confidence.

FURTHER EDUCATION

The puppy should be taken out and about as part of its socialisation training. The sights and sounds of the outside world are less frightening if introduced slowly when there is someone familiar to provide support. Introduce the puppy regularly to new situations. Some puppies take everything in their stride, others tend to be cautious and must be introduced more slowly to new conditions.

Exposure to unfamiliar situations will help to prepare the young puppy for adult life. Be careful of heavy or fast-moving traffic, even on quiet roads and on country lanes. Keep the puppy on a loose lead – even if an area appears safe – until you have checked for escape routes leading to roads. Some areas worth taking your puppy to are:

Pubs/bars: These contain a lot of new sights and smells. Even more important, most persons will want to talk to and make a fuss of a young puppy, especially if kept in the owner's arms.

Lead training can start in the garden, so the puppy is walking confidently on the lead by the time the inoculation programme has been completed.

Every puppy should be exposed to as many different situations as possible in order to develop into an adaptable, well-behaved adult.

This type of socialisation is encouraged as the puppy learns that most strangers are friendly.

Lifts and elevators: Here the puppy is in a totally enclosed space, and there are strange sounds and strange sensations of gravity change to get accustomed to.

Road works and construction sites: Again, a lot of noise, strange smells, often a deviation in the normal pathway used.

Crowds: Pups get used to being hemmed in, but make sure that if the dog sits its tail does not protrude, as it is easily trodden on in a crowd where the dog's presence is not realised.

Escalators: The pup must be carried. Guide dog owners are instructed to carry their dog on an escalator, or to summon help to stop the moving staircase before using it. Many guide dog owners get to know rail routes where there are stairs or lifts to use.

Telephone kiosks: Here again, the puppy gets used to a confined space and hopefully avoids getting its tail injured.

Unusual walking surfaces: Slippery surfaces can frighten a dog later in life. Open staircases are particularly disliked by most dogs. Some adult dogs may refuse to negotiate metal fire escapes. Try to find this type of staircase and play a game with the puppy on the first few low steps.

Loud noises: Thunder can be a particular problem, as dogs probably sense a change in the atmosphere long before the noise is heard by humans. A similar explanation is used for earthquake prediction by dogs. Take care of a dog when there is a loud noise. Many gun dogs are trained on the reward system, so that a loud noise is followed by the reward of retrieving an object, then a lot of praise is given. If a door slams or a car backfires, use your voice to praise and reassure the dog in a confident way.

Travel and Railway Stations: You may not use the train yourself, but a railway station is an excellent place to introduce a puppy to many new conditions and there is usually plenty of space. Some puppies are exposed to air journeys very early in life and seem to travel unharmed. It is a good idea to obtain an air travel box and get the puppy used to going into it and even sleeping in it for a few days, before an air journey is planned.

Visiting the veterinary surgery: Like humans, many dogs have a fear of the surgery situation: unusual chemicals, the pheromones left by other fearful dog visitors and the anxiety of the people with the pets – all produce apprehension in the puppy. If the visit is made to 'register' the new puppy, try to talk to the reception nurse at a quiet time; she may then come out from behind the desk and make a fuss of the puppy. This will help to associate the first visit with a warm welcome, rather than a wait among strangers, a yank on to the table, a quick jab and goodbye, perhaps followed by a feeling of being slightly unwell from the vaccine for the rest of the day.

Do not put your puppy down on the surgery floor until the first vaccine has been given. If you have one of the very heavy breeds that you cannot carry, book an appointment at a time when the floors will have been recently disinfected, e.g. the first appointment in a session.

Night work: Take the puppy out in the dark, remembering that its eyesight and night vision is probably better than that of the handler. Some dogs can show unusual worries when first taken out after sunset. Many guard dogs will do most of their patrol work after dark.

This list is not complete but gives ideas of the conditions that are useful to the puppy for a wider experience of the adult world. A puppy is better able to face a new situation when its familiar handler is there than later in life when a dog may be on its own. Avoid the risk of a puppy being attacked by another loose-running dog, as this unprovoked hurt may have a permanent effect on that dog's relationships with other dogs throughout the rest of its life.

If a pup shows signs of worry at a situation, be sensible yourself. Words of reassurance given in a confident manner will help a lot. This can be a situation where small titbits are perfectly permissible for reward training. Food helps to overcome worry in many situations, so, with the minimum of fuss, you can offer flavoured tablets or squares of dried meat or offal. If you have used a lot of food, you can adjust the quantity of food given at the next scheduled feed. The food reward should be abolished as soon as the worry disappears, so the pup will not become dependent on a reward every time; but continue the verbal praise.

Some local dog clubs have puppy classes and they are well worth attending. Make sure your dog has had its first vaccine, and check if there is any kennel cough, parvo virus or gastro-enteritis infections in the locality before you mix with others of the same susceptible age-group. Many veterinary practices run puppy parties where a few hand-picked puppies, all known to have been adequately vaccinated, are brought together on a regular basis to help socialisation. Again, this gets the dog used to being handled in the surgery, an experience which occurs, on and off, for the rest of its life.

Finally, allow plenty of people to talk to your puppy, children in particular. Use common-sense to prevent the puppy being over-fussed. Do not hide a puppy away during these important first months. Remember, if you have chosen a puppy that is genetically sound and has good temperament, then give it the best start by socialising it properly. You will dramatically increase the chances of owning a dog that is reliable in all conditions and a pleasure to own.

WHEN TO CALL THE VETERINARY SURGEON

1. CALL IMMEDIATELY & ARRANGE TRANSPORT TO THE SURGERY

Bleeding
All severe bleeding from a major limb or neck artery or vein is an extreme emergency. Apply pressure to the site, as any way of reducing this sudden loss of blood may help to save the dog's life. Haemorrhagic gastro-enteritis with visible blood in the vomit and faeces, is another emergency situation.

Bloat
Sudden distension of the left side of the abdomen, accompanied by attempts to vomit and then difficulty in breathing are signs that the dog requires urgent veterinary attention.

Choking
Look for the tongue turning blue or purplish in any presumed choking situation. The dog will be distressed, extending its neck, pawing at its mouth and have noisy breathing.

Collapse
The dog may show signs of collapse for many reasons, not all of which are extreme urgencies. Again, look for any abnormal tongue colour: purplish or white. The character of the breathing is important to notice. The legs may be stiff, paddling frantically or limp.

Continual straining
Attempting to pass urine or to defecate (pass a motion) with little or no result. See also the whelping bitch (page 58) to decide when to ask for veterinary assistance.

Convulsions or 'fits'
Unless there are signs of poisoning or the dog appears to be choking, it is often better to wait for a fit to pass off before stimulating a dog by bringing it to the veterinary surgery. Fits due to poisons need urgent veterinary attention. Dogs with suspected Rabies should not be handled at all.

Ear problems

Any sudden response of head shaking, particularly if a dog has been out in a field with ripening grass, could mean a foreign body, such as a grass seed, in the ear. If the violent head shaking continues for over 30 minutes, notify the veterinary surgeon that you have a dog with a possible foreign body in the ear.

Eclampsia

A bitch feeding puppies that starts twitching or goes 'stiff' may require emergency treatment. (See also pages 68 and 163).

Eye problems

Damage to the eye may be as severe as a cut into the cornea with the iris protruding, or a prolapsed eyeball when the lids cannot close over the bulging eye. Less obvious internal injuries to the eye are equally damaging to sight, and so all eye conditions should be treated as potentially serious Eyelids partially closed, excessive tear streaming and haziness of the cornea are all signs to watch for.

Injury

Any deformity of a limb, skin laceration, severe continuous pain, a cut with bone or joint exposed, or a puncture wound affecting the chest or abdomen requires immediate veterinary attention.

Pain

The amount of pain a dog feels is difficult to assess. Some distressed dogs will cry out for what would seem minor injury, while larger breeds are more stoical or perhaps have a higher pain threshold, showing little vocal evidence of pain.

Paralysis

A displaced intervertebral disc may cause sudden loss in the use of the back legs. If a disc ruptures after a relatively minor jump or fall, then emergency treatment may be needed.

Poisoning

Accidental or deliberate poisoning will require veterinary attention. Any chemical, plant or other substance should be retained to help the veterinary surgeon identify the cause and, perhaps, use an antidote.

Shock

Fluid loss from the body as with severe diarrhoea, dysentry or other haemorrhage may turn into irreversible shock. Some internal diseases, such as acute pancreatitis, will cause severe shock and abdominal pain although there is little to see from the outside of the dog. The prevention of shock is important and veterinary attention should be given as soon as possible.

Staggering

Vestibular disease and the 'stroke' condition may cause a dog to stagger, pace round the room endlessly, walk with stiff or crossing-over legs and fall over when attempting to turn round.

NOTE: Triage is the name given to the sorting of cases in a surgery, depending on the seriousness of the injuries and an assessment of the clinical signs shown. This system is used in busy veterinary clinics when two or more urgent cases arrive at the same time, as in road accidents or other major traumas. The veterinary surgeon and nurses should be involved in a continuous process of monitoring breathing, blood losses and all the other signs that indicate that a patient may be suffering from a life-threatening condition.

2. CALL THE SURGERY TO BOOK THE NEXT AVAILABLE APPOINTMENT

Abscesses, infected wounds

Not urgent, but cause distress to the dog and may have to be treated with surgical drainage or antibiotics as appropriate. Anal sac disease is another example of bacterial infection.

Aural haematoma

A sudden swelling in the ear should not be left untreated too long.

Bladder obstruction

Although most dogs with bladder stones do not have a complete obstruction with the signs of straining, there may be instances of a total obstruction of the urethra and urgent attention is needed.

Constipation

Repeated straining with attempts to pass faeces can be distressing, and if simple remedies have not worked, the dog should be examined for the possible presence of a bony impaction or an enlarged prostate.

Coughing

Any repeated or deep harsh cough would require attention. The possibility of an infectious condition such as kennel cough or bronchitis should be considered. An appointment time, when there are no other dogs to infect, should be discussed with the receptionist at the surgery when booking the appointment.

Diarrhoea

If there is no response to withdrawal of food for 24 hours and the use of electrolyte replacement fluids to drink, veterinary attention should be requested. In the event of the condition clearing up in 48 hours, the appointment could always be cancelled.

Ear problems

Not all ear conditions are urgent, but any unusual discharge, constant head shaking and scratching with the hind legs so that the toes dig at the ear may quite urgent. Swelling, irritation or other problems should be attended to as soon as practical.

Fever

Unless the owner is able to use a clinical thermometer, it is difficult to measure how bad a dog is that has an infection that affects the body's temperature regulation. Some virus infections cause temperatures of 40.5 degrees Centigrade (104.6 degrees Fahrenheit), but any temperature over 39C (102.2F) requires attention.

Increased thirst

This is one of the most commonly reported symptoms at the surgery, and there should be some measure of how much and how often the dog is drinking to help the veterinary surgeon. A urine sample taken in with the dog helps to make for a quick check for diabetes and kidney disorders.

Injuries

Many wounds that are not bleeding but are liable to become infected should be seen within the first 24 hours. A small cut through the full thickness of skin that needs stitching, a puncture wound of the foot, or a broken toe-nail with some blood showing are other examples of non-urgent injuries.

Jaundice

Any yellow colour in the skin, the whites of the eyes, the gums or the ear flaps should be reported, and treatment given once the cause is found.

Lameness

Any swollen joint, painful area on the legs or stiffness on rising.

Not eating

A dog that refuses food but shows no other signs, such as vomiting or raised body temperature, may have something as severe as a foreign body in the intestine or it may be suffering from some behaviour change. Discretion is needed to interpret the dog's problem. Look for other signs, such as a dog that lies down a lot, laboured breathing, less frequent defecation and altered thirst and urine output.

Scratching and biting the skin

Pruritus may develop suddenly as when a flea jumps on to the dog, or there may be a slower response as when the atopic dog enters a dusty room or a new home.

Swellings

Any sudden hot painful or discharging swelling needs attention. Swellings in the mammary glands of bitches need looking at. All unexpected lumps or black-pigmented warts need inspection as well.

Vomiting

When this has happened after each meal has been fed, or sickness has been continuous through the day, an investigation is needed.

Worms

Segments of tapeworms on the tail, roundworms vomited or passed during an attack of diarrhoea need reporting. In the absence of other signs, it may be decided to administer a routine worm dose without having to see the dog at the surgery.

3. THINGS TO MENTION AT THE TIME OF THE ANNUAL BOOSTER OR ANY OTHER NON-URGENT CHECK-UP

• Any of the above items in the urgent list that did nor seem worth bothering the veterinary surgeon with when they happened.
• Anal sac distension or irritation.

- Any unexpected behaviour change to other dogs or persons.
- Bad breath.
- Breathlessness or rapid breathing after moderate exercise.
- Excessive moulting, bare skin patches.
- Eye disorders: opaqueness, itching or tear overflow.
- Flea control – newer methods?
- Increased thirst.
- Lameness that appears after rest or excessive exercise.
- Limping or paw holding in the air.
- Loss of weight.
- Lumps like lipomas that have been present for some time.
- Nails that are too long.
- Scratching, especially if at one time of the year or in a new situation.
- Smells that are not usual.
- Weight increase and reduced capacity to exercise, as measured by how far the dog walks each day.
- Worms presumed present.

SIMPLE FIRST AID MEASURES

It is worth remembering that the principles of 'first aid' for dogs are to preserve life, prevent pain and suffering, and generally to prevent the situation getting worse for the dog. In the absence of a veterinary surgeon any owner or bystander has the right to administer first aid to an injured dog, bearing these three principles in mind. There has to be a limit as to how far the first-aider should go with treatments and, in most cases, the dog should be transported to the surgery premises where skilled and technically supported treatments can be given.

CARING FOR DOGS INVOLVED IN ACCIDENTS

1. Try to assess the wound by looking at the injured areas, and looking at the whole dog. Some wounds will be so smeared with blood or road dirt that it may be impossible to see what part has been damaged. However, you can check the dog's breathing, the colour of its tongue and lips if the mouth is open, and also look at the dog's eyes. You are looking for signs of shock, extensive blood loss – internal as well as external – and for head and neck injuries. If the dog is moving about, a swinging leg may suggest a fracture or dislocation.
2. Ensure the dog can breathe freely. If it is unconscious pull the tongue forward. If present, loosen a tight collar/chain round the neck.
3. Stop any further blood loss by pressure on the wound. A pad of sterile gauze is best, but any reasonably clean material can be placed over or wound round an exposed wound.
4. Make contact with the veterinary surgeon. Be prepared to describe the wounds you can see, how long it is since the accident occurred and how long it will take to transport the injured dog to a place where further veterinary care is possible. If the accident is away from home, an accurate description of the location is essential, especially if an ambulance vehicle is being sent out to pick up a casualty – valuable time will be lost if the driver has to search for the dog.

WOUND DRESSINGS AND TREATMENT

Where the wounds are only small cuts on the skin surface, washing with sterile saline is preferable to using antiseptics. Antiseptics based on phenols should not be used at all on open wounds. Wound powders may clog up a clean but raw surface

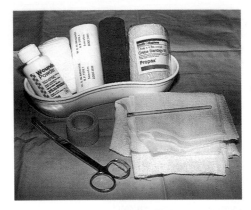

*First aid kit
required
for
treatment
of wounds.*

*First aid kit
required
for
preventing
blood loss.*

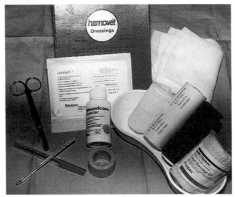

making it more difficult for the veterinary surgeon to inspect the wound later.

When dealing with larger wounds, often the first requirement is to stop excessive blood loss. The second is to inspect the wound to decide on the nature of the injury and how far to go as a first-aider. Simple lacerations may have tearing of the skin or flesh underneath, but there may be little contamination in the first six hours, so the dog can be brought to the surgery in this interval where it can then be prepared for cleaning up and stitching when appropriate.

Puncture wounds may appear small on the surface but can penetrate deeply and, in the case of bites from other dogs, may be more in the nature of laceration below the skin, as the muscle and fat becomes crushed by the chewing of the other dog's jaw action. Infection, any foreign matter in the wound, any tissue loss will all complicate the healing of such wounds.

Wounds with extensive skin loss are not uncommon after those road accidents where a dog is dragged along the road surface. These type of wounds are known as abrasions. A special type of skin loss on the leg is known as a 'degloving injury' where the whole skin is pulled down the leg and lost, leaving a raw bleeding area, anything from the size of one toe to a large area the length of the leg.

Burns of the skin are not common as dogs will avoid hot surfaces and live electric cables. If hot fat or boiling liquid is spilt on a dog in the kitchen, death of the skin and the underlying tissues may occur depending on how long a contact with the hot substance was made. Try cooling the wound with copious quantities of icy water as soon as the incident occurs, but then the first aid worker should take the dog to the veterinary surgery for pain relief, followed up by cleaning dead tissue with the aim of reconstructing any lost skin.

WOUND CARE

The first-aider should only attempt to clean up the wounds if the bleeding has stopped – you will worsen matters by removing clots of blood sealing a wound. A combination of cutting away the hair around a wound, and gentle stroking of the wound edges with a swab of cotton-wool, soaked in a mild antiseptic, will be the best approach. Do not go straight to the centre of the wound as this may be where major blood vessels or nerves are exposed and too vigorous a cleaning movement could make matters worse.

Look for exposed bone fragments, any holes in the chest that may be sucking air in as the dog breathes, or large bulges in the abdominal wall. All of these indicate trouble far beyond the skill of a first aid worker and they are best left alone until a veterinary surgeon can attend. The one exception is the air sucking wound in the chest wall. In this case, apply a pad of wet cotton-wool, a sheet of polythene from an opened food bag, then bandage over the chest wound to try to stop further air movement from the chest.

It is better not to attempt to apply splints for broken bones in a first aid situation. If necessary, pick the dog up for transport with the injured leg unsupported and let its weight stretch it downwards. The exception is any injury to the neck or spine, where vital nerve trunks may be damaged by unwise lifting. In this case, slide a plywood board or, for the smaller animal, a tea tray under the dog so as to be able to move the dog in as rigid a manner as is possible.

Grit from the road and hair from the body may be stuck on the wound surface. Occasionally foreign bodies can be seen projecting from the wound: a broken fragment of wood when a dog has run on to a stick thrown in play, grass seed awns between the toes, or sharp slivers of glass or metal may be seen on the pad surface. Most of these are best left in place until the veterinary surgeon can remove them. Often a general anaesthetic needs to be used to make sure that all of the foreign body is removed. After stick injuries to the throat, fragments may remain. It may be one or two years before the wood splinters work through to the skin surface of the neck, and swellings known as granulomas appear.

BANDAGING HINTS

Suitable bandages for first aid in dogs are stretch or 'cotton conforming' bandages, as these can be made to fit the awkward shapes of dogs' legs and bodies better than the semi-stiff open-wove bandages. Cotton crepe bandage 7.5 cm wide is also useful, or the semi-plastic Vetband can be used to shape over a tapering leg or tail. Do not apply cotton-wool direct to wounds as the cotton fluff may stick and become embedded. Gauze soaked in medical paraffin or the porous plastic wound dressings are safest to use directly on the wound.

When applying cotton crepe bandage try to overlap each turn by two thirds, bandage in a clockwise direction to cover above and then below the wound. Apply bandages with firm, even pressure. If they are too tight the leg will swell below it; if they are too loose the dog will remove it quite quickly. Adhesive tape strips can be used to support the bandage, and this will still allow air to get through the bandage and allow fluids to drain outwards. An over-tight plaster covering the whole wound may stop the dog pulling it off, but may result in a wet, sweaty wound if not changed daily. Safety pins are not approved to fix leg bandages, but there are times when they can be useful to fix

An ear bandage.

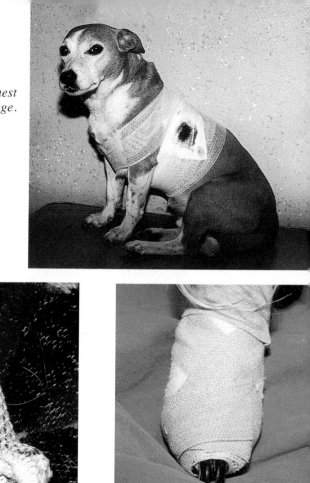

A chest bandage.

A tail bandage.

A foot bandage.

an encircling head bandage in place. Avoid tight bandages over bony prominences, such as those found on the dog's carpus (wrist joint). A dew claw bandaged tightly on to the fore leg may cause a painful wound unless padding is first placed between the toe and the skin.

POISONINGS

Fortunately, accidental poisonings are now less common – but sudden deaths do occur and a dog may not be known to have eaten a poisonous compound. Try to find out anything a dog could have got hold of. If rat bait has been put down, find out which of the three groups of poisons may have been used.

Some poisons have a specific antidote and this can be used if the poison has been identified, otherwise the treatment will have to be that for shock in general, as there is no such thing as a 'universal antidote'. It has been known for dogs to steal tablets prescribed for human use, left within their reach. Some anti-depressants, iron tablets and arthritis tablets can be very damaging to dogs, especially as they will tend to eat any sugar-coated tablets in large quantities.

A demulcent can be given by the first-aider at home in the treatment of irritant or some corrosive poisons. This is a substance that coats the mucous membranes and soothes. Mix a beaten raw egg with a tablespoon of cold milk and add a teaspoon of glucose or sugar. The egg proteins coagulate on raw surfaces and the sugar substance helps the shock. In some situations it is better to give nothing by mouth, especially if there is any difficulty in swallowing.

The use of an emetic or a substance to make the dog sick is very effective if the 'theft' of the tablets can be found within the first hour. A large crystal of washing soda (sodium carbonate) is the very best remedy to make the dog sick. When pushed down the throat, it will make most dogs empty their stomach contents within ten minutes, or often more quickly. Apomorphine or Xylazine can be injected to make a dog sick, and as washing soda is not often found in the home, the other household remedy to try when nothing else is available is two teaspoons of fresh mustard in a cup of warm water. Salt water seldom makes a dog sick and may make any dehydration much worse.

If a poisoned patient is semi-comatose it is quite easy to pass a stomach tube down the throat. Using a smaller tube passed down the inside of the bigger one, a gastric lavage can be carried out with a wash of warm water or of normal saline, followed by a charcoal suspension or Fuller's earth to absorb any poisons left inside the body.

COLLAPSE (SHOCK)

Syncope or 'fainting' is a poorly understood condition in the dog which may be due to the brain being suddenly deprived of blood. Both oxygen and glucose are needed in large quantities to keep the brain working. This sort of collapse is usually associated with heart or lung disease that leads to decreased blood-flow to the fore brain, but nervous and emotional factors may play a part as well.

Collapse may also be seen when a dog is out running and it drops down on the ground, or it may be the dog that has been lying in its bed at home and then fails to get up and walk. It is often difficult to find out why a dog has collapsed, and some dogs will be walking again by the time the veterinary surgeon sees the dog in the home or at the surgery. Shock is a term widely used, but it has a more definite meaning to the surgeon as a failure of the blood circulatory system that will usually require the use of intravenous fluids, and cortisone-type drugs may be injected.

The first aid treatment of a collapsed dog is to ensure that breathing can take place freely without obstruction. Gently massage the dog's side to stimulate it and talk to the dog in a reassuring voice. The dog should next have a full clinical examination, and blood tests etc. taken at the first opportunity, to find out any reason for the collapse.

HOW TO GIVE MEDICINES

The first-aider should give as little by mouth as possible, as the animal may need to have a general anaesthetic for wound repair, an X-ray or some other procedure.

The aftercare of the dog may require liquid or solid medicines to be given. Liquid medicines can be poured into the side of the mouth using the loose lower lip to make a groove. Many medicines supplied have a suitable-size plastic spoon. It may be easier to use a 5 or 10 ml syringe obtained from the veterinary surgery to suck up then squirt the liquid into the side of the mouth. Always keep the dog's nose raised up until the liquid is seen to be swallowed.

Tablets may be 'palatable' to mix in with the food, or some drugs in gelatine capsules can be scattered on the food once the

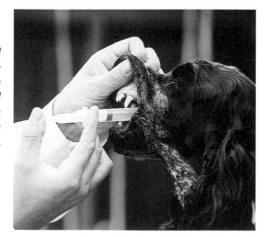

Liquid medicine can be administered using a plastic syringe.

capsule is part opened. If the dog is reluctant to take in medicated food, then a direct approach to tablet swallowing is necessary. Slightly open the dog's mouth by pressing the cheeks into the space between the premolar teeth. Insert the thumb on to the roof of the dog's mouth and, with the thumb pressing upwards, the dog is unable to bite but opens its mouth wider. Now drop the tablet centrally at the back of the tongue, still keeping the thumb on the hard palate, tilting the head upwards even more, when the dog will have to swallow the tablet.

Administering drugs by injection is a method often used by the veterinary surgeon as it is quick, efficient in giving a full dose, and usually painless. Injections can be given under the skin (subcutaneous), into the muscle (intramuscular) or into the vein (intravenous) or, rarely, intra-articular (into a joint space). The type of drug to be given and the disease to be treated will decide which method is used. Normally such injections will only be given by the veterinary surgeon or registered veterinary nurse. The one exception is the diabetic dog needing insulin at home at 24-hour intervals. The injection technique can be demonstrated in the veterinary surgery, and most dog owners can become proficient in measuring out the very small quantities of insulin needed and safely injecting their own dog.

SECTION II

SIGNS OF DISEASE AND HEALTH PROBLEMS

SOME of the leading signs of illness are listed here, and their significance in the early detection of disease is emphasised where possible. More information on associated signs and possible diagnosis is given in the last section: Treatment of Diseases and Health Problems.

ABDOMINAL PAIN

Pain is not always easy to detect: the dog may appear 'tense', move cautiously and will not wish to be disturbed. A dog will often seek as cool a surface as possible to lie on in an attempt to relieve the pain. Abdominal pain will often be accompanied by sickness, straining or diarrhoea. The size and contents of the abdomen can be a useful guide when diagnosing disease.

Possible causes: Bloat (see page 135), Colitis (see page 148), Cystitis (see page 153), Diarrhoea (see page 159), Gastro-enteritis (see page 177), Intussusception (see page 195), Pancreatitis (see page 226), Poisoning (see page 237), Pyometra (see page 243).

ABDOMINAL ENLARGEMENT

By far the commonest cause of abdominal enlargement is the accumulation of fat, but this must be distinguished from fluid accumulating in ascites (see page 128), also known as dropsy. Diagnosis of conditions in the abdomen may involve palpation, radiography, ultrasound, blood analysis, and analysis of the fluid from the abdomen. Palpation deep into the abdomen is a skilful procedure that is best left to the qualified veterinary surgeon.

Abdominal palpation may detect enlargement of organs, the presence of foreign bodies, abnormal masses e.g. a tumour of the spleen, or an intussusception. Gastric tympany produces a drum-like distension of the left side of the abdomen, which is readily diagnosed. A rigid abdominal wall, known as

Spleen tumour: A Beagle with haemangiosarcoma.

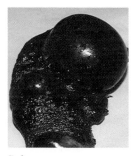

Spleen tumour removed after surgery.

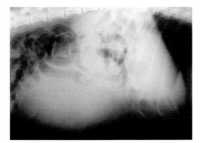

An X-ray of a tumour shows a spleenic mass.

'boarding', is a sign of abdominal pain – the abdominal wall muscles are tensed up as the dog tries to guard against further pain. This sign should always be seen as a warning of a major problem inside the cavity and veterinary examination should be sought urgently.

Possible causes: Ascites (see page 128), Cushing's disease (see page 152), Foreign bodies (see page 174), Malignant tumours – liver or spleen (see page 207).

BLOOD LOSS

This may be due to an external injury, and a haemorrhage can be fatal when a major artery or vein is severed. This may be seen after a dog has jumped at a glass door or window and landed on the broken glass edge, cutting the base of the neck or the armpits. This is the most extreme case, with death occurring in a matter of minutes, even though an attempt to compress and close the wound is made. Most blood losses are much slower and, although a lot of blood seems to have been spread around, the circulation of the dog is maintained in response to the haemorrhage and shock. Measures such as compresses and tight bandaging will help to slow down the blood flow and give the dog a better chance of recovery. In all except the minor cases, the dog should be kept warm and quiet and transported to the veterinary surgery where the haemorrhage can be stopped, the wounds repaired, and any shock treated with intravenous fluids and other measures, as necessary.

Bleeding may result from an ulcerating tumour.

Wound on the toe, with bleeding.

Greater skill is needed to detect internal blood losses. Bleeding from the nose, from the ears, from the mouth, from the anus or from the openings of the urinary tract at penis or vulva indicate specific problems which require investigation. Haemorrhagic gastroenteritis (HGE) is a severe illness, often of smaller dogs, where the blood in the vomit or faeces may be bright red (fresh) or dark (digested blood). Blood may be lost from other causes such as clotting defects (coagulpathies), dysentry, and bleeding tumours.

Possible causes: *Anaemia (see page 125), Colitis (see page 148), Cystitis (see page 153), Haematoma (see page 182), Haemophilia (see page 183), Malignant tumours (see page 207), Parvo virus (see page 230), Poisoning – Warfarin (see page 238), Penis injuries (see page 233), Pyometra (see page 243), Wounds (see page 278).*

BREATHING DIFFICULTIES

Rapid breathing or 'panting' has to be distinguished from shortness of breath. Dyspnoea is the term used by veterinary surgeons when an animal has any form of difficulty in getting sufficient air to the lungs. The colour of the tongue and mucous membranes will indicate if there is a serious shortage of oxygen reaching the body tissues. Any colour change from pink to pale mauve or deep purplish-black that can indicate a breathing problem may be the cause.

Possible causes: *Bronchitis (see page 137), Cardiac failure (see page 142), Collapse (see page 149), Heart disease (see page 184), Pneumonia (see page 236), Respiratory distress (see page 247), Shock (see page 254) Strokes (see page 258).*

CHOKING

Repeated coughing, as if something was stuck in the dog's throat, will, most frequently, be due to gagging and retching after a kennel cough infection. Choking and salivating may be due to a stick or bone wedged across the roof of the mouth betwen the molar teeth. Foreign bodies, such as lengths of cane or stick or wood, may be lodged in the back of the mouth – the object enters the throat but cannot be propelled futher down. Round objects, such as squash balls, pieces of bone or plastic toys, may become stuck in the throat, the stomach or the small intestine depending on the width of the object. Needles, pins, fish-hooks can become stuck in the tongue or the throat; sometimes string, plastic net or cloth may cause an obstruction. The wedged object which causes a dog to choke may be anything in size from an inch-length of stick to a tennis ball.

Dogs often chew and mouth toys, sticks and other foreign bodies. Chewing is probably at its worst between six weeks and six months of age as the teeth are erupting, and it is at this age dogs are most likely to swallow foreign bodies and either choke or have obstructions in the intestines. Some older dogs never give up this infantile habit of chewing; it may be continued as the result of boredom.

A complete obstruction of the throat is the most serious sign to look for: the dog cannot swallow, gulps repeatedly and will dehydrate quickly as saliva drools from the mouth and no fluid can be swallowed to replace the losses. Choking and gagging, breathing in deep gasps may all be signs of an obstruction or choke. Blueness of the tongue and mouth may be due to difficulty in breathing. A foreign body that is eventually swallowed may enter the stomach and if solid, may lie there for six weeks or more and perhaps cause little trouble except occasional vomiting. Less commonly swollen glands or abscesses in the neck may cause choking for the same reason.

Possible causes: *Fainting (see page 170), Fits (see page 172), Foreign bodies (see page 174), Kennel cough (see page 198), Megaoesophagus (see page 211), Pharyngitis (see page 235), Vestibular syndrome (see page 273).*

CONSTIPATION AND STRAINING

Unless the dog has consumed a large quantity of bone which passes through undigested, or the enlarged prostate is pressing into the rectum, constipation is fairly uncommon in the dog. Straining (see Tenesmus p262) may occur with a number of abdominal diseases. The obstruction of the urethra, with straining to empty the bladder, has been confused with the straining of constipation, especially when there has been no close supervision of a sick dog.

Possible causes: *Calculi (see page 139), Constipation (see page 150), Cystitis (see page 153), Foreign bodies (see page 174), Prostate disorders (see page 241), Tenesmus (see page 262).*

COUGHING

Acute (rapidly repeated) coughing may be a sign of airway

irritation as may be caused by smoke or dust inhalation. Any injury to the airway – as from pressure from a choke-chain, an injury after a fight, or a road accident – may similarly cause deep and distressing coughing; haemorrhage into the lungs will aggravate the cough further. A foreign body, such as an accidentally inhaled plant seed or ear of corn, will also produce this type of acute coughing, but it may be difficult for the dog to bring anything back up into the mouth. A further problem is that the dog tends to swallow whatever mucus etc. that is coughed back up into the mouth so no evidence is seen externally. Kennel cough or infectious tracheobronchitis is one of the most frequently seen causes of repeated and 'deep coughing'. An allergic pneumonia, or the inhalation of stomach contents during or after anaesthesia will cause a severe acute coughing response.

The more persistent low cough is known as a chronic cough. Heart disease and lung congestion are quite frequent causes of such a cough. Chronic bronchitis may be a cause of a cough – often in the older dog – as a result of exposure to irritants in the air such as prolonged exposure to smoke or fumes. The tracheal worm *Oslerus* is found rarely in Greyhounds and other infected dogs, will cause a chronic cough due to the nodules at the base of the airway. Any pressure on the airway such as a tumour or an enlarged heart will cause a continuous cough that is not relieved by a change in temperature or humidity.

Possible causes: Bronchitis (see page 137), Heart disease (see page 184), Kennel cough (see page 198), Lungworms (see page 205), Tracheitis (see page 268).

DIARRHOEA

'Looseness' or soft liquid faeces is a very common problem in the dog and has many different causes. The dog is by nature a scavenger, so it may be the quickest way that the dog can get rid of unsuitable things eaten such as decayed matter or the food poisoning types of toxins. The skilled dog owner will be able to distinguish between transient mild attacks that often commence with vomiting followed by 48 hours or so of watery or mucoid faeces, and those attacks of a more severe kind. Persistent attacks of frequent diarrhoea can result in excessive fluid loss and shock (see page 254). If diarrhoea persists for more than 24 hours, the veterinary surgeon should be consulted if one of the life-threatening conditions associated with diarrhoea is present. Dysentry – when blood is present in the faeces – may be either fresh blood from the large intestine or dark, digested blood from the stomach or small intestine. This is another sign of more serious disease.

Possible causes: Campylobacter *(see page 140), Diarrhoea (see page 159), Dysentry (see page 162), Exocrine pancreatic insufficiency (EPI) (see page 168), Gastro-enteritis (see page 177), Giardia (see page 178), Malabsorption (see page 207), Parvo virus (see page 230), Salmonella infection (see page 251).*

EAR PROBLEMS
Any sudden irritation of the ear may be due to a foreign body, such as a grass seed, in the ear canal. There will be a very rapidly developing intense irritation, with frantic head shaking and attempts to rub the face along the ground. Ear infections are usually slower to cause irritation and will be accompanied by discharge and an unusual smell from inside the ear. Swelling of the ear flap is often due to an aural haematoma (see page 130). It is considered that irritation of the ear flap and the visible part of the ear canal may follow an allergic reaction (see atopy page 129). If the inflammation with wax and discharge that is coming from the deeper or horizontal part of the ear canal is from an infection, it may be associated with a perforated ear drum and otitis media.

Possible causes: Atopy (see page 129), Aural haematoma (see page 130), Foreign bodies (see page 174), Sarcoptic mange (see page 252), Otitis externa (see page 222), Otitis media (see page 224).

Otitis showing dry crusts.

EYE PROBLEMS
Various signs of eye problem may be seen, and it is important to distinguish those that are likely to lead to serious disease or even the loss of sight.

1. The red eye is when the white of the eye is harsh red, or sometimes the conjunctiva may droop and expose a bright-red colour unlike the paler pink colour of a healthy eye.

Possible causes: Glaucoma (see page 180), Conjunctivitis (see page 149), Ectropion (see page 163), Scleritis (see page 253), Uveitis (see page 272).

Glaucoma seen in the right eye.

An allergic reaction shown by difficulty in opening the eyes.

2. The itchy eye is one where the dog paws repeatedly at its face and may rub its face on the floor or grass to relieve the irritation.

Possible causes: Conjunctivitis (see page 149) is the most common reason, but insect stings, Allergies (see page 123), Foreign bodies (see page 174) and dermatosis – periocular (see page 157) are possible causes. Both types of mange: Sarcoptic (see page 252) and Demodectic (see page 156), and Auto immune disease (see page 131) will also cause skin irritation near the eyelids.

3. The painful eye, where the dog screws up its eyelids and cannot bear to have bright light shone on the eye.

Possible causes: Glaucoma (see page 180) or a Keratitis (see page 199), perhaps with a deep ulcer, Uveitis (see page 272). Orbital pain may also occur with a tooth root abscess, an orbital abscess or a bone fracture.

4. The bulging eye.

Possible causes: Prolapse of the whole eyeball (see page 240), or more likely to be seen are Glaucoma (see page 180) or undue prominence of the eye as with Thyroid disease (see page 264) and other disorders.

Corneal opacity, possibly the first sign of an eyelid tumour.

Prominent eye (left) in an eight-year-old black Labrador. The third eyelid is prominent and there is a tear overflow in the cornea, caused by a tumour of the optic nerve.

Entropion with discharge from the eyes.

5. The watery eye, often with a wet face or a tear-stained streak down the face.
Possible causes: Distichiasis (see page 161), Entropion (see page 167), blockage of the lacrimal duct, any painful corneal disorder, ectopic hairs in the lids or inhalent allergic dermatitis – Atopy (see page 129).
6. The prominent third eyelid is seen as a white film in the cornea of the eye nearest the nose. Sometimes it will bulge from the lymph gland underneath the eye being swollen, when it is known as cherry eye.
Possible causes: Allergies (see page 123), Chemosis (see page 145), Cherry eye (see page 146), any loss of fat behind the eye, or ocular pain in the eye.

FAINTING AND FITS
If a dog collapses, it may lie down appearing weak in its limbs, or there may be jaw chattering, salivation, convulsive movements of the legs and great distress to dog and owner. If the blood supply to the brain is temporarily lost – and the faint

is less than five seconds – the dog may simply stagger or 'flop' with relaxed limbs. However, if the lack of oxygen continues longer, there may be brief convulsive movements and urinary incontinence. Convulsions due to epilepsy are often quite violent and once seen will be easily recognised. The bitch with eclampsia will have prolonged tremors and a glazed look in its eye.

Possible causes: Eclampsia (see page 163), Epilepsy (see page 167), Fainting (see page 170), Fits (see page 172), Some forms of poisoning will cause similar attacks that may be fatal if untreated (see Poisoning page 237).

FEEDING PROBLEMS

Changes of food intake, either more or less, may be the first sign of disease and should be reported. Loss of appetite is common in most infections where the body temperature is raised, but may also be seen with many other diseases, particularly those involving the gastrointestinal system. If intestinal obstruction is present the dog may refuse all food but still drink without necessarily vomiting. A sudden increase in appetite may be due to lowered blood glucose, as in cold weather, but it can occur in diseases such as Cushing's disease, diabetes and malabsorption and Exocrine Pancreatic Insufficiency (EPI). Investigation by the veterinary surgeon will often involve blood tests, after which a change in diet may be advised.

There are some dogs that are 'shy feeders' and such dogs may have behaviour problems from their early development. Puppies develop from a complete dependency on their mother's milk to solid feeding at the time of weaning. Most activities of sucking and eating are done in competition with other puppies in the litter. Feeding provides an opportunity for a close relationship with the mother, and there is reciprocal interaction with the bitch cleaning the puppies and responding to their cries and the puppies rooting for milk from the teats. Later in development, the puppy in a new home will become a single feeder and the human becomes the new provider of food, responding to the puppy's demands. Psychogenic vomiting can occur in the puppy of five months or older when it shows spontaneous involuntary vomiting of food, often as late as three hours after a meal. Feeding disorders later in life may also develop through too great a dependency on one adult, and food is repeatedly refused until a new flavour or consistency of food is produced. Over-frequent feeding 'treats' or offering snacks at repeated intervals may also lead to problems when a main meal is placed in front of the dog.

Possible causes: Cushing's disease (see page 152), Diabetes (see page 158), Exocrine Pancreatic Insufficiency (EPI) (see page 168), Malabsorption (see page 207), an advanced Nephritis (see page 216), Pharyngitis (see page 235), a variety of behavioural problems.

FLATULENCE AND BOWEL STASIS

Constipation may be a sign of an inadequate fluid intake or an inappropriate diet. Many dogs cannot produce enough gastric acid to dissolve bones that have been eaten in anything but small quantity, and for this reason feeding bones is discouraged in many situations. Any change of diet, intestinal disorder or obstructing foreign body may lead to delayed passage of intestinal contents, and this stasis is often associated with excess gas production.

Flatulence (Gas) is more of an annoying problem for the owner of the dog that lives indoors than a disorder of the dog itself. The unpleasant smell from the anus may be due to air that was gulped down by the greedy dog that swallows its food too rapidly. Some vegetable protein diets cause excessive fermentation of gas in the intestine, spicy foods, and eggs have all been blamed for strong smelling gas emissions. A deficiency of digestive enzymes may also be a cause of undigested residues entering the large intestine to ferment (see Malbsorption p207). Coprophagia, where the dog eats its own or other animals' faeces, may also cause digestive disturbances and gassy intestines.

Possible causes: Flatulence (see page 173), Malabsorption (see page 207), Coprophagia (see page 150).

HAIR LOSS

Excessive moulting and shedding the hair may follow after any major illness or, more often from inappropriate housing with temperatures that do not stimulate a 'natural' moult twice a year. Hair loss may occur at various sites on the body. The bitch feeding puppies will lose hair from the abdomen around the mammary glands before the puppies are born, and later on in the lactation period she may lose hair from the flanks as well. Hair loss in symmetrical patches usually indicates one of the hormone disorders. Pituitary gland failure and dwarfism, hypothyroidism, Cushing's syndrome, testicular abnormality, ovarian imbalance with hypo-oestrogenism are all such examples that may need to be investigated.

Injuries as from burns and scalds where the hair follicles have been destroyed will cause permanent hairlessness. Demodectic mange and some bacterial skin diseases will also cause

A Yorkshire Terrier suffering from Cushing's disease.

permanent bald areas. There are some hereditary alopecias that have a characteristic loss of hair. The Dachshund may have a flank baldness; it is seen in other shorthaired breeds and may be genetic. The colour mutant alopecia, seen especially in blue Dobermanns as well as other breeds, has an hereditary basis.
Possible causes: Alopecia (see page 124), Bacterial skin diseases (see page 132), Burns and scalds (see page 138), Cushing's disease (see page 152), Demodectic mange (see page 156), Hormonal alopecia (see page 190).

HEATSTROKE
Distress and a rise in the dog's temperature, flushed mucous membranes and weakness then collapse are known as heat stroke. It is usually caused by over-exposure to the sun, followed by an inability to keep the body cool by panting, resulting in an increase in body temperature. Dogs left in poorly ventilated cars are at greatest risk, but a dog left in a concrete yard with neither shade nor water can easily become hyperthermic. Affected dogs show severe distress and will die if treatment is delayed.
Hyperthermia see page 192

LAMENESS
A dog that does not put its full weight on its leg as it walks or runs will be described as 'lame'. There are many degrees of lameness, from the slight stiffness seen as an older dog rises to its feet that vanishes once the dog walks a few paces, to the

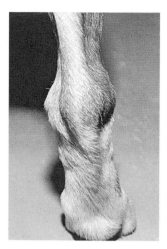 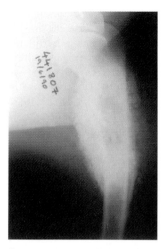

A swollen hock will result in lameness.　　*Osteosarcoma: X-ray of a dog's leg bone.*

very severe pain of a fractured leg or an acute arthritic joint. Some lameness may originate in the spine rather than in the legs themselves, and a thorough veterinary examination is needed to assess the degree of pain and find a cause. It is important to know how and when a lameness developed, and whether the dog is most lame after a long rest period, or whether it is lameness that develops on exercise, often becoming worse as the dog tires after a long walk on a hard road surface. A dog will often 'favour' a leg after minor injury and this is a key to the importance of rest in the treatment of lameness.

There are specific treatments for joint and bone inflammation. Usually an X-ray picture will be required before the veterinary surgeon will confirm the presence of the disorder and then give the appropriate surgical or medical treatment. In

A foot infection causing soreness and bleeding.

some conditions, complete 'kennel rest' is required. In others, restricted exercise on the lead for specified time is advised. Rest may mean controlled exercise to keep joints mobile without producing any extreme joint movement as will happen when free exercise is permitted.

Possible causes: There are many specific causes of lameness: Arthritis (see page 127), Barlow's disease (see page 133), Cruciate ligament injury (see page 151), Hip Dysplasia (see page 187), Intervertebral disc disease (see page 194) Juvenile bone disease (see page 197), Malignant tumours (see page 207), Nail disorders (see page 216), Osteo-arthritis (see page 220), Osteochondrosis (see page 221), Panosteitis (see page 227), Rheumatoid arthritis (see page 248), Spondylosis (see page 257).

LUMPS AND SWELLINGS

Swelling can be seen or felt under the skin – they will be more easily noticed in the thin coated breeds than in the dogs that are long coated. Swellings may be hot and painful such as those from abscesses or foreign bodies). Lumps may be soft and

Tumour: An immunocytoma of the upper lip.

easily moveable under the skin such as lipomas or thick and attached to the underlying body part. All such growths are potentially dangerous and should be brought to the attention of a veterinary surgeon as soon as they are discovered. A haematoma may cause a sudden swelling of the ear, but a haematoma can occur in a muscle mass or in a joint.

Possible causes: Abscess (see page 121), Foreign bodies (see page 174), Haematoma (see page 182), Lipoma (see page 204), Malignant tumours (see page 207), Poisoning – Warfarin (see page 238).

NASAL DISCHARGES

A slight watery discharge from the nostrils is normal, but an

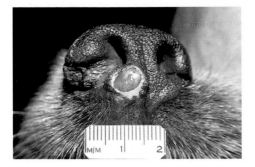

Carcinoma tumour on the nose of a Cocker Spaniel before irradiation treatment.

increase in the amount of discharge, and the discharge crusts on the nostril, may be an early sign that disease is developing within the nose. If the fluid becomes thick, cream or green-coloured, this can indicate an infection of the nasal cavity. Infections can be caused by viruses, bacteria or fungi, and it may be secondary to a tumour or a foreign body in the nose. Fungal infections and foreign bodies often cause a blood discharge or bleeding from the nose. The discharge may be from one or both nostrils, and can be difficult to detect if the dog licks its nose frequently. Dogs with nasal discharge may have difficult, noisy breathing and often sneeze and snort. They may also gag and cough if the discharge is draining down the throat. Veterinary attention to the cause of a discharge is necessary; this may include examination of the nasal cavities, often with a general anaesthetic using an endoscope. Samples may be required for laboratory examination before a definite diagnosis is possible.

Treatment following aspergillosis – an infection of the nasal sinuses.

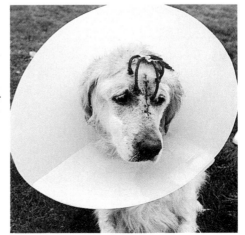

Possible causes: Foreign bodies (see page 174), Malignant tumours (see page 207), Rhinitis (see page 248), Sinusitis (see page 254).

NERVOUS SYSTEM DISORDERS

It is very difficult to detect some nerve and brain disorders until the condition has become quite advanced, and often irreversible changes have taken place. Any unexpected change in behaviour, appetite or loss of vision may indicate some disturbance in the brain. Nerve paralysis often results from injuries, and may affect the motor neurones that control the muscles and/or the sensory neurones that perceive pain etc. Prolonged unconsciousness may be seen as coma and it is difficult to get a dog to respond, although sometimes the dog will still swallow food. Epilepsy and other toxic conditions affecting the brain cause signs of convulsions. Loss of balance and staggering may be due to the Vestibular syndrome.The dragging of the back legs may be due to a Intervertcbral disc disease (see page 194), Spondylosis (see page 257), or the progressive and, at present, incurable condition of Chronic Degenerative Radiculomyelopathy CDRM (see page 147).

Behavioural problems such as depression, a condition not well documented in veterinary practice, is known to occur in dogs – sometimes after the death of a person or animal to which the patient was closely 'bonded'. A depressed pet is unusually quiet, has little appetite and a lack of interest in events that previously would have aroused the animal's attention. Hyperactive dogs are those that have boundless energy, but are

Toe dragging associated with chronic degenerative radiculomyelopathy (CDRM).

physiologically normal. Signs such as constant and restless motion, poor learning, lack of attention, a tendency to easy distraction and sometimes aggression may be seen in dogs with hyperactivity. Veterinary examination of the hyperactive dog is advised to investigate the presence of an underlying disease. Blood analysis to include the test for an overactive thyroid gland, and then possibly a challenge with a low dose of a stimulant such as dextro-amphetamine may be advised to diagnose a hyperactive dog.

Possible causes: Chronic degenerative radiculomyelopathy CDRM (see page 147), Epilepsy (see page 167), Horner's syndrome (see page 191), Hyperactivity (see page 191), Intervertebral disc disease (see page 194), Nerve injuries (see page 217), Malignant tumours (see page 207), Spondylosis (see page 257), Vestibular syndrome (see page 273).

ODOURS AND UNUSUAL SMELLS

Most unusual smells are attributed to skin secretions, to breath odours and to discharges from the other natural orifices: the ear, rectum or vagina. The condition of the skin is responsible for some of the dog odours. Sarcoptic mange does not have the characteristic odour that is associated with Demodectic mange which will fill a closed room with a smell of the 'mange'.

The mouth may have an impossibly offensive odour from foetid labial eczema characteristic of the Spaniel, where the smell comes from the lower lip fold. Many gum and dental disorders can produce an equally strong or unpleasant breath odour. Even when the teeth and gums appear to be healthy an offensive breath may be present: this is often attributed to tonsil infection or more infrequently to liver disorders. The odour of the breath with kidney failure is quite characteristic as a 'uraemic' breath odour. A slightly sweaty odour to the breath may be detected in untreated diabetic dogs. Another area to investigate are the ears, as they may be responsible for other smells coming from the head region; ear canals should always be inspected for discharges that may then stick to the hair on the face.

Anal sacs can over-secrete and sometimes the substance leaks out on to the hair around the tail and over the back legs. Usually the source of the obnoxious gland secretions will be revealed when pressure is applied to the anal sacs. As a scent gland, the greasy material clings to carpets and bedding and will persist long after the dog's own sacs have been expressed to remove their contents. Flatulence causes a readily recognised smell – this will vary with the type of food in the intestinal tract.

Possible causes: Anal sacs disease (see page 126), Demodectic mange (see page 156), Diabetes (see page 158), Eczema (see page 164).

PALE GUMS AND CONJUNCTIVA

Any paleness may be due to a change of blood supply from the extremities to the more central or core organs of the body. Some stressed dogs will show a colour change due to sympathetic nervous system control. Traditionally, paleness is a sign of anaemia: the anaemic dog would be weak and lethargic and have a poor appetite. Blood-sucking parasites will cause anaemia. Anaemia is not a disease but a sign of something else destroying blood cells or stopping them forming, and it is important to find the cause. Usually a blood sample will need to be taken and this may be followed by a bone marrow biopsy or other tests. Faeces samples should also be examined at the time of an investigation.

Possible causes: Anaemia (see page 125), Lice (see page 203), Ticks (see page 265).

PARASITIC DISEASES

1. External Skin changes with parasitic infestations may vary from a mild irritation and no noticeable change in the skin surface as with *Cheyletiella* (p146) to a severe thickening and oozing of red skin with a generalised demodectic mange infection and a secondary pyoderma. Most parasites such as fleas, lice, harvest mites, etc., cause an intense skin irritation as soon as the parasite attacks the skin. The exception is the UK common tick, which attaches itself to the dog as a tiny 'seed tick', engorges itself with blood until it is bloated to the size of 1cm before dropping off the dog's body ready to deposit eggs. Throughout this time the tick seems to cause minimal irritation and, apart from any infection it can introduce into the dog while attached, the most severe effect seems to be the hard nodule left in the skin after the tick has dropped off. A parasite

Demodex patch under the eye.

in the 'wrong place' may also cause the dog more severe problems: the cat's *Otodectes* that transfers to the dog's ear may cause a sudden otitis externa, while the migrating hookworm larva *Uncinaria* may cause a dermatitis of the legs if it is unable to migrate to the dog's intestines.

2. Internal Worms are considered to cause poor coat condition, diarrhoea, increased appetite, and sometimes coughing if they have to migrate through the lungs. In the British Isles there are no life-threatening internal parasitic infections, although some such as *Giardia* can cause severe diarrhoea in the dog, but the greatest fear is if there is a zoonotic transfer of an infection to the human handler. Severe roundworm infections causing diarrhoea and poor condition can cause death by an intestinal obstruction. The common tapeworm infections may cause increased appetite, unthriftiness and diarrhoea but the *Echinococcus* tapeworm is the most important from the zoonotic risk again.

See also: Cheyletiellosis (see page 146), Fleas (see page 173), Giardia (see page 178), Hookworms (see page 189), Lice (see page 203), Lungworms (see page 205), Mange (see page 210), Mites (see page 213), Ringworm (see page 248), Roundworm (see page 249), Tapeworms (see page 261), Whipworm (see page 277), Yeasts (see page 279).

SCRATCHING

Itching (pruritus) is one of the most common manifestations of skin disease and, in many cases, it is the signpost to some allergic reaction in the skin. The presence and the amount of scratching is one of the most important signs when first examining a dog with a skin disorder. Possible causes to consider are allergic responses to the presence of parasites especially fleas, lice, and sarcoptic mites. *Malasezzia* yeast infection of the outer skin causes scurfiness and scratching. Harvest mites *Trombicula* (Chiggers in North America) cause scratching and biting at the legs. *Cheyletiella* mites cause some irritation and scratching but most of all will cause the owner or person handling the dog to scratch or itch.

Atopy is a very common cause of scratching in some breeds. Bacterial folliculitis may be a secondary infection of the atopic dog and often causes the dog to scratch even more. Infection and hypersecretion in the external ear will cause scratching at the head and neck. The anal sacs also will sometimes cause an acute moist dermatitis from self-trauma of the hindquarters, but here the teeth are used, rather than scratching with the back legs. Adverse drug reactions often after an injection may cause a dog to scratch at the site or develop a general skin itchiness.

Possible causes: Atopy (see page 129), Allergies (see page 123), Bacterial skin diseases (see page 132), Fleas (see page 173), Lice (see page 203), Mange (see page 210).

SKIN CONDITIONS

Problems of the skin may be the most frequent reason for veterinary consultation, but the signs of skin disease are very varied and often two very dissimilar diseases mimic each other's symptoms. Scratching is probably the commonest complaint, but hair loss and excessive coat shedding leading to bare patches are almost as frequent a reason for consultation. Some skin problems can lead to the dog having a bleeding wound such as from mast cell tumours or from anal furunculosis.

Close examination of the skin under a bright light should be undertaken to look for skin parasites. Parting of the hair and the inspection of the skin of the abdomen, between the toes, the armpits and under the chin is necessary, as these areas are not always inspected for skin abnormalities. Broken hairs may suggest a dog is biting at itself or, possibly, ringworm will cause bare patches with hairs broken off near their base. Any loss of hair, scaliness of the skin or unusual pigmentation may be a sign of skin disease. Hair loss on either side of the body as symmetrical patches may indicate a hormonal cause for the skin disease. Short-haired dogs are more likely to suffer from infection of the hair follicles where yellowish crusts of dried

Atopy seen in a Golden Retriever.

serum accumulate on the skin surface. The condition of atopy is more frequent in some breeds than others (see page 129).

Possible causes: Allergies (see page 123), Atopy (see page 129), Fleas (see page 173), Eczema (see page 164), Furunculosis (see page 176), Hormonal alopecia (see page 190), Malignant tumours (see page 207), Mites (see page 213), Mange (see page 210), Staphylococcus infection (see page

Spotted nose and loss of pigmentation which can be associated with vitiligo.

258), Vitiligo (see page 274), Zinc (see page 280).

STIFFNESS

The most common cause of stiffness when the dog moves is osteoarthritis. Other diseases such as the autoimmune disorder systemic lupus erthematosis (SLE) may be seen as stiffness accompanied by loss of appetite and tiredness. Rheumatoid arthritis is another autoimmune disease with similar signs that include a reluctance of the dog to move. Any feverish condition such as tonsillitis or hepatitis may be seen in the dog as stiffness, lameness and rapid breathing. Many conditions of the dog where there is abdominal pain may make the dog look as if it is stiff, since the back is slightly arched and the dog is reluctant to move for fear of increasing the pain in the abdomen. Sometimes a pain in the neck region or the chest may first be mistaken for general stiffness, but the dog will move when encouraged to walk, and it can be seen that the stiffness is in one part of the dog, not all over the body. Tetanus is, fortunately, very rare as a dog disease, but it would be recognised by a stiff-legged walk and an inability to prize open the jaws due to muscle spasms.

Possible causes: Abdominal pain (see page 96), Arthritis (see page 127), Auto immune disease (see page 131), Hepatitis (see page 185), Rheumatoid arthritis (see page 248), Tonsillitis (see page 266).

SWOLLEN LYMPH GLANDS (LYMPH NODES)

The filtering 'glands' of the lymphatic system are situated at various places in the body, and those just below the skin are only recognised when they become enlarged or swollen. This swelling can be an important sign of a disease. At the same time, the tonsils at the back of the throat may be swollen, causing difficulty in swallowing, and the internal lymph glands of the chest and abdomen may cause other disturbances due to pressure on nearby internal organs. The most common cause of enlargement is a response to infection: streptococcus, mycobacterium, actinomyces, nocardia. Fungal infections due to aspergillus, parasite infections with demodex or toxoplasma are less likely reasons for glands to be found enlarged. Immune-mediated conditions, such as rheumatoid arthritis and systemic lupus erythematosis (SLE), are other conditions affecting lymph nodes. The most serious problem is when there is a neoplastic enlargement of one or many lymph glands. The degree of cancer present may vary from the lymphoma to others such as lymphosarcoma, malignant histiocytosis, leukaemia, multiple myeloma and systemic mast cell disease.
Possible causes: Auto immune disease (see page 131), Leukaemia (see page 202), Malignant tumours (see page 207).

TOOTH DISEASE

Some puppies have misshapen teeth, or sometimes temporary teeth may be retained in the mouth long after the permanent teeth have erupted. Apart from the mild disfigurement that affects the dog's showing career, these dental problems rarely cause disease. Periodontal disease is very common in older dogs, affecting the gums at their junction with the teeth. At first, the exposure of tooth roots will not cause obvious pain – but it will lead to loosening of the teeth and eventually to teeth

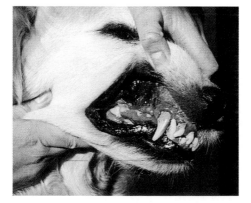

Gingivitis and receeding gums, with a heavy build-up of tartar.

dropping out. Calcium salts forming a deposit from the saliva on the teeth is known as dental calculus or plaque. A build-up of the calculus will cause constant gum pressure and hasten the periodontal disease process. Food often becomes trapped between the ledge of calculus on the tooth and the gum margin below. The teeth should be inspected for any reddening of the junction between the gum and the tooth, and for brown spots in the molar back teeth which may indicate caries. The smell of the breath will often be the first guide to some unhealthy process taking place inside the mouth. A full veterinary inspection is then called for.

Possible causes: Gingivitis (see page 179), Periodontal disease (see page 234).

TEMPERATURE

The dog's normal temperature is between 100.9 to 101.7 degrees Fahrenheit (38.3 and 38.7 Centigrade). Dog owners should know how to measure the temperature with a rectal thermometer and also how to take the dog's pulse from the artery inside the thigh. Pulse rates will be found to increase or decrease with temperature changes. An increased temperature is known as fever or pyrexia (see page 244). A raised temperature can be a good sign, as it shows that the dog has a good resistance and may be fighting an infection. Such a febrile response means that many bacteria and viruses will be unable to multiply in a body where the temperature is higher than normal. Dogs with heat-stroke may have temperatures well above 106 F (41.1 degrees C) and with a dangerously high temperature, they will need total body cooling as an urgent measure.

A low or subnormal temperature is also a worrying sign and can be the result of severe illness or toxaemia affecting the metabolism of the whole body. Inadequate food intake after an illness may also reduce the dog's temperature, especially if it is taken during the recovery period. Keeping the dog in a warm area and offering foods or fluids containing nutrients may help in the nursing care. In the pregnant bitch, a drop in the temperature is used as a sign of closeness to birth. (See *The Birth of Puppies and Aftercare*, page 58).

VAGINAL DISCHARGE

Any discharge that appears, other than when the bitch is on heat, can be considered a sign of disease. A discharge that is usually creamy or yellowish in colour indicates a vaginitis. The discharge that is coloured brown and liquid indicates an endometritis; a thick, more tarry, black discharge indicates a dead puppy, or if the discharge is the more greenish-black, it could be a pyometra.

Possible causes: Endometritis (see page 166), Pyometra (see page 243), Vaginitis (see page 273).

VOMITING

Vomiting is a reflex action triggered by nerve impulses causing the expulsion of the stomach contents. This may take the form of repeated sickness of mucoid fluid after a dog has been out to eat roughages such as grass. Sickness may be more severe, such as the repeated vomiting as in kidney failure or abdominal cancer, where little food is eaten but the dog tries to be sick repeatedly through the day. Vomiting may occur just before or soon after diarrhoea, and this needs reporting to the veterinary surgeon. Repeated vomiting will need investigation involving blood tests, X-rays and endoscope examination. Blood in the vomit should always be reported – but it is not always as serious as it would first seem – especially if it only occurs the once, as healing takes place quickly. Short-term vomiting can occur after stomach overload, and the dog seems unperturbed by vomiting in this way and will sometimes even attempt to eat some of the same food again.

Possible causes: Foreign bodies (see page 174), Gastro-enteritis (see page 177), Malignant tumours (see page 207), Parvo virus (see page 230).

Vomiting caused by the presence of foreign bodies.

WEIGHT LOSS

Any unplanned weight loss should be reported to the veterinary surgeon, as it may be one of the earliest signs of a major disease. Some diseases cause a reduced food or water intake and this shows as weight loss. Dogs entering kennels or puppies leaving home for the first time may show a temporary loss of weight (See *Feeding Grooming and Exercising*, page 31).

Conditions affecting the intestines such as EPI and malabsorption syndromes, cause weight loss from inadequate nutritional intake; these are fairly rare and found in certain breeds. Malignant tumours cause loss of weight, but only in the later stages is the appetite lost. Investigation at an early stage will help to avoid an untreatable tumour being found to be the cause of the dog's thinness. Kidney disease is probably the second most common cause of weight loss. The damaged kidney leaking out protein forces the body to draw on reserves of muscle protein to keep up the necessary levels of albumin and globulins in the circulating blood. The toxins that accumulate in kidney failure also will reduce appetite and may cause vomiting with further weight loss.

Possible causes: Exocrine pancreatic insufficiency EPI (see page 168), Malabsorption (see page 207), Malignant tumours (see page 207).

YELLOW GUMS AND CONJUNCTIVA

Staining of the visible membranes with the pigment bilirubin does not always indicate liver disease, as the pigment is the result of the breakdown of haemoglobin, a normal blood pigment. Jaundice, the name given to the yellow coloration, most often will come from the liver, but sometimes the type known as 'prehepatic jaundice' is the sign of excessive breakdown in the blood cells. Incompatible blood transfusions may cause a transfusion reaction with haemolysis of the blood cells, but this will not happen the first time blood is given. Destruction of red blood cells may occur in autoimmune disease, in leptospirosis, sometimes in renal failure, or in febrile diseases.

Jaundice from the liver cell damage may occur with viral hepatitis, leptospirosis, liver tumours and in cirrhosis (scarring) of the liver. Many poisons cause liver damage – the yellow colour develops several days after poisonous substances have been taken. Tumours pressing on the bile ducts may cause another sort of jaundice; an obstruction of the bile ducts can occur with pancreatitis, and with tumours of the duodenum, the bile duct or the pancreas. Gallstones and bile duct internal blockages are very rare in dogs.

Possible causes: Cirrhosis (see page 148), Icterus (see page 193), Jaundice (see page 196), Leptospirosis (see page 202), Malignant tumours (see page 207) Pancreatitis (see page 226), Poisoning (see page 237).

SECTION III

TREATMENT OF DISEASES AND HEALTH PROBLEMS A–Z

ABSCESS

A swelling containing pus which may cause an illness with raised body temperature.

SIGNS
Abscesses in internal organs such as the liver are uncommon in dogs and most abscess swellings will be seen in or just below the dog's skin.

CAUSE
A special form of abscess is produced by penetrating foreign bodies. Grass seeds migrating through the skin between the toes are commonly seen in the summer.

TREATMENT
The use of antibiotics and sometimes surgical drainage.

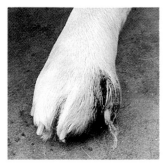

A foot abscess with swelling.

ADDISON'S DISEASE

A disorder due to an underproduction of hormones by the adrenal cortex.

SIGNS
The usual signs are of vague ill health with weakness, lethargy, gastro-intestinal upsets and weight loss. A blood test may show an increase in the eosinophil cells and potassium level.

CAUSE
This is a rare condition of under-activity of the adrenal cortex known as hypoadrenocorticism.

TREATMENT
Treatment with replacement doses of the two adrenal cortex hormones in tablet form can be successful.

Addison's disease (Bedlington Terriers). The normal dog is pictured left.

AGEING DOGS

See Geriatric dogs page 178

AGGRESSION

This is essentially a behaviour problem where the dog reacts to a presumed threat by making an unwanted attack and biting.

SIGNS
Any unprovoked attack on humans or other dogs may be interpreted as aggression. Exposure of the teeth and flattening the ears down may be accompanied by other body and tail carriage signals before an attack is made. Rewarding, as used in the training of guard dogs, will reinforce these aggressive tendencies, while the sudden withdrawal of the praise or a treat may then produce another form of aggression through frustration.

CAUSE
Aggression is often the result of a territorial challenge, but it often develops after a dog has been attacked when least anticipating pain (touch pain is an important stimulus). It is possible that a dog that has been punished harshly will subsequently show aggression when approached incautiously. Aggressive tendencies can be made worse by hormone changes. In false pregnancy some bitches will become excessively protective and will bite when at other times no aggression has been seen. Cocker Spaniels with a solid colour, e.g. Goldens, were known to show more unstable behaviour with fear biting than roan colours. Aggression may have an inherited cause, but one cannot rule out the influence of the mother rearing the puppies on behaviour later in life, as in some breeds strains of animals possess an inherited tendency to react in a more aggressive way than others. Hormone level

changes may also be a contributing cause in both males and females.

TREATMENT

Training a dog in a consistent manner can be used to reduce aggression and an attempt should be made to extinguish fear of a situation, by building up a dog's confidence. There are some drugs available that can be used for any 'hostile' behaviour, as well as medication to lower a dog's awareness of threats. A common suggestion for any aggression in the male is to castrate the dog, so as to remove the major source of testosterone, the hormone associated with the 'macho' dog. There may be situations where spaying a bitch will improve behaviour subject to mood swings due to hormone levels.

ALLERGIES

Disorders produced as a result of previous exposure to an allergen where the body reacts in an exaggerated manner. The allergen may be a protein or non-protein substance that induces allergy or specific hypersensitivity.

SIGNS

A frequently diagnosed condition for a variety of disorders ranging from diarrhoea to skin irritations such as dermatitis.

CAUSE

Essentially an allergy is a response of the dog's body to a foreign substance or allergen. The dog's immune system reacts

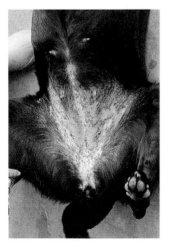

An allergic reaction.

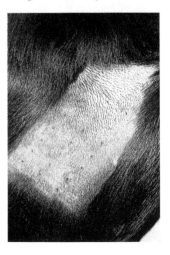

A prick test may be used when testing for allergies.

as if this were an unwanted invader and puts up an excessive reaction to something that is probably relatively harmless. Immune systems have 'memories' and a similar reaction can be expected every year or whenever the allergen is encountered or a suspect food is eaten. Eventually after five or seven years there seems to be a tailing off of the response, and older dogs often suffer less than previously with their allergies.

TREATMENT

Once the cause has been recognised, avoidance of the allergen, as far as practical, will help to reduce the signs. There is a wide range of drugs used in treating allergies either in tablet form, by injection or for topical application. The veterinary surgeon will advise on which antihistamine or corticosteroid is most appropriate. Desensitising vaccines may be used, and sometimes avoiding glutens, with a single protein dietary food, will be recommended in the treatment of some allergies.

ALOPECIA

Loss of hair from any part of the body can be a sign of skin disease or hormone imbalance.

Alopecia.

SIGNS

This may be seen as a thinning of the coat with hair loss becoming more noticeable all over the body.

CAUSES

Hormonal alopecia does not cause hair loss from the head and neck but from the inside of the thighs, the abdomen and flanks, and then the rest of the body is affected as the hair is loose and the dog does not grow a replacement coat. Patches of hairless skin are seen with some parasitic diseases such as Demodectic mange (*see page 156*) or when a dog has bitten hair away as after a flea-bite irritation. The effect of diet on hair growth is often discussed, but only in a severe dietary deficiency would the hair fail to grow. Signs of hair loss should be investigated by a veterinary surgeon to find out a specific cause.

TREATMENT
There are no specific treatments, unless the cause of the condition has been found. Parasitic baths, hormone therapy and diet supplements may all have a place in therapy.

ANAEMIA

A condition in which there are fewer red blood cells than normal to carry oxygen around the body.

SIGNS
The affected dog shows pale mucous membranes of the eyes and gums and may seem lethargic and weak.

CAUSES
The main causes of anaemia are: blood loss, red blood cell destruction (usually autoimmune) or failure to produce adequate red cells from the bone marrow (usually caused by iron deficiency, toxins, or tumour cells invading the marrow). Blood loss may be external or internal and is often caused by accidents (trauma). Serious internal haemorrhage can occur if an intestinal tumour bleeds, or after Warfarin poisoning.

TREATMENT
Investigation of anaemia involves a full veterinary examination followed by blood tests and possibly X-rays and bone marrow biopsy. Treatment is dependent on the cause and, in severe cases, blood transfusions may be necessary. It can be helpful to feed a high-protein, iron-rich diet including liver, kidney or heart during recovery from the anaemia, although most diets are not deficient in iron. Emergency treatment is required in the case of serious internal haemorrhage.

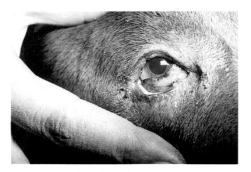

Anaemia (and haematoma).

ANAL ADENOMA

A disease seen in older male dogs as a tumour under the tail.

Anal adenoma.

SIGNS
Bleeding growths appear around the anus.

CAUSE
Growth of the tumour is dependent on male sex hormones produced out of balance in the older dog. It is a benign tumour, but, by growing large and ulcerating, it may lead to death from haemorrhage.

TREATMENT
As it is a benign tumour, surgical excision to remove the growths before they enlarge is successful. Castration is usually performed at the same operation.

ANAL SACS DISEASE

Dogs have ways of recognising each other: the glands that line the anal sacs produce the strongest distinctive scent of the dog. When a dog defaecates, a small part of the sac secretion is deposited with the faeces as an identifying smell.

CAUSE
If the dog cannot get rid of all the secretion in the sacs, they may become swollen and painful, causing discomfort. An abscess may develop.

SIGNS
In extreme cases of anal sac disease, the dog will bite into the skin near to the root of the tail trying to relieve the irritation. Milder distension causes dogs to 'toboggan' or scoot across the floor to try to press the gland area to empty the sacs out.

TREATMENT
A higher-fibre diet will often help a dog to empty its own sacs. In some cases it is necessary to squeeze out the glands, at regular intervals, using gloved fingers and a pad of cotton-wool.

ANOESTRUS

Defined as the absence of heat, the failure of a bitch to come on heat at all is very rare. The word is usually used to describe the time in the breeding cycle between the end of false pregnancy (or a pregnancy) and the first signs of the next heat. Some breeds do not start oestrous cycles until nearly 18 months of age and many older bitches revert to less frequent heats, perhaps only once a year.

SIGNS
Some younger bitches show little or no vaginal discharge and the owner may miss the signs of heat.

CAUSE
The cause of late development may be partly genetic, partly nutritional, and the temperature and hours of daylight (photoperiodicity) are known to affect the breeding cycles of other species.

TREATMENT
Investigation of hormone levels through blood tests may be considered. Where there is a suboestrus and the bitch shows no signs of being on heat, a small dose of an oestrogen given at the right moment has allowed a bitch to breed puppies.

ARTHRITIS

This can be simply defined as an inflammation of the joint.

SIGNS
This is usually seen in the older dog that is stiff or chronically lame. The joint(s) may be swollen.

CAUSE
There are many different types of arthritis depending on the cause of the joint inflammation: e.g. the traumatic arthritis due to damage of a joint surface; infectious or septic arthritis which may result from a bite or blood-borne infection such as Lyme's disease; or immune-mediated arthritis such as rheumatoid arthritis. Arthritis may involve one or more joints simultaneously. The most common form of arthritis is osteo-arthritis, the result of degenerative joint disease (DJD), shown on X-ray by the appearance of frightening bone 'spurs' and bony nodules around the joint.

TREATMENT
Management of arthritis involves diet to avoid the dog becoming overweight, as this puts undue strains on the joints. Moderation in exercise, as a series of controlled short walks

through the day, is preferable to violent play and chasing exercise, which strains the joint ligaments and causes excess wear of the joint cartilages. Fortunately a number of new medical and surgical treatments will give relief to dogs and allow a return to better mobility. *See Hip dysplasia (page 187), Osteochondrosis (page 221).*

ARTIFICIAL INSEMINATION

This method of breeding from bitches has only quite recently been studied and successfully employed. In the UK, the Guide Dogs for the Blind Association has the greatest practical knowledge of the techniques involved and the export and import of dog semen has allowed guide dog puppies to be born from the most successful stud dogs in the world. The Metropolitan Police now operate a similar scheme at their breeding centre based on the guide dog development work in this field. At present, the only reservation is over the identity of semen collected and stored, so that pedigrees can be accurately compiled for the puppies born by the use of this method.

ASCITES

The accumulation of excessive amounts of fluid in the abdominal cavity.

SIGNS
The enlargement of the abdomen from fluid distension is slow to develop and may not be recognised by the person who is with the dog every day. Shortness of breath may be noticed due to pressure of the diaphragm. A fluid feel on palpation may be detected, but care should be taken not to rupture a tumour by unwise squeezing of the dog's abdomen.

CAUSE
The condition is often the result of diseases of the heart, liver or kidneys. Different sorts of fluid are known as transudates and exudates. Examples are blood, urine, intestinal fluid or, most commonly, a clear fluid, like serum.

TREATMENT
The veterinary surgeon may withdraw some of the fluid by a needle in a process known as paracentesis to help diagnose the type of fluid and the reason for its accumulation. In simple cases the use of diuretics, and an adjustment in diet, may help.

ATOPY

A clinical syndrome involving hypersensitivity where the dog has a hereditary predisposition to the condition.

SIGNS
The condition causes skin irritation with licking and scratching resulting in self-trauma and secondary infection. The skin of the face, ears, limbs, feet and lower abdomen is most often affected, showing in pale-coated breeds as a tear-streaked face from the watery eyes, orange saliva stained paws in pale-coated breeds and bare forefeet from licking as well as red and itchy ears. The skin of the abdomen may be red and hair loss is not uncommon. Some dogs show only the inflammation of the ear canal as an otitis externa.

A tear-streaked face caused by atopy.

Saliva staining as a result of atopy.

CAUSE
An allergic disorder in the dog caused by an inherited predisposition to develop antibodies (IgE) to allergens in the environment. Atopy is more common in certain breeds, notably English Setters, Terriers, Boxers, Labradors and Golden Retrievers. The most common allergen for atopic dogs is the

household dust mite and its excreta. These mites multiply in warm, damp rooms and, thus, the problem is greatest when working breeds such as Labradors and Golden Retrievers are housed indoors as pets and then get limited exercise periods in the fresh air. There may be a seasonal incidence that varies with breeds.

TREATMENT
Management of the problem involves reducing exposure to the allergen. This can be assisted by avoiding centrally-heated, carpeted living quarters where open windows for ventilation are few. Outdoor housing will often reduce the challenge. Dogs in colder conditions will grow thicker coats which may also be of help to reduce exposed areas of skin. Any veterinary treatment will involve reducing allergens by parasite control, feeding single or uncommon protein foods, and skin sedation with the use of antihistamine tablets. Essential fatty acids (Gamma Linoleic Acid GLA) food supplements are advised and sometimes corticosteroids will be used cautiously. Antibiotics may be required to treat secondary skin infections. The use of desensitising vaccines may take many months to obtain a response but can be beneficial in some dogs if used for at least a year.

AURAL HAEMATOMA

A condition of the ear where blood collects in the space between the skin of the ear flap and the ear cartilage.

SIGNS
Extensive shaking and scratching leading to blood loss between the skin and ear cartilage. This may be extensive enough to bulge out the whole ear so that the flap feels like a bag of blood or haematoma. Sometimes only minor bleeding may occur and a thickening at the edge of the flap will not spread across the whole ear.

CAUSE
Any ear irritation may cause shaking and scratching of the ear leading to burst blood vessels within the pinna or 'ear flap'. The ear seems a point of weakness in the dog's healthy outside surface.

TREATMENT
Prevention is by inspection of the ear canals, removing wax or foreign bodies such as grass seeds promptly and treating inflammatory disease so that the dog does not get into the habit of ear-scratching and violent head-shaking. Any discs or identity tags on the collar should be removed if a dog starts

head-shaking, as the metal contacting the ear may aggravate the bleeding. Treatment at the veterinary surgery is either by sucking out the haematoma blood and injecting a steroid or by surgical drainage and stitching of the pinna to preserve its shape.

AURAL RESECTION

This is a surgical procedure used successfully to deal with ear disease that does not respond to normal medication and cleaning routines. There are several variations of the operation which is designed to open up the ear-canal tube. Ventilation of the lining surface of the ear tube helps to resolve chronic otitis. In some cases, the diseased ear canal requires total removal and the aural ablation operation is performed. A veterinary surgeon will discuss which operation is most appropriate. In all cases, careful nursing for the first week after surgery is essential for healing, before stitches can be removed.

AUTO IMMUNE DISEASE

A disease produced by the dog responding to the presence of its own cells or antibodies with an excessive immune reaction.

SIGNS
Many different types of auto immune disease occur: e.g. Pemphigus which affects the skin producing blisters, pustules and ulcers, and Systemic Lupus Erythematosis which involves many body systems such as the skin, kidneys, joints, and blood.

CAUSE
A disease where the body's defence system produces auto-antibodies which are directed against healthy parts of the dog's own body. When antinuclear antibody is formed, cells of the many internal organs and the blood may be destroyed. Such diseases may also be described as 'Immune Mediated Diseases'.

TREATMENT
Specific treatments require close veterinary supervision but may include steroids at high doses and similar suppressive drugs.

B

BACTERIAL SKIN DISEASES

A common disorder due to bacteria that may normally be present on the skin surface producing an inflammatory response in the surface layers of the skin, or sometimes, as in pyoderma, in the depth of the skin.

SIGNS
The skin appears red and causes itching, especially when the skin of the abdomen and perineum become infected.

CAUSES
The underlying causes may be flea bites, atopy or demodectic mange and secondary infection.

TREATMENT
Treatment with mild shampoos helps to remove crusts and some of the surface bacteria but, in the majority of cases, a prolonged course of antibiotics is needed together with topical ointments. Laboratory tests on swabs from the skin may help in the selection of the most appropriate antibiotic.

Bacterial skin disease.

BALANITIS

The inflammation of the glans penis; balanoposthitis is the term when the prepuce and the penis are infected.

SIGNS
The condition is seen as an infection of the prepuce. The

discharge, that apparently comes from the end of the penis, may cause excessive licking by the male dog. The sticky discharge may be sufficient in quantity to leave stains on the floor or furniture used by the dog.

CAUSE
Herpes virus infection is often the cause of the initial infection, but bacteria such as *Pasteurella* may be found in swabs taken for culture.

TREATMENT
Treatment with antibiotics may be only partially successful. In dogs that develop the habit of licking to remove the discharge, castration may be resorted to as a way of reducing the size of the exposed penis and often the condition will resolve.

BARLOW'S DISEASE

This is a condition affecting the growing ends of the bone, more correctly termed 'metaphyseal osteopathy'. It is seen in rapidly growing puppies, mainly of the larger breeds, between three and seven months of age.

SIGNS
A puppy will show hot, painful swellings around the end of the long bones, causing lameness and reluctance to move. The legs may be so painful that the puppies show collapse, and, often, the body temperature may be as a high as 40 degrees Centigrade (106 degrees Fahrenheit). The condition is diagnosed by veterinary examination and by the typical changes seen on X-ray films.

CAUSE
The cause of the disease is unknown, although over-supply of minerals may be responsible. In the past Vitamin C deficiency had been suggested as one of many causes, but a daily supplement may cause hypercalcaemia and therefore should be avoided.

TREATMENT
A controlled food intake and the use of medication for the painful joints may be all that is required in the growing puppy. Anti-inflammatory and pain-relieving drugs may be prescribed.

BENIGN TUMOURS

Skin tumours are very common in the dog and approximately two-thirds of these are benign. Roughly 50 per cent of mammary tumours are benign.

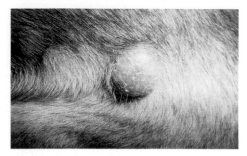

Benign skin tumour.

SIGNS

Growths may occur at various places in the dog. Benign growths are those that do not spread by invading healthy organs, nor by 'seeding' of cells that travel by blood vessels and lymphatics to other parts of the body. Benign tumours grow by 'expansion', often within a capsule, and may be quite moveable if they occur under the skin. The most harmful effect of a benign growth is to put pressure on adjacent structures. The lipoma under the armpit may force a dog to walk with one leg swinging very wide, or similar pressure can restrict an airway to the lungs.

CAUSE

There are no specific causes. Some 'growths' may be the result of repeated injury to the body at the site where the tumour develops. Mammary tumours may grow if milk is retained in the glands after repeated false pregnacies. Viruses are known to cause warts and canine oral papillomatosis.

TREATMENT

Treatment should be by surgical removal whilst the tumours are still small, although, in some cases, experience may indicate that some small tumours can be ignored.

BILIOUS VOMIT

Sickness where the gastric contents brought up by the tongue are coloured due the presence of bile from the liver.

SIGNS

Sickness experienced by dogs, often on an empty stomach. The vomit usually appears green, or brown occasionally.

CAUSE

Bilious vomit may be due to the release of bile from the gall bladder that passes forwards in the small intestine and causes vomiting when it enters the stomach. Bilious vomit is often associated with gastritis, or a condition known as the 'bilious vomiting syndrome'.

TREATMENT

Dogs may benefit then from having a small feed prior to settling at night. Diets rich in fats stimulate the flow of bile from the liver, so providing a low-fat, carbohydrate-based diet may also be beneficial. Diagnosis of any persisting vomiting problem may require an extensive veterinary examination and associated tests.

BLOAT

The name for the condition where the stomach is distended with gas. It also applies to any distension of the abdomen, as with severe over-eating, and after a dog has been gorging dried food.

SIGNS

The gas-filled stomach presses on the diaphragm restricting breathing, resulting in frequent shallow breaths and a purplish discoloration of the tongue. The weight of the enlarging spleen, attached to the greater curvature of the gas-filled stomach, can make the stomach twist in a clockwise direction. The signs of discomfort become more noticeable as the stomach's connection to the oesophagus is pinched off by a 180 degree rotation.

CAUSE

Accumulation of gas in the stomach may be due to fermentation of cereal products when there is insufficient gastric acid present – but most gas is thought to be air that is swallowed during the eating process. Bloat may be followed by 'torsion' or twisting of the stomach, especially in the larger breeds. It is particularly associated with feeding regimes where a highly digestible food can be swallowed rapidly, followed by drinking large quantities of water. Feeding immediately before or after strenuous exercise has been blamed as well. When the bloated stomach rotates a 'torsion' or volvulus often results.

Gastric dilation: X-ray of gas in the abdomen.

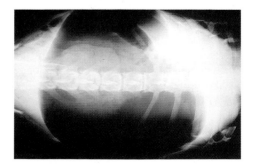

TREATMENT

The condition of gastric dilation and volvulus (GDV) is an acute emergency, requiring the dog to be rushed to the veterinary surgery. If the stomach twists, and its connection to the oesophagus is pinched off by a 180 degree rotation, it will be found that when a stomach tube is passed through the mouth down the oesophagus, it can be pressed down no further than just beyond the entrance level of the oesophagus into the abdomen. No gas can pass back up the tube, even though the stomach is still tight, filled with gas.

Emergency treatment at the veterinary surgery will usually necessitate setting up an intravenous drip to deal with the shock. Decompression of the stomach will possibly be attempted by passing a stomach tube. A more successful, but bolder, method, is inserting a wide bore (18G needle) canula at the point behind the left rib arch that shows the most distension with the gas. Frequently a laparotomy operation will still be necessary to empty and reposition the stomach, and/or to provide a means of fixing the stomach to the abdominal wall so that an adhesion will form. This will reduce the chance of a recurring problem. GDV is always a serious problem and the sudden gas distension will sometimes be fatal despite all efforts at treatment.

BLOOD CLOTTING DISORDERS

See Haemophilia page 183

BONE TUMOURS

The majority of bone tumours in dogs are highly malignant osteosarcomas which occur in the long bones of the legs. Osteosarcoma is most commonly seen in the large and giant breeds in mid to old age.

SIGNS

The tumour produces pain, local swelling, heat, and lameness which often occurs suddenly. Obvious swelling may not be present when the lameness is first noticed.

CAUSE

There are no specific causes, but there does seem to be a genetic predisposition to cancer of the long bones in the giant breeds of dogs.

TREATMENT

Dogs showing these signs should be examined without delay by the veterinary surgeon, who will use X-rays to help in diagnosis. The appearance of a malignant bone tumour is quite typical on X-ray, but it may be necessary to take repeat X-rays two to three weeks apart to follow the characteristic bone changes. A biopsy may be required to confirm a diagnosis. The outlook for dogs with osteosarcoma is poor as the tumour spreads rapidly to cause secondaries at other sites, principally the lungs. Amputation of the affected limb relieves pain and usually gives a good quality of life for a period of time. Unfortunately, 90 per cent of dogs develop secondary tumours within one year of amputation, and the average survival time is only three to six months. Improvement in survival time has been seen in dogs receiving chemotherapy after amputation, so this should be considered. Early diagnosis and treatment will produce the best results. Benign thickenings of the bone, known as osteomas, are very rare and cause only slight lameness. If they interfere with a joint movement, they can be treated by surgical removal.

BRONCHITIS

Inflammation of one or more of the bronchial tubes as they enter the lungs. It may take the form of either acute or chronic bronchitis.

SIGNS
Bronchitis produces coughing which may be dry or moist (the sputum is not seen but swallowed) and intermittent gagging. The breathing rate is fast, and there may be shortness of breath with exercise and wheezing after exertion. Dogs that are short of air show a purplish colour to their tongues and sit with their chest raised and elbows turned out. Coughing dogs can exhaust themselves. This can progress to collapse and unconsciousness.

CAUSES
Bronchitis is an inflammation of the bronchial tubes which results in airway obstruction, and excessive sputum production. The disease may be produced by infectious agents, viruses or bacteria, or non-infectious irritants and allergens such as inhaled dust or smoke and mould spores. Allergic bronchitis, sometimes called bronchial asthma, causes spasm of the bronchial muscles producing narrowing of the tubes and further airway obstruction. Bronchitis may become a chronic (long-standing) condition, particularly common in older dogs of the small and medium-sized breeds. Kennel cough can lead to chronic bronchitis, even in young dogs.

TREATMENT
Diagnosis of bronchitis by the veterinary surgeon involves a full clinical examination, and such additional tests as X-rays,

endoscopic examination of the airways and analysis of sputum as obtained by washings from the bronchial tubes. Management of the problem is dependent on the cause. It may include weight reduction, exercise restriction and the use of a harness rather than a collar. Affected dogs should avoid under-ventilated rooms that have a high content of dust-mite debris, tobacco smoke and any chemical or boiler fumes as well as moulds. Under veterinary supervision, antibiotics, broncho-dilators and drugs to liquify mucus may be prescribed. An even temperature should be insisted on for the dog's comfort, and sometimes moistening the air will help. Steam inhalations can be used after veterinary consultation on the type of bronchitis. Cough suppressants are not always advised.

BURNS AND SCALDS

These are infrequent injuries in dogs. Even when electric cables are chewed, the dog usually senses the current in live wires before burning of the mouth and electrocution take place. The most common scalding injury occurs when hot fat or other cooking liquids are spilt on the dog in the kitchen. If the scalding fluid remains in contact with the dog's skin surface too long, the skin layers become badly damaged sometimes resulting in permanent scarring and hair loss. A rotund animal with a flat back runs a greater risk of hair loss.

Burns seen on a terrier's flank.

TREATMENT
First aid treatment involves cooling the skin at once by flooding it with copious amounts of icy water. Fats and oils are a greater problem since they adhere to the slightly greasy skin of the dog and continue burning. A very mild detergent may also be needed in these cases, to remove matted fat in the hair, followed by more cold water. Badly affected dogs will need veterinary treatment for shock, followed by careful wound management to promote healing. Antibiotic cover is used to prevent secondary infection. Skin grafting may be necessary where extensive skin damage has occurred.

CAESAREAN SECTION

This operation, also known as a hysterotomy, can be a life-saving procedure for a bitch with birth problems. It may well result in a greater proportion of live births than if a prolonged whelping has been allowed to continue without veterinary help. The operation is best performed at a time when the bitch shows that she is ready to whelp by the presence of milk in the mammary glands and, preferably, at a time of the day when adequate nursing help is available to the veterinary surgeon. Some form of deep sedation or ultra short anaesthesia is preferred to ensure the birth of viable puppies. Many veterinary surgeons have perfected their own routine to obtain live births and ensure that the bitch is able to feed her newborn puppies. *(See The Birth of Puppies and Aftercare, page 58).*

CALCULI

The word calculi describes a chalky deposit. It is most commonly applied to the bladder 'stones' that may occur in some dogs and bitches.

SIGNS
Frequent urination, straining to empty the bladder, and often blood in the urine. Calculi can lodge in the urethra, particularly in the male dog's prostate region or the base of the penis bone. There will then be repetitive, unproductive straining as the urine flow is obstructed.

CAUSE
The cause of calculi is an excess of dietary magnesium, protein, calcium and phosphorus, reduced water intake and abnormal acidity or alkalinity of the urine.

TREATMENT
Bladder stones irritate the bladder lining and produce secondary infection. Adequate fluid intake and an adjustment in the diet may sometimes be sufficient to dissolve the calculi and avoid major surgery. The obstructing calculi can sometimes be dislodged with a catheter and 'reverse flushing'. Where there is pain or a complete blockage, surgical removal is essential to extract calculi lodged in the male dog's urethra

at its narrowest in the os penis, or in the bitch the bladder itself will have to be opened as a cystotomy.

DENTAL CALCULUS: The word calculus is also used when dental plaque is followed by a stone-like concretion of minerals on the teeth. The chalky deposit on the teeth is also known as tartar. Preventive action by brushing the dog's teeth and providing hard chews and special rusks to clean the teeth is

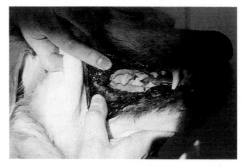

Dental calculus.

effective. Routine scaling of teeth, followed by polishing, is the best care that the veterinary surgeon can give to preserve a healthy mouth in the dog. The condition has become more common in dogs in the last 20 years, but some dogs still retain clean teeth into old age when they are allowed to chew tough meat and to gnaw at bones.

CAMPYLOBACTER

The name of a bacterium found in the dog's intestine.

SIGNS
This organism does not always cause diarrhoea but, in some circumstances, it can be associated with a fairly violent watery diarrhoea, often bloody. Vomiting may occur early on in an attack.

CAUSE
The source of infection may be from raw poultry offals, or from seagull or other wild birds' droppings. The bacteria is a potential threat to humans, although experience suggests that different strains affect humans from those found in dogs. *See diarrhoea, page 159.*

TREATMENT
Oral fluid therapy, and the use of appropriate antibiotics, may be needed. In all cases precautions such as hand-washing after grooming, and the disposal of diarrhoeic faeces, should be enforced to prevent transfer to humans.

CANCER
See carcinoma (below), malignant tumours page 207.

CARCINOMA

A carcinoma is a malignant tumour arising from epithelial tissues.

SIGNS
These tumours or 'cancers' may be found in the skin, the mouth, the glands and the intestinal body systems and organs. They may invade local surrounding structures and can spread to form 'secondary' tumours at distant sites (often the liver or the lungs). Carcinomas often grow rapidly and may develop a bleeding or very red surface. In the dog, carcinomas involving the tonsils or thyroid gland are examples of very invasive malignancies. Mammary gland tumours are common in the older, unspayed bitch and between 40 and 50 per cent of these tumours are carcinomas.

Squamous cell carcinoma on a black Labrador's face.

CAUSE
The causes of cancer are still uncertain, but there are now examples of viruses, radiation damage and carcinogenic chemicals that may 'trigger off' a cancer.

TREATMENT
Some mammary carcinomas will spread to form secondary tumours earlier than others, so veterinary inspection and surgery is essential for the older bitch with lumps in the mammary gland. For mammary gland growths, a number of treatment methods are available including surgery, radiotherapy, and chemotherapy. The veterinary surgeon will advise on which treatment is most appropriate for each case, depending on the type and extent of the tumour, and the dog's general health. In some cases treatments may not be possible, nor beneficial. The earlier the diagnosis, and the treatment, the better, so any unusual lumps or sore patches or bleeding from body orifices should be assessed as soon as possible.

CARDIAC FAILURE

Heart failure is a condition where the dog's heart does not work properly due to the presence of disease affecting the heart. Many different types of heart disease exist (*see page 184*), which may then lead to heart failure.

SIGNS
Affected dogs usually show tiring when they are walked, plus weakness on exercise because of the poor circulation. Coughing, spells of rapid breathing, and sometimes a rapid heart beat can be seen or felt as the lungs are congested. The pulse in the arteries may be fast but weak, and the tongue may show a slight purple tinge to a darker-blue colour, which indicates that the oxygen in the blood is insufficient to give the mucous membranes their healthy pink colour. Poor appetite and weight loss is also frequently seen due to a swollen liver and the ascites in the abdomen.

CAUSES
Some of the most common causes can be divided into congenital heart defects, degeneration of old age (*see endocardiosis page 165*), heart muscle disease (cardiomyopathy) and infectious and toxic agents affecting the heart (*see heart disease page 184*). The heart failure may be sudden, as with a cardiac arrest, but often the condition develops gradually as chronic heart failure (CHF). Dogs which have suffered progressive heart failure may suddenly deteriorate into an acute heart failure. The signs of chronic heart failure develop gradually as the blood circulation from the heart worsens. As a result, fluid accumulates in the lungs and sometimes the abdomen (*see ascites page 128*).

TREATMENT
Treatment and prevention mean exercise restriction, and the avoidance of any excess weight by dieting. Depending on the type of heart disease, diuretics may be used to remove excess fluid through the kidneys. Other drugs, which act on the heart muscle, blood vessels and airways, may be given, depending on the severity of the condition.

CARDIOGENIC SHOCK AND HEART FAILURE

One of the causes of collapse is a failure of the heart to keep the blood circulating. Irreversible shock may develop and death can ensue.

SIGNS

The dog shows signs of collapse, with rapid breathing, and pale – almost white – mucous membranes and tongue. The tongue will often be dropping out from the open mouth. Panting cools the body, but it also allows for a better intake of air to reach the lungs. The pulse in the arteries is weak, and the feet may feel cold.

CAUSE

Shock, then cardiac arrest, can develop when the heart fails to pump enough blood around the body. It leads to rapid deterioration and sudden death.

TREATMENT

The first aid treatment is to force the dog to rest by talking calmly and soothing it. Immediate treatment also involves ensuring the airway is clear, cleaning the nostrils and mouth, and pulling the tongue well forward, with the neck outstretched, if the dog is semi-conscious. Veterinary attention at the surgery is urgent: oxygen may be administered by a loose face mask, or an airway can be introduced by a tube down the trachea. Mouth-to-mouth resuscitation, and providing an airway to give oxygen-rich air, is best left to the trained nurse, as is cardiac massage. Further treatment involves specific drugs. Diuretics to remove fluid though the kidneys is one of the first veterinary measures used.

CARIES AND DENTAL DISEASE

Decay of the teeth is not common in dogs on approved diets. Calculus on the teeth and periodontal disease are more frequent tooth problems in dogs.

SIGNS

Dental caries is a destruction of the tooth enamel, due to mouth bacteria, leading to tooth cavities in the dentine and eventually an abscess.

CAUSE

Excess biscuit in the diet and lack of chewing to produce saliva that washes the teeth.

TREATMENT

Cavities may be filled in molar teeth but extractions are normally the most appropriate for dogs that no longer need to chew hard foods. New diets with harder fibre have been introduced to help tooth cleaning as the dog eats. Routine scaling and polishing the teeth may be advised as a preventive measure.

CASTRATION

The operation of surgical removal of both testes is usually performed as a method of controlling breeding, but it has been widely used to make dogs less dominant, reduce their roaming tendencies, and remove signs of undesirable sexual behaviour *(see balanitis page 132)*. When one or both testes are retained in the abdomen *(see cryptorchidism page 152)*, castration is advised as a positive health measure to prevent the formation of testicular tumours in later life. Prostate disorders *(see page 241)* are also quite common in the older male, and routine castration can help to prevent these conditions. The operation is invariably performed under general anaesthesia and should take no more than 15 minutes. Any stitches used will be removed about 10 days after the operation.

There are no side-effects other than the tendency to put on weight, and strict dietary control should be followed, with the dog weighed at the time of operation to act as the 'base line' weight. A guideline for the age for operation is that used by the Guide Dogs for the Blind Association: as soon as the male puppy is mature enough to show male behaviour by lifting his leg when passing urine. At this time the castration can be undertaken, and the dog will retain some masculine characteristics afterwards. Usually dogs are castrated at between 6 and 10 months, but the operation can be successful on much older dogs as well.

CATARACT

The condition in the eye where the lens appears opaque. Some forms of cataract are recognised as a small opacity on the lens capsule and do not interfere with a dog's sight – some affected dogs have been able to continue to work as guide dogs.

SIGNS
A cataract is an opaque area or milkiness in the lens of the eye which may first be seen when the dog stands in a bright light. Opaqueness of the lens is known as cataract because it was thought it was similar to a waterfall, where clear water suddenly became white. Older dogs may have cloudiness due to crystals in the fluid of the eye, and examination with an ophthalmoscope is necessary to confirm whether cataract is present or not in the eye.

*Cataract in the
lens of the eye.*

CAUSE

Cataract may be due to degeneration of the lens as part of the ageing process, or it may develop as secondary to other eye conditions Diabetes produces a particular type of clefting opacity seen in both eyes. Cataract may be an inherited eye disorder. The dominant gene cataract of the Golden Retriever was seen in very young puppies, often soon after their eyes opened. However, the Boston Terrier had a late onset cataract that was often undetected until seven years of age. Regular inspection of the lens, especially in animals intended for breeding, can be used to help to eliminate the hereditary type of eye disease with a selective breeding programme.

TREATMENT

Treatment by surgical removal of the lens can be successful, but due to the delicate nature of the operation, it is quite expensive. Home treatment for a dog with cataract is minimal, but it may help to keep the eye surface moist, and to watch for any signs of uveitis – a painful condition with reddening of the white sclera of the eye.

CHEMOSIS

A condition of the dog's eyelids where the inner surface becomes puffy with oedema.

SIGNS

A prominent lower eyelid that droops showing a pinkish balloon-like swelling.

CAUSE

A foreign body such as a grass particle or grit may start off the swelling, and the dog rubbing at the eye often increases the amount of fluid in the lids.

TREATMENT
The eye should be inspected for any obvious foreign body, and artificial tears can be used to flush the eye out repeatedly. The veterinary surgeon may use anaesthetic drops and have the eye searched before using medication reducing the oedema present.

CHERRY EYE

A popular descriptive term for an eversion of the third eyelid where there is prolapse of the nictitans gland over the eyelid margin, causing a small cherry-shaped blob to appear.

SIGNS
A prominent red swelling in the corner of the eye nearest the nose.

CAUSE
The lymph gland behind the third eyelid becomes enlarged and, by bulging out, it may evert the lid exposing a large lymphoid tissue mass rather like a large 'tonsil'. The swelling may be the result of chronic infection or a sudden allergy.

TREATMENT
Moistening the eye with artificial tears is the best first aid. The veterinary surgeon will wish to inspect the eye fully and may use steroid eye drops, or suggest operating to remove the swollen gland of the third eyelid.

CHEYLETIELLOSIS

A parasitic disease of the dog's skin, commonly known as 'walking dandruff'.

SIGNS
Mild skin irritation can occur, but the mites often cause scaly areas on the back towards the tail. Owners may show the first signs, with an intense irritation on the arms, chest, trunk and buttocks. Fortunately, the human response does not last unless there is further infection from a pet.

CAUSE
The small mite *Cheyletiella yasguri* does not burrow, but lives on the skin surface. It feeds by piercing the outer skin layer, and gorging on the clear, colourless serum below. The mites are quite plump and can just be seen moving in the coat. The eggs are very small, attached to the base of the dog's hair. Female mites can live off the host for ten days at least, and can infect other dogs. Two other species of *Cheyletiella* are more specific to cats and to rabbits.

The cheyletiella yasguri mite (magnified).

TREATMENT
Treatment with prescription shampoos or with Ivermectin injections is usually quickly effective, but normal treatments for flea control do not appear to be successful.

CHRONIC DEGENERATIVE RADICULOMYELOPATHY (CDRM)

A disease causing weakness in the hind legs of German Shepherd Dogs.

SIGNS
At first a dog may be slow to pick up its toes and may wear down the central two toe nails of the back legs more than might be expected. Later there is progressive loss of motor control, loss of sensation in the back legs and a swaying walk.

CAUSE
The cause is unknown but, as it is mainly seen in certain strains of German Shepherds, a genetic factor may be involved. The nerve roots from the spinal cord are affected: some dogs deteriorate quickly while others are able to manage to keep walking for several years.

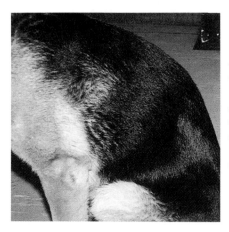

Muscle loss experienced in a German Shepherd Dog suffering from chronic degenerative radiculomyelopathy (CDRM).

TREATMENT
The dog should be X-rayed to rule out any other causes such as spondylosis, disc protrusion, or hip dysplasia. Once the condition is confirmed there is no specific treatment, but products such as Vitamin E and corticosteroids may be of limited benefit to the dog.

CIRRHOSIS

A liver disease characterised by the fibrous tissue replacing normally functioning liver cells.

SIGNS
The dog shows signs of chronic liver failure which may include ascites *(see page 128)* jaundice *(see page 196)*, and weight loss.
CAUSE
Cirrhosis is a chronic liver condition in which the liver is damaged or 'scarred' with fibrous tissue. The condition can be the end result of many liver diseases, including damage by toxins, drugs, infections and immune-mediated inflammation.
TREATMENT
Blood tests are available to assess liver damage and liver function and, provided the fibrous change has not gone too far, the liver has great powers of repair and recovery. Blood proteins are also low in chronic liver damage. Depending on the degree of damage, the veterinary surgeon will prescribe appropriate supportive treatment and recommend a suitable diet. This will usually be a low-fat, high-carbohydrate diet, with a good-quality protein source in specified amounts, fed several times through the day.

COLITIS

Colitis is an inflammatory disease of the large intestine.

SIGNS
Affected dogs often show frequent straining to pass faeces, fresh blood and an over-production of mucus. The increased mucus produced may be seen as slime coating the soft faeces, or sometimes a firm motion coated in an egg-white membrane – like a sausage with a thick skin – is produced. The jelly-like slime may be streaked with pink blood, or sometimes darker clots and blood streaks are obvious, especially near the end of the straining. Straining may be painful, causing the dog to cry out suddenly. A third of affected dogs vomit – often a day before changes are seen in the faeces. Nausea may be shown by a grass eating habit, as if to make the dog sick. The frequent

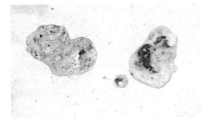

Faeces produced by a dog suffering from colitis.

passage of small quantities of faeces, or sometimes diarrhoea, is expected with colitis in the dog.

CAUSES
The causes are not fully known, but certain diet changes, food allergies, parasites and bacteria may set off an attack.

TREATMENT
Investigation of the condition involves analysis of the faeces and blood, and possibly an endoscopic examination that may involve taking a biopsy of the intestine wall. A high-fibre diet is often advised, and no titbits from the table should be fed. Some dogs need a low allergenic diet: one containing a single 'new' protein will have to be fed, then another protein may be fed after six weeks. Specific treatments are used against any bacteria or parasites. Where symptoms persist and inflammation is severe, anti-inflammatory drugs and the long-term use of Sulphasalazine tablets may be advised.

COLLAPSE

A general term for any sudden loss of consciousness or limb weakness that prevents the dog from rising. A special type of collapse may occur in the lungs after a chest injury when air enters the pleural space.

SIGNS
Inability to walk, little or no response to the human voice, sometimes dilated pupils and a glazed look to the eyes.

CAUSES
Any failure of the circulation such as that caused by shock, heart failure or damage to the brain and spinal cord.

TREATMENT
Treatment for shock is needed, ensuring the tongue is pulled forward to provide an airway. If the collapse lasts more than a few minutes, urgent veterinary attention may be needed.

CONJUNCTIVITIS

This is one of the commonest eye conditions seen in dogs.

SIGNS

The inner lining of the eyelids is affected, and, being very itchy, it often causes the dog to rub at the eyes making the condition much worse. The pink lining membranes of the eyes are often a harsh red, and a sticky or dried-on discharge will be seen on or around the eyelids.

CAUSE

The possibility of a foreign body, such as a seed or a hair on the eyeball surface, should be considered. Often a fine injury, such as a cat's claw scratching the cornea, will cause a sudden onset of conjunctivitis. Infections are another common cause.

TREATMENT

Bathing the eye with contact lens fluid, or with sterile water (produced by boiling water in the kettle and allowing it to cool to below blood heat), may provide immediate relief. Usually a full veterinary inspection and specific drugs will then be used.

CONGENITAL

The word means a condition that is present at birth. Congenital diseases may not always be inherited as, for example, after toxic damage to the unborn foetus. Congenital diseases may not be recognised until weeks after birth. For example, a congenital cataract would not be found until the puppy's eyes open after 10 days.

CONSTIPATION

SIGNS

Straining and difficulty in passing faeces.

CAUSES

A condition caused by impaction of dry or solid faeces in the colon and rectum. Lack of fluid intake, too much bone or dry matter in the diet, or rectal strictures, prostate enlargement, perineal hernia, anal tumours and furunculosis can lead to this problem. Prostate disorders *(see page 241)* should always be considered in the older uncastrated male seen to be straining a lot to pass faeces.

TREATMENT

This would involve lubricants such as medicinal liquid paraffin and faecal bulking agents such as methyl cellulose. An enema may be used or, in extreme cases of impaction, a general anaesthetic has to be given to extract the solid masses.

COPROPHAGIA

The abnormal habit of a dog eating its own faeces or, in

some instances, faeces lying on the ground produced by other dogs.

SIGNS
Foul breath and poor condition may be due to the ingestion of the dog's own, or another dog's faeces.

CAUSE
This is an example of abnormal behaviour, often seen when dogs are confined, become bored and have the opportunity to smell and investigate the composition of recently voided faeces. The possibility of malabsorption *(see page 207)* should always be investigated, but some meat-based diets still have a flavour left that is attractive to the dog – even after the food has passed through the whole length of the digestive tract.

TREATMENT
A change of diet, and exercising on the lead until faeces have been passed, can help to prevent the habit. The use of fresh pineapple in the feed has been successful in some kennels, and there are many other methods which attempt to make voided faeces less palatable.

CRUCIATE LIGAMENT INJURY
Two of the ligaments that support the knee joint cross over the centre of the joint in a cruciform shape and provide a major stabilising effect in this poorly constructed joint. Rupture of the anterior ligament is most common in heavyweight dogs that are made to flex their joints excessively.

SIGNS
The signs of injury may be only a slight lameness at first that does not improve with rest and tends to get worse when more exercise is given. The dog will stand with only its toe touching the ground. If there is a complete tear or rupture of the ligaments, then the joint will be much more painful and no weight can be carried at all on the affected leg.

CAUSE
The cruciate ligaments, which stabilise the stifle or 'knee' joint, are particularly liable to twisting injury. Such injuries were traditionally more common in gundogs, due to jumping or sudden turning. Larger breeds of dogs and overweight animals are more susceptible to cruciate ligament damage. At one time, it was thought that dogs who travelled in the back of shooting-brake cars were susceptible as the rear bumper made the dog stretch out and land heavily, after first being let out at the end

of a journey. Certain breeds, such as Labrador Retrievers and Rottweilers, may be affected by a weakness of the ligaments, which makes them more prone to rupture at an early age.

TREATMENT

Although most ligaments should repair naturally with rest, surgery is advised for those dogs weighing more than 10Kg in order to stabilise the joints and speed the recovery process. A number of different surgical operations have been developed to stabilise the stifle joint after cruciate ligaments damage, facilitating a quicker return to work.

CRYPTORCHIDISM

The hidden testis may be the result of a failure of one or both testes to descend from the abdomen to their adult site in the scrotum.

SIGNS

A cryptorchid is a term used to describe a dog with both testes undescended. Sometimes the dog has only one testis that can be found in the scrotum, and such a dog is more often called a monorchid, even though this implies there is not a second testis hidden in the abdomen. More correctly, the dog is a 'unilateral crytorchid'. Some puppies have both testes descended at birth, but in others, the testes may not pass down into the scrotum until several weeks after birth. In the normal puppy, both testes can be felt in the scrotum by 8 or 10 weeks of age, but often vets are asked to examine much younger puppies to see if they are 'entire'.

CAUSE

Certain breeds seem more susceptible than others to this genetic failure. It is thought to be an example of 'threshold inheritance'. The normal puppy development process is to have two testes in the scrotum, but if the descent passes a development threshold, then one or more are held back in the abdomen. Bilateral cryptorchids are sterile, but if their sisters are used for breeding, they may produce puppies also with the same defect.

TREATMENT

Castration is advised, as the testis kept in the abdomen is at a higher temperature and may later become diseased, sometimes resulting in a higher incidence of testicular cancer.

CUSHING'S DISEASE

Cushing's Disease is due to an excess production of hormone from the adrenal gland.

SIGNS
Cushing's Disease is mainly seen in middle-aged and elderly dogs, but may be difficult to recognise in the early stages. The usual signs shown are increased thirst and urination, increased appetite, tiredness due to muscle weakness, and a 'pot belly' covered with hairless skin. The pendulous swollen abdomen may be due to an enlarged liver, and the muscles stretching with the fat deposited in the abdomen, resulting from the increased appetite and increased stomach size.

CAUSE
This condition is caused by a tumour in the adrenal gland or, more commonly, by a tumour in the pituitary gland which stimulates the adrenals. Some dogs become 'Cushingoid' after long-term or excessive doses of a cortisone drug used to manage a chronic skin or respiratory condition.

Calcified ulcer on a Boxer's foot as seen with Cushing's disease.

Cushing's disease seen in a Yorkshire Terrier.

TREATMENT
The disease is diagnosed with veterinary tests specific for the condition. Treatment for the pituitary tumour type is often quite successful, but the outlook for dogs with adrenal tumours is not as good.

CYSTITIS

Inflammation of the lining of the urinary bladder.

SIGNS
Affected animals often show frequent attempts to urinate. They will spend longer than usual passing urine, and trying to void

urine long after the bladder seems to be empty. Blood streaks may be seen in the urine. Wetting in the house and apparent incontinence may be the first sign of cystitis noticed.

CAUSE

An inflammation of the bladder lining, most commonly caused by a bacterial infection. Bacterial infection is more common in the bitch due to the shorter length of the urethra, and the time of oestrus may be when infections are first recognised.

TREATMENT

Cystitis is diagnosed after a full veterinary examination and tests performed on the urine. A fresh 'mid-stream' sample should be brought for the veterinary surgeon to examine. Urine tests often demonstrate blood and protein present, with an alkaline pH in cases of cystitis. Microscopic examination of the urine and bacterial culture will be performed to investigate the cause of the problem. Long-standing cases of cystitis may require further tests including X-ray examination. Cystitis can be due to the irritation of bladder 'stones', and this possibility should be examined for, especially if more than one attack occurs in a dog or bitch. First aid treatment can be to encourage the dog to drink more water, and to give frequent walks to encourage bladder emptying. Usually specific antibiotics, such as those drugs that are excreted in the urine (after leaving the blood stream through the kidneys to produce a high level) will be prescribed. The veterinary surgeon may prescribe a special diet to alter the pH of the urine.

DEAFNESS

Deafness is not uncommon in the old dog. The loss of hearing is slow, and adaptation with the greater use of the other senses, especially of smell, allows the dog to lead an almost normal life. The high-pitch dog whistle can be used to attract the attention of many dogs with a hearing defect. This is especially useful for loose recall.

CAUSE
Deafness may be due to loss of nerve function and there is a hereditary form of deafness in some breeds. The Dalmatian breed has both unilateral and bilateral deafness. Other dogs become deaf due to injury. A veterinary examination with a deep-tube auroscope is necessary to look for a perforated ear-drum or a deposit of wax across the ear drum. Specialised hearing tests are available to investigate the type of inherited deafness in Dalmatian puppies. Such tests in the Guide Dogs for the Blind Association's Labrador Retrievers and German Shepherd Dogs have shown no hereditary or other deafness in younger dogs.

TREATMENT
Cleaning the ear canals with a non-irritant cleaner may help some dogs with wax build-up in the ears. The frequency of cleaning depends on the individual, but it may be done on a weekly basis, or less frequently.

DEHYDRATION

The condition where the body loses water at a faster rate than water can be taken in and retained.

SIGNS
The signs of fluid loss may be recognised in the eyes, skin and mouth. The eye will be look dry and lustreless and, in severe cases, the whole of the eyeball will sink into the head. The skin will stay in a ridge when lifted up, and the degree of 'tenting' can be used to assess how dehydrated a dog is. The inside of the mouth will appear dry, with stringy mucus around the teeth. Eventually a dog will show signs of shock, with cold extremities, and a thin, thready pulse.

If a dog is dehydrated, the skin will stay in a ridge when lifted up.

CAUSE
Dehydration may be recognised in dogs deprived of water or, more commonly, in dogs that have lost large quantities of fluid through diarrhoea and sickness. Serious dehydration can occur when excess fluid is lost through the kidneys in renal failure, and with diabetes.

TREATMENT
Treatment for dehydration aims to correct the fluid loss, and restore the body fluids. Dogs should be coaxed to swallow small quantities of fluid, often with salts (electrolytes) and glucose added to make an 'isotonic solution'. A simple household remedy is a mixture of a teaspoonful of salt with dessertspoonful of glucose in two pints of water. Alternatively, there are number of proprietary powder mixtures that can be obtained through the veterinary surgeon. When there is severe water depletion, as in heatstroke, intravenous water can be given as a five per cent dextrose solution. Blood tests taken will accurately measure the degree of dehydration, and specific electrolyte mixtures, such as Hartmann's, can be given intravenously.

DEMODECTIC MANGE

This is a form of skin infection caused by the Demodex parasite, The disease is more correctly known as demodecosis.

SIGNS
Demodecosis can cause localised or more generalised skin disease. The localised form is seen in young dogs (less than 12 months old) as hairless patches on the face or legs; 90 per cent of these clear spontaneously without treatment. The generalised form may develop in both young and old animals, producing many hairless skin-scaling patches. This form is often complicated by secondary bacterial skin infection,

sometimes known as 'red mange', which usually causes irritation and scratching. The parasite can often be identified by examining skin scrapings under the microscope.

CAUSE

Demodecosis is a form of skin infection caused by a burrowing parasite *Demodex foliculorum* which lives in hair follicles and sebaceous glands. Some dogs seem to be more susceptible to infection than others, and there may be a predisposition in certain breeds to develop more severe forms of Demodectic mange. There may be an inherited defect in their immune system's response to the Demodex mite, so allowing the mite to multiply and spread through the skin. Older dogs developing generalised demodecosis may have some other disease that is suppressing the immune system, e.g. pyoderma *(see page 242)*. There is evidence to suggest that bitches that regularly produce puppies affected with mange should not be bred from. The parasite may be transferred from the skin of the bitch's mammary glands to the suckling puppy, as the first signs in younger dogs are bare areas on the face and fore legs.

TREATMENT

Treatment of the affected skin with washes containing Amitraz is generally the most effective – but a variety of different treatments are in use, depending on the severity of the condition. Generalised forms, where the dog's skin is red and oozing, may require intensive treatment including long-term antibiotic use. A total body-clip may be advised to assist in penetration of medicated washes into the skin.

Demodectic mange seen in a Scottish Terrier.

DERMATOSIS

Dermatosis is a term used for any skin disorder. The word dermatitis describes an inflammatory skin condition. All skin conditions require investigation – it is usually necessary to find an underlying cause before treatment and

advice can be given. Pyoderma, allergic dermatoses and hormonal alopecia are three examples of widely differing conditions of the skin that come under the general heading. *(See pyoderma page 242).*

DIABETES

A term in common use that describes a number of disorders where there is increased urine output as well as an increased thirst.

SIGNS
The two forms of diabetes found in the dog are both associated with a noticeable increase in thirst and the output of increased quantities of watery urine.

CAUSE
Diabetes mellitus is the more common 'sugar diabetes' that results from the endocrine tissue of the dog's pancreas producing little or no insulin. The insulin of the healthy dog is produced in the largest quantity just after a meal. It ensures that the sugars absorbed after the meal is digested can be stored in the liver and in the muscles as glycogen. A failure of insulin production by the pancreas gland means that, after a starchy meal has been eaten, sugar flooding into the blood-stream is not stored by the tissues. Blood-sugar levels therefore become abnormally high, and the excess sugar has to be removed by the kidneys, pulling the water with it. In this sort of diabetes the dog may fail to store the urine, with a constant dribble of urine and wetting indoors – especially overnight.

Diabetes insipidus is characterised by the dog producing great quantities of watery urine, with no glucose excess. The cause may be due to a failure of the pituitary gland in the brain to produce enough anti-diuretic hormone (ADH), or a failure in the kidneys to respond to the need to concentrate the urine.

A Jack Russell Terrier suffering from diabetes.

TREATMENT
Tests on urine samples are needed for the veterinary surgeon to confirm a diagnosis and frequently blood samples will also be taken for analysis. In the case of diabetes mellitus, insulin can be injected on a once or twice a day basis once the diabetic dog is at home, after the dog has been stabilised at the veterinary surgery and the treatment regime marked out. Regular urine samples may be needed for checking the dosage of insulin; this can now be done with a simple home kit. Attention to diet with a fixed daily routine of exercise and feeding help to stabilise the dog. The type and quantity of food will be advised: more soluble fibre and less starch foods are recommended and a number of commercial diets are designed for this purpose.

Treatments for diabetes insipidus are available but it must be emphasised that a definite diagnosis is needed before commencing treatment for either type of diabetes *(see water deprivation page 277)*.

DIARRHOEA

Diarrhoea does not mean the frequency with which faeces are passed but, by definition, it is the passage of soft or sloppy faeces of increased bulk and water content.

SIGNS
Frequent passing of loose motions. Diarrhoea may be acute where the dog does not seem ill in between frequent voiding of the liquid faeces. More severe diarrhoea causes vomiting as well, and the dog appears ill and shocked due to the continued loss of fluids. There are some forms of diarrhoea associated with parasitism or malabsorption where the dog seems thin and passes frequent liquid faeces, and progressive weight loss may be expected.

CAUSES
Diarrhoea is a very common problem in the dog and has many different causes. There are those that directly affect the intestines, such as infections, food intolerances, 'worms', toxins, inflammatory bowel disease and tumours. Diseases elsewhere in the body can also affect the guts and cause diarrhoea. The dog is, by nature, a scavenger, so an attack of diarrhoea may be the quickest way that the dog can get rid of unsuitable things eaten, such as decayed matter or the food poisoning types of toxins. The skilled dog owner will be able to distinguish between transient, mild attacks that often commence with vomiting followed by 48 hours or so of watery or mucoid faeces, and attacks of a more severe kind. Persistent attacks of frequent diarrhoea can result in excessive fluid loss

and shock *(see page 254)*. In all dogs, if diarrhoea persists for more than 24 hours or if blood is present in the faeces, the veterinary surgeon should be consulted in case one of the life-threatening conditions associated with diarrhoea is present.

TREATMENT
For the first aid treatment, food should be withheld for 24 to 48 hours, and fluids should be given by mouth to avoid dehydration. Balanced electrolyte mixes are preferable to water to replace the losses of the diarrhoea. Specific treatments may be given to overcome the sickness, to stop undue straining and for intestinal spasms, or appropriate antibiotic drugs used if these are called for. As the dog recovers, a bland low-fat diet, such as boiled chicken and rice, can be offered. Dairy products should be avoided, although at the end of an attack fresh yoghurt may be considered beneficial. The normal food ration can then be gradually reintroduced once the problem has improved.

The dog that has repeated attacks of 'looseness' or diarrhoea can be a difficult problem. Sometimes these attacks seem to clear up after appropriate simple measures, only for another attack to develop as soon as the dog returns to full rations of food. Such cases of chronic diarrhoea will need investigation through the examination of faeces samples, and blood samples may also be required to look for intestinal digestive problems. Faeces samples can be examined under the microscope for parasites, and then used for bacterial culture, with sensitivity tests made on any intestinal micro-organisms present. An endoscope may also be used for an intestinal biopsy, and sometimes X-rays may be helpful as well.

DISTEMPER

An historic description for a severe disease in man or animals, it is now used for a specific infection of the dog that is caused by a morbilivirus.

SIGNS
The virus has an incubation of 7 to 21 days, which is followed by a rise in temperature, loss of appetite, a cough and often diarrhoea. Discharges from the eyes and nose may be watery at first, but often become thick mucoid, with a green or creamy colour, due to secondary infections. The enamel of the teeth may be damaged when the puppy of under six months of age is infected; enamel defects appearing as brown marks last for life and are known as 'distemper teeth'. In some dogs affected with

distemper, the injury to the nervous system is seen as fits, chorea (twitching of muscles) or posterior paralysis. Old dogs who were infected with the distemper virus in their youth may develop encephalitis (ODE) due to latent distemper virus in the nervous tissue.

CAUSE
This virus disease has become rare where distemper vaccine is used on a regular basis. It is seen in larger cities where there is a stray or roaming dog population, and this may lead to infection of show or other dogs that may have had contact but do not have a high level of immunity against distemper.

TREATMENT
Prevention by the use of vaccines is very effective, as most of the injections used are modified live vaccines and are efficient in providing solid immunity. The age for a first injection will partly depend on the manufacturer's instruction sheet, and partly on a knowledge of the amount of protection passed by the mother to the young puppies. Maternally derived immunity (MDI) might block the effect of the vaccine in the young puppy, but blood-sampling bitches during their pregnancy can be used as a method of estimating how much protection the puppy has. The use of a first vaccine at six weeks is often advised, as the puppy should then be able to respond to vaccine. A further vaccine dose for distemper can be given at 12 weeks, although some veterinary surgeons still use a 12 and 14 week routine. All vaccination programmes should be followed by a booster after 12 months.

DISTICHIASIS

The condition of the eye caused by a double row of eyelashes, one or both grow inwards to rub on the surface of the cornea.

SIGNS
This eye condition may first be noticed by a strong tear flow. Hairs rub on the cornea causing excessive watering and sometimes keratitis and ulceration may develop. In many cases the hairs do not cause a major problem and may cause only occasional conjunctivitis.

CAUSE
Distichiasis is a condition of the eyelids seen in young dogs, where an extra set of eyelashes is present. They grow on the eyelid margin, and if the lashes turn inwards they will cause an intense irritation, with the dog rubbing at its face.

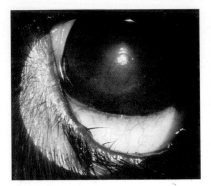

Distichiasis: Note three ectopic cilia that show against the white sclera on silhouette. A corneal ulcer (stained green) is also present in the eye of this Pekingese.

TREATMENT
Close inspection with a magnifying lens will confirm these lashes are present and their surgical removal will be advised.

DYSENTRY

The presence of blood in the faeces usually associated with diarrhoea.

SIGNS
Straining by the dog to pass moist or mucoid faeces, either with streaks of fresh blood or darker blood that has been partly digested. This will often be accompanied by a high temperature, and if the blood and fluid losses are severe, shock will develop.

CAUSE
Chemical irritants, bacteria *(Salmonella infection, see page 251)*, parasites *(Giardia, see page 178)*, viruses *(Parvo virus, see page 230)* or worms *(Hookworms, see page 189)*.

TREATMENT
General nursing for fluid losses: give solutions of electrolytes by mouth or intravenously. If a specific cause can be found or suspected, then specific drugs can be administered.

ECLAMPSIA

This medical condition occurs in lactating bitches when the blood calcium levels fall.

SIGNS
The bitch will appear restless, with a raised body temperature, then may start to twitch and show convulsions. These signs need to be treated as an extreme emergency and the puppies removed temporarily.

CAUSE
Eclampsia is a condition of blood calcium deficiency seen in the bitch feeding puppies. It more commonly occurs with a large litter at three to five weeks of age. The demand for calcium in the milk is enormous, and sometimes the bitch cannot extract the calcium from the food, or from her own bones, in sufficient quantity to keep her blood calcium at the correct level. The advice on feeding supplements has changed, as it is possible that the calcium supplements given to the lactating bitch may pose an increased risk of eclampsia developing. The parathyroid gland mobilises calcium from the bones, and a high calcium intake from food depresses the gland's activity. High-fibre diets, where the lignin interferes with calcium absorption, may also be to blame. Some strains within a breed seem particularly liable to eclampsia. The small breeds may be genetically predisposed, and puppies from affected bitches should not be used for subsequent breeding.

TREATMENT
Calcium by mouth does not correct the situation. Intravenous 10 per cent calcium will need to be injected by the veterinary surgeon as soon as possible. Prevention involves early feeding of puppies with supplementary food, especially puppies in a large litter.

ECTROPION

Ectropion is a condition where the lower eyelids droop and turn outwards.

SIGNS
Inflammation of the exposed areas of the eye and tear overflow.

Ectropion seen in a Cavalier King Charles Spaniel puppy. Both upper and lower lids are swollen. The muzzle is also swollen with a juvenile pyoderma.

CAUSE
The condition of drooping lower eyelids is produced by a lower eyelid that is too large for the size of the eyeball. It can be an inherited fault, but it may develop due to different growth rates of the skull and the skin of the face. Ectropion may be seen secondary to facial nerve paralysis or eyelid injury. As a polygenic inherited condition it can be bred out, but it is not as severe a condition as entropion *(see page 167)*.

TREATMENT
Exposure of the mucous membrane may lead to conjunctivitis that can be treated with ointment. Several surgical techniques have been used to correct the slackness in the lower lid.

ECZEMA

Eczema is an old-fashioned term for some types of skin disorder. Nowadays, the term is better reserved for atopic eczema *(see atopy page 129)*.

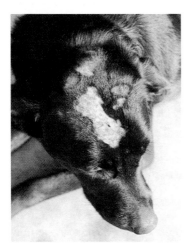

Eczema: In this case, the hair regrew within six weeks after treatment.

SIGNS

Any skin irritation will cause a dog to scratch, usually more so in warm rooms, but the scratching produces further skin damage and a secondary infection.

CAUSE

The dog scratches at various points in the body after exposure to allergic substances in the environment.

TREATMENT

It is advisable to seek diagnosis by the veterinary surgeon to ascertain the type of skin disease.

EHLERS-DANLOS SYNDROME

A congenital condition of fragility of the skin and of over-extensibilty of the joints, also known as hereditary collagen dysplasia.

SIGNS

This is a very rare condition where the skin becomes thin and very elastic. Wounds can tear almost as readily as tissue paper. They heal badly with a very fragile scar. There are other signs such as weak legs due to soft tendons.

CAUSE

The cause is unknown, but it may have a hereditary basis.

TREATMENT

There is no known treatment but injury to the skin should be avoided.

ENDOCARDIOSIS

This is a common disease in which the heart valves degenerate progressively.

SIGNS

The condition may be first detected by the veterinary surgeon who hears a 'murmur' when listening to the heart with a stethoscope. The murmur noise is due to an abnormal blood flow through the affected valve.

CAUSE

The valves may become shortened and thickened, which prevents them from working to seal off the heart chambers tightly at each beat. Heart failure may be the result. Although the valve changes may begin quite early in life, the signs of heart failure are usually not seen until middle or old age. The condition is more common in small breeds. In the King Charles Cavalier Spaniel heart failure may develop at an earlier age than in other breeds, but often it may not be detected until three to five years of age.

TREATMENT
Specific drugs for heart disease can be given according to the heart's failure in pumping the blood.

ENDOCARDITIS

This inflammatory condition of the endocardium of the heart is most important as it causes disease of the valves used in the vital pumping action of the heart.

SIGNS
The signs are vague: fluctuating temperature, depression, poor appetite, and sometimes shifting lameness.

CAUSE
This is an uncommon, acquired heart disease due to bacterial infection of the heart valves. It can occur at any time of life and could be the result of bacteria entering the blood-stream after a simple throat or tooth infection.

TREATMENT
Any source of infection needs treatment with antibiotics as it is a serious condition. To reduce the risk of endocarditis developing, routine dental care of the older dog is helpful.

ENDOMETRITIS

An inflammation of the lining of the uterus.

SIGNS
Blood-stained discharges from the vulva, often accompanied by a rise of body temeprature, refusal to eat and sickness.

CAUSE
Puerperal endometritis can be a cause of illness after whelping *(see The Birth of Puppies and Aftercare, page 58)*. Bacterial infection may lodge in the uterus if an afterbirth has been retained or the uterus fails to close down leaving a fluid-filled cavity. This is most likely in the older bitch or the bitch that has had a large litter. The persisting corpus luteum is the cause of the hyperplastic endometritis, which then becomes infected to cause the illness known as pyometra *(see page 243)*.

TREATMENT
Antibiotic treatment is urgent for the bitch with endometritis after whelping. Surgery is usually the method used to deal with pyometra.

ENTERITIS

Inflammation of the large or small intestine *(see colitis page 148, gastro-enteritis page 177)*.

ENTROPION

A condition where the eyelids turn inwards.

SIGNS
Affected dogs show a continuous watery discharge from the eye, and the eyelids are screwed up because of severe pain and irritation.

CAUSE
An inward turning of the eyelid causing the eyelashes to rub on the surface of the eyeball (cornea) and irritate it. If left untreated, the cornea may ulcerate and this could lead to an opacity and blindness. Some puppies are born with an inherited tendency to this condition, but it may only become a problem as the puppy grows and the skin on the face becomes tighter.

TREATMENT
Soothing creams applied to the eye may help to reduce irritation. Eye ointments will be prescribed by the veterinary surgeon. However, most cases will need an operation to evert the eyelids and thus prevent continuing damage to the cornea.

Entropion seen in a German Shorthaired Pointer puppy. Inflamed third eyelid with the lower lid in-turned so that the eyelashes rub on to the cornea.

EPILEPSY

Often defined as a short lasting but devastating disturbance of the nerve activity of the brain. The seizures are paroxysmal and may be repeated at intervals.

*Epilepsy
experienced
by a Yorkshire
Terrier.*

SIGNS
Fits in dogs have to be distinguished from other sorts of
convulsions, as well as faints and 'funny turns'. From time to
time, many dogs may have short periods of abnormal
behaviour, altered alertness, or abnormal movements. Most of
these will be due to a non-epileptic 'paroxysmal ' disorder. The
distinction from epilepsy is important and you should be able
to describe the type of fit to the veterinary surgeon, or even
video-record it if possible. Epileptic fits are characterised by
recurrent, unprovoked seizures.

CAUSE
Epilepsy is a disease caused by abnormal electrical activity in
the brain leading to recurrent fits also known as 'attacks',
'seizures' or 'convulsions'. Some epilepsy will develop after
there has been a head injury, but most epilepsy is described as
'idiopathic' which means there is no known cause. Idiopathic
epilepsy is more common in certain breeds such as the
Miniature Poodle, Cocker Spaniel and Golden Retriever, and is
assumed to be inherited – although it has not been proved from
pedigree analysis. The 'idiopathic' epileptic attacks are more
common in males and usually appear between six months and
five years.

TREATMENT
Dogs displaying fits should be fully assessed by the veterinary
surgeon. Most veterinary surgeons will not think it necessary to
treat fits that occur less frequently than once a month, but if the
intensity worsens or the number of days between the fits grows
less, there are a number of medications that can be used.

EXOCRINE PANCREATIC INSUFFICIENCY (EPI)

A disorder where there is a failure in the production of the digestive enzymes normally produced by the exocrine tissues of the pancreas gland.

SIGNS
This is a disease responsible for causing partial digestion of the food with resulting weight loss and grey, greasy faeces *(see pancreatic insufficiency page 225).*

CAUSE
The condition is related to the low output or absence of digestive enzymes produced by the pancreas.

TREATMENT
The diet should be a highly digestible, low-fat and low-fibre, mixture. Supplements of pancreatic extract may be given, often combined with a method of suppressing stomach acidity.

FADING PUPPIES

A condition where puppies are born and appear to feed well at first but then decline in general condition, become less active, and then may weaken and die.

SIGNS
The Fading Puppy Syndrome affects puppies in the first few weeks of life causing weakness, poor weight gain, dehydration, and finally, death. The problem develops when new-born puppies apparently feed well at first, but then become weaker as they suck before refusing all nourishment.

CAUSES
Many bacteria and virus infections have been identified as causes, but Herpes virus should be suspected when there is no response to warmth, antibiotics and supplementary feeding. Other factors include congenital abnormalities, low birth weight, trauma at birth, too much or too little milk supply, and poor immunity to disease.

Some puppies do not develop properly and they are unable to walk out of the nest once their eyes open. These are popularly known as 'swimmers' as this describes the movement made with their front legs as they try to pull themselves along. These puppies are often overweight, and they have loose-fitting shoulder-joints that do not allow the puppy to support its own weight. Some of the more mildly affected puppies will improve, but badly affected cases may have to be euthanased.

TREATMENT/PREVENTION
One of the most common causes of death is hypothermia, and an ambient temperature of 25 to 30 degrees Centigrade (85 Fahrenheit) is essential for the puppies, especially when the bitch is not as caring as she should be in providing her own body warmth. Preparation of the whelping area and scrupulous cleanliness at birth will help the bitch to look after her puppies and transfer immunity to the newborn animals. *(See The Birth of Puppies and Aftercare, page 58)*.

FAINTING

A term in general use, especially when referrring to people, for any temporary loss of consciousness.

SIGNS
A brief, temporary loss of consciousness. If the faint is less than five seconds, the dog may simply stagger or 'flop' with relaxed limbs. If the lack of oxygen continues for longer, there may be brief convulsive movements and urinary incontinence.

CAUSE
Fainting is caused by a fall in the blood flow to the brain. This results in insufficient oxygen supply to the brain tissue (cerebral anoxia). There is nothing equivalent to the emotional cause of the human faint, but dogs are known to collapse for brief periods where there is no underlying disease. The Boxer breed is prone to repeated fainting attacks, probably due to reflex activity of the vagus nerve.

TREATMENT
First aid treatment involving loosening the collar and providing plenty of fresh air should be all that is necessary. If the unconsciousness persists, or there are repeated attacks, then professional advice should be sought. Heart disease may be one cause of inadequate supply of blood to the brain and this possibility should always be investigated if there have been several attacks.

FALSE PREGNANCY

The term describes the behaviour pattern, and production of milk, found in some bitches that are not in whelp.

SIGNS
The non-pregnant bitch produces milk six to eight weeks after her season. Behaviour abnormalities may also be seen, including bed-making, excitability and protective aggression at, or about the time, that milk is formed and fluid can be squeezed out of the teats.

CAUSE
The bitch has an unusual breeding cycle in that the hormone changes after oestrus are very similar in both pregnant and non-pregnant bitches. The non-pregnant bitch has a corpus luteum that persists, and there are many still present in the ovary at the time false pregnancy develops. This unusual feature – and the associated behaviour patterns – would have allowed the ancestral bitch, living in a pack of dogs, to provide for any other puppies whose own mother might have had no milk to feed them, either as a result of disease or accidental death.

TREATMENT
A reduction in protein intake and more exercise may be sufficient to stop a bitch with false pregnancy being too

distressed but, in many cases, treatment with diuretics or hormone preparations may be needed as well.

FERTILITY

A high rate of conception and live births is expected when free-access mating is available during the breeding bitch's heat. Some of the problems of infertility may be due to single or restricted mating of the bitch, especially when there is a delayed release of eggs from the ovaries, as with late ovulation. The average bitch ovulates 12 days after the beginning of proestrus bleeding and should be mated by the 14th day, but ovulation may occur as early as the 8th day or as late as the 21st day. Blood tests from the bitch can be used by the veterinary surgeon to identify when ovulation occurs. Evaluation of the dog's semen may also be necessary if fertility is to remain high, especially in the older dog. *(See Breeding and Health, page 44).*

FITS

A fit is defined as any temporary but sudden loss of consciousness, accompanied by severe involuntary contractions of the jaw and body muscles.

SIGNS
A fit can vary in intensity, but a full fit is seen when the dog falls on its side, the legs become extended and the neck arches back with an involuntary champing of the jaws, usually with frothy saliva at the lips. The eyes remain wide open, breathing is fast, and often urine and faeces are expelled in an uncontrolled manner.

CAUSE
Fits, seizures and convulsions are caused by a disorder of the electrical activity in the brain. This can be caused by diseases, toxins, or injury affecting the nervous system, or more generalised diseases, such as liver failure, can affect the brain. Epilepsy does occur in dogs and is characterised by recurrent, unprovoked seizures, but there are many conditions in dogs best described as 'nervous attacks' that can be mistaken for epilepsy.

TREATMENT
The dog 'in a fit' should not be touched, but left in a quiet darkened room. Usually the attack will pass of in less than five minutes. In order to avoid accidental damage or injury, objects should be moved away, as low furniture may be knocked over and ornaments broken. Open fires should have guards put in

front of them. Following an attack, a dog will get up and wander round looking dazed and confused but will then return to normal behaviour. Calm handling will help to reassure the dog until all signs of the fit have passed. It is best not to try driving in a car with a dog that has been having fits unless specifically requested after contacting the veterinary surgeon. It is better to wait until the fit has passed before moving or stimulating the dog.

FLATULENCE

The excessive accumulation of gas in the stomach or the intestines. Uusually gas will be voided through the anus as 'flatus'.

SIGNS
Flatulence is an unpleasant, but seldom harmful, condition of the dog's digestive tract where gas is voided quietly but with a strong enough smell to inform all those in a room what has occurred.

CAUSE
Fermentation in the large intestine is encouraged by vegetable carbohydrate and fibre residues, but some dogs swallow quantities of air as they eat greedily and this will pass on through from stomach to large intestine.

TREATMENT
Several small meals, followed by exercise will help to get rid of the gas out of doors. Diets containing pea and bean meal should be avoided, though some all-meat diets will also cause excessive gas waste-products. Dairy products should also be avoided, although changes of diet may be tried until a suitable highly-digestible, low-residue diet is found for the dog.

FLEAS

The group of wingless insects, belonging to the order *Siphonaptera,* can live away from the animal but in order to multiply they will need a host to feed from. They do this by biting and then feeding from the blood which they have sucked out, and which has dried on the host.

SIGNS
Fleas can infest the skin surface of the dog. Allergy to flea bites and flea saliva can produce long-lasting itching and scratching, even when all the fleas have apparently been removed from the dog.

Fleas on the skin resulting in abdomen dermatosis.

CAUSE
With an increase in the domestic cat population, and the greater number of dogs housed indoors, the flea has become one of the most common causes of chronic skin disease.

TREATMENT
Effective flea control involves removal of flea larvae from the environment as well as 'on the dog' treatment for fleas. There are numerous preparations now available for flea control, and the most appropriate product to use can be recommended by the veterinary surgeon or nurse.

FOLLICULITIS

A generalised skin disorder with infection of the hair follicles.

SIGNS
Folliculitis is an inflammation of hair follicles, seen as small, raised red spots on the skin. Yellow serum sometimes covers the spots as little crusts or scabs.

CAUSE
This condition is more common in short-haired breeds as an infection of the hair follicles with bacteria, usually staphylococcus *(see staphylococcus infection page 258)*. Folliculitis is sometimes associated with Demodex parasite infection of the skin *(see demodectic mange page 156)*.

TREATMENT
There is no specific treatment other than an appropriate antibiotic and cleansing skin washes that will help to remove surface crusts *(See pyoderma page 242)*.

FOREIGN BODIES

This is the name given to objects that enter the dog's body.

SIGNS

The signs will vary with the type of substance entering the body. An air-gun pellet or gunshot may produce only small entry holes in the skin and, if fired at low velocity, the shot may remain in the body without great harm, only to be discovered later on by X-ray. Penetrating foreign bodies such as grass seeds in the foot will produce an intense irritation, often with a bleeding entry-point or hole, and a swelling above it as the seed moves forwards. Foreign bodies may become inhaled into the lungs or may lodge in the digestive tract – the signs will vary with the affected organ's function. The eyes and nose may also show severe reactions if a foreign body should enter either organ.

CAUSE

Foreign bodies may range from a swallowed squash ball in the stomach or a grass seed up the nose, to a splinter of glass in the foot pad.

TREATMENT

Treatment requires these objects to be removed, once their exact location has been found.

FRACTURES

Any break in the bone surface is described as a fracture.

SIGNS

The classical signs of fracture are deformity where the bone has broken, pain, swelling and warmth. At the fracture site there is unusual movement, a noticeable loss of function, and the grating of broken bones may be noticed if the leg is handled unwisely.

CAUSE

Most are the result of accidental injury. Fragments of bone are sharp, and an injury can be made worse by unwise attempts to manipulate or 'set' a fracture.

TREATMENT

First aid care involves disturbing the broken bone as little as possible. Often a dog will adopt its own position, and only when moved unwisely will pain be experienced. After an accident it is more important to ensure there is an adequate airway, cover any open wounds to prevent further contamination, and control blood loss to reduce the amount of shock. Splinting and bandaging make make the dog worse, and it is best to wait for a full examination, including X-rays, before fracture treatment is attempted.

FURUNCULOSIS

The pus forming in the skin after an infection leads to small abscesses and tunnels running just under the skin.

SIGNS

The discharge of pus on the skin surface from deep tracts, most often seen around the anus, on the nose, muzzle, flanks or legs.

CAUSE

Some bacteria have power to invade tissue better than others, but there is also the resistance of the dog to infection that may be reduced so that furunculosis will develop. The German Shepherd Dog breed has a particular tendency to develop a peri-anal furunculosis which is difficult to treat. There may be a genetic predisposition in some strains within the breed to develop furunculosis.

TREATMENT

Skin cleanliness is important in controlling the problem. Hair should be removed with scissors to allow any discharges to be wiped away, and anti-bacterial skin washes applied. Long courses of antibiotic tablets may be needed, and sometimes surgical excision of the tracts under the skin. In the treatment of anal furunculosis, wide excision and possibly cryosurgery may be needed to freeze out and destroy all the pus tracts.

Furunculosis of the nose.

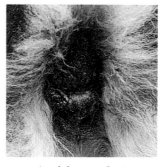
Anal furunculosis.

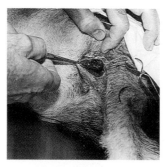
Surgical treatment for anal furunculosis.

GAMMA LINOLEIC ACID (GLA)

GLA is considered to be one of the essential components of the fatty acid supplements that are frequently used in dogs with skin disease. Certain fatty acids cannot be manufactured by the dog and these EFAs are essential items of the diet. They include linoleic, alpha-linoleic and arachidonic acids. The amount of gamma linoleic acid present is considered to be the most important factor when using a supplement. It works at a cell membrane level and is especially useful in atopic eczemas.

GASTRIC DILATION/VOLVULUS (GDV)

See Bloat page 135.

GASTRO-ENTERITIS

Gastritis is an inflammation of the stomach which is often accompanied by enteritis – an inflammation of the intestines.

SIGNS
Gastro-enteritis typically produces signs of vomiting accompanied or followed by diarrhoea.

CAUSE
This is a common problem in the dog and may be caused by many conditions that affect the digestive tract, either directly or indirectly. Bacteria or viruses (e.g. parvo virus), diet factors, toxic substances and certain medications may all produce gastro-enteritis. Other body organs' disorders, such as the liver, kidneys, or drug toxicity on the brain, may all show with signs of a gastro-entritis.

TREATMENT
The condition may vary in seriousness from a mild inconvenience to a life-threatening condition where fluid loss and toxaemia can lead to death in 24 hours. The passing of blood is a further cause for concern, and veterinary advice should be sought urgently. The basis of home treatment is dietary rest for 24 hours, and the supply of small quantities of

fluids by mouth as soon as vomiting is reduced enough to make this possible, so as to replace fluid already lost. Electrolyte-based balanced fluids are preferred for diarrhoea cases. The preparation of a teaspoonful of salt and a dessertspoon of powdered glucose in two pints of water as an isotonic fluid is widely used for home treatment.

GERIATRIC DOGS

Some dogs appear active and well at 13 years of age, while others can be considered to be geriatric soon after seven years. Regular exercise and attention to diet to avoid obesity are important in slowing up the ageing process. The larger and 'giant' breeds seem most subject to premature ageing.

SIGNS
Apart from heart, joint and urinary tract disorders, some of the worst aspects of ageing are seen as mental alterations. These may include dogs that avoid bright lights by hiding in corners, show disorientation and bark at night. Some dogs will eat voraciously while, more often, dogs become fussy about food and require frequent changes of flavour and consistency to keep up their interest in eating. Urinary and faecal incontinence may also be a problem of the senile dog.

TREATMENT
A complete physical examination, including a screening blood test, is advised before giving specific treatment to the geriatric dog. Adjustment to the diet and medication can be used to improve the life of the geriatric dog kept as a pet.

GIARDIA

This parasite is extremly small and has flagellae to propel itself in a liquid environment. The cysts passed in the faeces are very resistant to many of the normal disinfectants used in kennels.

SIGNS
Persistent diarrhoea, often with light-coloured greasy and soft consistency. Blood and mucus are seen less often in the diarrhoea unlike some other chronic diarrhoeas.

CAUSE
Giardia is a small Protozoal parasite of the dog's small intestine. These parasites attach themselves inside the dog with an adhesive disc, and the faeces produced contain fragile trophozoites and very resistant cysts. Contaminated water and

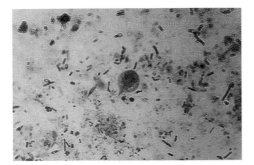

The giardia parasite.

wet areas may be the source of the first infection for a dog, but after giardia have become established in one dog, licking the coat during grooming and other activities, may account for the rapid spread throughout a kennel.

TREATMENT

Treatment with antiprotozoal drugs may have to be used over several weeks to get rid of an infection. As the parasite can cause illness in humans, cleanliness is vital when handling dogs suspected of carrying this infection. Attention to any wet areas in exercise runs where Giardia may live away from the dog, should be part of a kennel hygiene routine.

GINGIVITIS

An inflammation of the gums, especially where the periodontal membrane of the gum margin and the teeth roots meet, is known as gingivitis.

SIGNS

This condition of gum inflammation is frequently seen in the older dog and is most often associated with disease of the tissues that surround the teeth.

Gingival recession of the incisor teeth .

179

CAUSE
Plaque or calculus builds up at the gum margin and the teeth, exposing the junction of the gum with the tooth root, allowing infection and inflammation to become established *(See periodontal disease page 234)*.

TREATMENT
Specific anti-bacterial treatment may be needed to control gingivitis together with dental hygiene measures to remove the calculus on the teeth. Jaw exercise involving chewing suitable tough material will keep the teeth and gums of many dogs healthy into old age. Regular tooth brushing after meals is also advocated as being the best way to prevent gingivitis.

GLAUCOMA

Glaucoma is an increase in the pressure of the fluid in the eyeball which can lead to blindness within 24 hours, in acute cases.

SIGNS
The signs of glaucoma are an eye that is painful, especially if the eyebrows are touched, with prominent blood vessels congesting the white sclera and a clouding of the cornea. The pupil is dilated and cannot constrict, even when a bright light is shone on it.

CAUSE
There are a number of different types of glaucoma, and certain breeds may develop 'primary' glaucoma without the presence of another eye disease. More commonly, glaucoma occurs after an injury or a lens cataract that causes uveitis, with a problem with the fluid drainage from the front part of the eyeball.

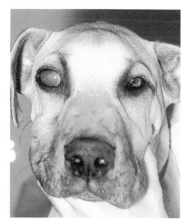

Swollen right eye due to glaucoma, seen in a seven-month-old Great Dane. The right eye is blue due to uveitis and secondary glaucoma.

TREATMENT
Urgent veterinary attention is required, especially in the terrier breeds where there could be a dislocated lens causing the glaucoma and blindness. Medical or surgical treatments may be needed to reduce the pressure within the eye and to treat any other disease.

GLOSSITIS

The inflammation of the mouth is known as stomatitis, but when the surface of the tongue is affected, the term glossitis is used.

SIGNS
The dog may have difficulty in eating. There may be more saliva present than usual, and if the tongue is inspected, raw areas and unusual marks may be present.

CAUSE
Virus infections may cause mouth ulcers, and chemicals licked by a dog may cause damage and erosion of the tongue surface. Some of the auto-immune diseases have extensive tongue ulceration as well as ulcers at other sites on the body. In advanced kidney disease, mouth and tongue ulceration will be associated with a strong breath odour.

TREATMENT
Antibiotics will be used when a bacterial infection is present – often this will include a drug effective against anaerobic bacteria. Nursing care involves mouth washes and feeding soft foods until healing takes place.

H

HAEMATOMA

Any accumulation of blood that has leaked out of the blood vessels and accumulated under the skin or in an organ is called a haematoma. Bruises after contusion of the tissues are another example of this condition.

SIGNS
Any swelling containing blood may be found after an injury to the body. The most common place to see a haematoma is in the ear pinna.

An example of a haematoma found in the ear.

CAUSE
The accumulation of blood under the skin is most often seen in the ear flap as an 'aural haematoma'. Blood vessels will become fragile after repeated ear shaking or scratching, then blood oozes into the space between the skin and the ear cartilage until a large sac of blood develops. The ears will appear uneven, as often the blood is heavy enough to pull down the ear due to this increased weight. Haematomas may occur at other parts of the body and these can result from bites or injuries caused by road accidents producing bruising.

TREATMENT
Initial treatment should be to apply an ice-cold compress to prevent further bleeding from dilated blood vessels. This will also help to control any irritation of the ear, relieving the dog's need to scratch or shake. Small haematomas may shrink as their contents are absorbed, but the larger ones, especially in the ear, need to be drained surgically and measures taken to prevent further bleeding.

HAEMOPHILIA

A blood disorder characterised by impaired coagulation and a tendency to bleed after even minor injuries.

SIGNS
Haemophilia causes a failure of blood clotting, noticeable as prolonged bleeding after small injuries or tooth loss.

CAUSE
By definition, an inherited disorder of blood clotting caused by deficiency of a factor required for the normal clotting process. Haemophilia A (Factor VIII deficiency) is the more common type seen in the dog, where it affects the German Shepherd Dog breed in particular. Sudden death of a dog due to rapid blood loss in major injuries may be the first knowledge of the disease. Bleeding can take place in the body cavities or into the joints without any outward signs of bleeding.

TREATMENT
Certain forms of haemophilia are managed by medical treatment and a controlled life style. Affected dogs should not be used for breeding if they survive to adult age.

HAEMORRHAGE

The loss of blood from ruptured blood vessels, often following some injury.

SIGNS
External bleeding is quickly recognised by the amount of blood found on or close to the body surface. Internal bleeding is less obvious – blood can accumulate in the abdomen or the chest without visible blood loss. If an internal organ is damaged in an

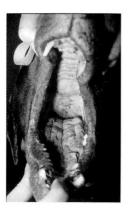

Petechial haemorrhage in the mouth.

accident or a tumour bleeds, the signs of panting, paleness of mucous membranes, weakness and of shock may be missed.

CAUSES
External injury, burst blood vessels or poor clotting ability may all lead to unexpected blood loss. (See haemophilia, page 183, warfarin poisoning page 238).

TREATMENT
The unnecessary loss of blood should be avoided by the use of first aid measures, and then by employing all the resources of the veterinary surgery if the haemorrhage is sustained and it threatens the dog's life.

HEART DISEASE

The heart acts as a muscle pump which moves blood round the body through the circulation. The healthy dog's heart has a pulse rate of between 70 and 140 beats a minute, but in times of exercise or stress the heart responds by speeding up to over 200 beats a minute as the cardiac muscle squeezes out more blood at each beat.

SIGNS
Tiredness and a low exercise tolerance may be the first signs reported. Rapid breathing that does not slow down after rest may be associated with a dog that stands most of the time and seems reluctant to lie down. Both signs indicate a failure of oxygen transport from the lungs to the body organs. The colour of the tongue and lips may be darker or even purplish-mauve in colour with advanced heart disease.

CAUSES
Heart disease may be present at birth or, more often, it develops later in life. Congenital heart defects often involve the valves or the blood vessels close to the heart which have failed to develop normally. The heart diseases seen later in life usually involve the heart muscle (myocardium) or the heart valves (see endocardiosis page 165, endocarditis page 166). The muscles of the heart will stretch in heart disease until they weaken. In cardiomyopathy of the giant breeds, the heart muscle becomes so thin and weak that the dog may collapse if the least stressed, and the heart rhythm will be irregular too. Heart disease can lead to signs of heart failure, which can be sudden as in cardiac arrest or slowly worsening as in 'chronic heart failure' (CHF).

TREATMENT
Diagnosis of heart disease involves a range of tests before any medication is given. Treatment involves exercise restriction

and strict rest. Weight control by dieting is equally important. A low sodium diet – avoiding salty foods and snacks such as crisps – is often advised. Diuretics such as Frusemide may be used to remove excess fluid through the kidneys. There is now a wide choice of drugs that modify heart contractions to help the blood flow, drugs that dilate blood vessels and also the airways, all of which can be used to reduce the signs of heart failure. Close monitoring of the dog's condition is essential when these drugs are used.

HEATSTROKE

(See hyperthermia page 192).
Never leave dogs in confined, airless spaces – such as cars on warm days or conservatories. Short-nosed breeds of dogs, hairy dogs and those who have inadequate supplies of drinking water are at greatest risk.

HEPATITIS

Inflammation of the liver may have a toxic or infectious cause.

SIGNS
Inflammation of the liver would not easily be recognised, but might be associated with sickness and a raised temperature; pain under the rib-cage where the liver lies, weight loss and jaundice may all develop during the course of the illness.

CAUSES
Hepatitis is an inflammation of the liver tissue which may result from chemical or other toxicity, and from bacterial or viral infections. Infectious Canine Hepatitis (ICH), caused by an *adenovirus 1* (CAV 1), is now quite rare because of effective vaccination. A different virus form (CAV 2) does not cause hepatitis, but is often found associated with 'kennel cough' infection in dogs. With a CAV 1 infection, the virus multiplies in the lymphatic system and then damages the blood vessels and liver cells. Severe infections with the virus were usually fatal, but in milder cases dogs would survive the disease. About 70 per cent of recovered dogs were found to have kidney damage. The eye injury following the immune response to canine hepatitis was known as 'blue eye' – most commonly it was seen in Afghan Hounds.

TREATMENT
There are no specific drugs; good nursing, antibiotics prescribed if indicated, and a low fat digestible diet can be offered. This

life-threatening disease can be prevented by vaccination at 6 and 12 weeks, using a reliable vaccine that contains the CAV-2 virus. Regular boosters through life are needed.

HERNIA

A weakness or unusual opening in the body wall may lead to the protrusion of fat or of an internal organ, with a resulting unexpected protuberance. Herniorrhaphy is the term for the surgical repair of the defect.

SIGNS
Any unexpected swelling in the groin (inguinal region), the umbilicus, or around the rectum (perineum) should be suspected as a hernia.

CAUSE
Any defect or weakness in the body 'walls' may cause bulging of contents, and this swelling is known as a hernia. Tearing of a muscle following an injury will cause a similar condition but, strictly speaking, this should always be called a 'rupture'. The commonest hernia is the umbilical hernia, seen in puppies as a swelling at the navel.

TREATMENT
Small hernias will seal up and not cause problems, although the bigger ones need surgery to reduce the swelling and repair the defect. Inguinal hernias are more common in bitches than in dogs. The swelling in the groin may contain the uterus, the broad ligament, the intestines or the bladder – all of these require urgent surgical attention. An inguinal hernia in the male may contain a loop of intestine which could strangulate, while the uterus caught in the bitch's hernia sac will develop pyometra *(see page 243)*. Perineal rupture is peculiar to older male dogs. It is usually associated with straining to defaecate, as a sequel to the prostate gland at the neck of the bladder being enlarged. This condition becomes an emergency if the bladder turns backwards and becomes trapped in the swelling. Any swelling round the anus needs examination to decide if it is a tumour, a distended anal gland sac, or a perineal rupture.

HERPES VIRUS

The group of viruses affecting dogs was discovered in 1965 as a severe and fatal infection of young puppies, with survivors likely to develop eye and brain damage. Infection of a bitch in pregnancy may cause abortion and stillbirths. Older dogs infected may develop respiratory disease as seen in kennel cough or infection of the genital system.

SIGNS
Herpes infection may be one cause of fading puppies *(see page 170)*, but it can also produce painful lesions on the male dog's prepuce or penis which can result in temporary male infertility. The herpes ulcers often heal after four to six weeks, but sometimes a persistent discharge from the prepuce continues as the only outward sign of a carrier of the virus.

CAUSE
A viral infection.

TREATMENT
In the absence of an effective anti-viral agent for dogs, nursing care and daily dressing may help the part to heal. Research into the disease in kennelled dogs is being undertaken to show that latent infections exist, and further investigations are needed to show how long the virus may persist after sores have healed. It has been suggested that herpes infection is very common in dogs not kept as domestic pets, and that cross-infection depends on the grouping together of dogs and on their housing conditions, so there is no effective control by restricting matings.

HIP DYSPLASIA

A degenerative joint disease that results from the abnormal development of the joint that forms the hip.

SIGNS
Affected dogs show abnormal sitting or an unusual way of walking, described sometimes as 'crabbing'. The back legs may seem stiff, and affected dogs are slow to sit, eventually developing stiffness and pain as well. The condition is most often seen in the larger breeds over 12 Kg, and can affect one or both hips.

CAUSE
The hip joint is a 'ball and socket' joint, and one of the best-known hereditary defects is where the joint does not develop properly. The condition of a shallow hip joint and a poorly fitting head of the femur (thigh bone) makes the joint unstable, leading to the development of bony changes and eventually arthritis. Although there is an inherited genetic basis, there are many other influences on the growing dog's joints such as exercise, nutrition, body weight, and the method of puppy rearing used.

Hip dysplasia is not a congenital disease as the condition rarely develops until 5 to 8 months of age. In the young dog the

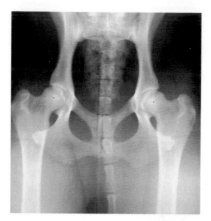

X-ray of a Labrador bitch (with a score of 12): Suitable for breeding.

A hip X-ray showing how tilting of the pelvis can alter the outline of the hip joints and affect the scoring adversely

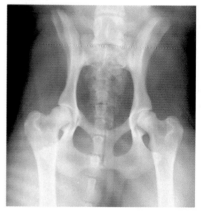

signs appear suddenly, with the dog showing difficulty in rising and an unwillingness to walk, run, jump, or climb steps. These signs may be due to pain from tiny fractures around the edge of the hip-joint socket (the acetabulum), often produced by the pressure from the loose femur head in the unstable joint. The fractures heal and the joint becomes more stable, so pain and lameness is reduced by 12 to 14 months. The joint surface responds to the instability by producing new bone (osteophytes) which can be detected on X-ray films. The osteoarthritis stage of the disease is seen in the older dog with hip dysplasia. Lameness is worse after exercise. Dogs prefer to sit rather than stand, and have difficulty in rising or jumping.

HIP TESTING
The BVA/KC scheme was set up in 1983 and is open to all breeds. Nine features of the hip X-ray are assessed by a panel

of radiologists, each one gets a score between 0 and 6 (but one feature is only 0 to 5) so that a dog can score between 0 and 53 on each of its hips giving 0 to 106 on both hips together. All breeders are encouraged to use the scheme as it is beneficial in determining which dogs to mate to produce the healthiest puppies. Breeders should aim to use the male dogs with the lowest scores for mating with low-scoring bitches. The X-ray

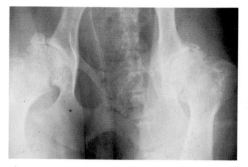

Hip dysplasia in an advanced stage, showing signs of osteo arthritis.

picture, which is normally taken at one year of age, is judged by a panel of radiologists and the score is recorded by the Kennel Club. In the USA, a similar scheme is operated by the Orthopaedic Foundation for Animals (OFA). A seven-point scoring system is used for hips ranging from 'excellent' to 'severe dysplasia'. Dogs must be at least two years old to receive a breeding number from the OFA, although preliminary evaluations will be made by the OFA on dogs younger than 24 months, to help breeders choose their future stock.

TREATMENT

With appropriate medical or surgical treatment, the majority of dogs with hip dysplasia can enjoy a pain-free active life. A proportion of dogs will need pain control for most of their life. A number of surgical techniques have been developed to treat different stages of the condition.

HOOKWORMS

Hookworms are a worldwide problem and can cause severe disease. *Ancylostomum*, the more dangerous parasite of the two types of hookworm, can inhabit the small intestine of dog, cat and fox.

SIGNS

Two types of hookworm can be found in the UK: *Uncinaria* is a hookworm that does not suck blood from the intestine wall but can cause damage leading to protein loss. Other signs are seen on the feet when hookworm larvae, which may lie in grass waiting for dogs to infect, migrate through the skin of the lower limbs. *Uncinaria* infections can cause a dermatitis, as they will not all migrate to proceed up the legs as far as the intestine. The other UK hookworm in the intestine, *Ancylostomum*, sets up a blood-feeding existence, but is very rare in UK bred dogs. *Ancylostomum* causes anaemia and debility, and emaciation may develop. Even after moderate exertion, exhaustion is soon evident.

TREATMENT
Control involves regular worming with proprietary preparations effective against hookworms, and good kennel hygiene is advised including the close mowing of grassed areas.

HORMONAL ALOPECIA

A group of skin conditions, characterised by hair loss, usually in symmetrical patches, are due to failure of the endocrine control of the dog's skin metabolism.

SIGNS
Each condition tends to start with hair loss in different sites on the body, and some can produce black pigmentation on the hairless parts.

CAUSE
Hair loss may be due to hormone imbalance: the thyroid, the adrenal cortex, or the gonads (ovary or testis) may be involved.

TREATMENT
Usually blood tests or skin biopsy will be needed to look for specific changes before treatment in the form of hormone supplements or possible surgery can be given.

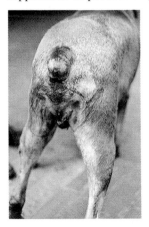

Hormonal alopecia.

HORNER'S SYNDROME

Nerve damage leads to a peculiar change in the appearance on one side of the face.

SIGNS

A drooping eyelid is accompanied by a tiny dark pupil and a slightly recessed eyeball. The third eyelid then becomes more noticeable and there may be an exposed conjunctiva.

CAUSE

The most common injury is one to the nerve that supplies the eye as it crosses over the ear tube. Any ear infection that causes inflammation of the surrounding tissues may affect the nerve. Less commonly the nerve is damaged as it runs lower down the neck. Here the nerve may be damaged by an injury caused by a severe choke-chain or some surgical interference. Thrombosis of the carotid artery is often recognised first as a drooping eye as one sign of Horner's Syndrome, due to pressure on the sympathetic nerve. Brain tumours are another cause, but these are quite rare in dogs.

TREATMENT

Phenylephrine drops in the eye will temporarily reverse the condition, and the time taken to dilate the pupil with these drops is used by the veterinary surgeon to study the cause. The majority of dogs seem to resolve the condition in three months or so, but steps should be taken to moisten or lubricate any exposed eye surfaces.

HYPERACTIVITY

Over-active dogs are those that have boundless energy, but are physiologically normal.

SIGNS

Signs such as constant and restless motion, poor learning, lack of attention, a tendency to easy distraction and sometimes aggression may be seen in dogs with hyperactivity.

CAUSE

Veterinary examination of the hyperactive dog is advised to investigate the presence of an underlying disease. Blood analysis should include the test for an over-active thyroid gland *(see thyroid disease page 264)*, which is a more specific illness, but rare in dogs.

TREATMENT

A challenge with a low dose of a stimulant, such as dextro-amphetamine, may be advised for a hyperactive dog. A low-grade diet, with more fibre and less protein to provide a lower plane of nutrition, may benefit some of these dogs.

HYPERTHERMIA

Any increase in body temperature if not caused by an infection is known as hyperthermia and can threaten the dog's life. When the temperature keeps on increasing it is known as malignant hyperthermia.

SIGNS
The ultra violet rays of the sun seldom produce the sunburn effects seen in humans with unpigmented skin. Affected dogs show distress, excessive panting, flushed mucous membranes. They may become weak, then collapse totally if treatment is delayed.

CAUSE
Hyperthermia or 'heatstroke' is usually caused by over-exposure to the sun, resulting in an increase in body temperature. Dogs left in poorly ventilated cars are at greatest risk, but a dog left in a concrete yard, with neither shade nor water, can easily become hyperthermic.

TREATMENT
Any dog thought to be affected by heatstroke should be cooled down, as soon as possible, with large quantities of cold water. Ice-packs applied around the body, and frequent sponging of the tongue and mouth with iced water also help to lower the body temperature. Intravenous fluids may have to be given by the veterinary surgeon when dehydration is contributing to the dog's distress. Rectal temperature should be checked very frequently at first, then every 15 minutes, until it has fallen to 102 degrees Fahrenheit (38.3 degrees Celsius).

I

ICTERUS

This term used for the discoloration of the body is of Greek origin. It is used by pathologists often in preference to the more easily understood word jaundice.

SIGNS
The condition icterus is seen as a yellow pigmentation of the skin, eyeballs and other parts of the body.

CAUSE
In the healthy animal, the worn out haemoglobin of the blood is broken down in the liver and spleen and reprocessed, so that necessary factors – such as iron – can be transported to the bone marrow for the production of replacement blood cells. The pigment from the blood breakdown (called bilirubin) is normally removed from the liver in the bile. Liver damage may result from toxins, bacterial or virus infection or from cancerous growths. A diseased liver cannot deal with all the waste products, and excess bilirubin is left in the blood circulating round the body. The pigment becomes visible in the mucous membranes and, soon after, in the skin as an orangey-yellow colour. Some thin-skinned dogs will appear almost buttercup yellow in colour. Jaundice can also occur in dogs that have a massive destruction of red blood cells, so that the liver cannot remove all the bilirubin at once.

TREATMENT
It is necessary to find the cause of the pigment retention in the tissues, then treat for liver or haemolytic disease as decided by the veterinary surgeon. A low-fat diet is always advised in any problem with the dog's liver.

IMMUNOSUPPRESSION

The state of a reduced immune response may occur after some infections (e.g. distemper), exposure to X-ray irradiations or toxic chemicals, or it is often deliberately produced for the treatment of some diseases by specific drug medication.

SIGNS
A lowered resistance may lead to secondary bacterial infections

and skin parasites such as *Demodex* becoming more active.

CAUSES

A number of drugs in use for the treatment of painful joint disease, or for skin irritation, may have wider effects over the body, causing immunosuppression. Immune-mediated diseases, such as polyarthritis, may need treatment with corticosteroids at high doses to suppress an abnormal immune response. Drug treatment for certain forms of cancer may also reduce the immune response by suppressing cell production from the bone marrow. Some virus infections, such as canine distemper, also have an immunosuppressive effect.

TREATMENT

The dog owner should be aware of the risks, and antibiotics may be needed to protect the dog from developing major infections when the normal resistance has been lowered.

INFERTILITY

A state of low fertility may be found in some stud dogs. Infertility can be found in the female as well *(See Breeding and Health, page 44)*. Veterinary advice should be sought when there is repeated failure after planned matings.

INTERVERTEBRAL DISC DISEASE

The pad of fibrocartilagenous material known as a 'disc', situated between the body of each vertebra bone is subject to degeneration, extrusion, protrusion and herniation to cause the disease known in humans as a 'slipped disc'.

SIGNS

Disc disease can vary from 'backache' signs in the dog to a sudden and severe paralysis.

CAUSE

The joints between vertebrae have a shock-absorber disc consisting of an inner soft nucleus and a fibrous outer ring, the annulus. Part of the ageing process is for the pulpy centre to be converted into harder, calcified material. Any unusual strain on the back, especially in long-backed breeds such as Dachshunds, may cause the fibrous ring to burst and some of the disc material to prolapse and press on the nerve fibres of the spinal cord.

TREATMENT

In severe, sudden onset of paralysis, intravenous injection of a corticosteroid and surgery to remove prolapsed disc material may be urgent. Milder cases can be treated conservatively with anti-inflammatory drugs and moderate rest. Particular attention has to be given to bladder emptying and bowel function, as often these may have been compromised.

INTUSSUSCEPTION

A difficult word to spell – and the idea of a length of intestine turning itself in, then out, is equally difficult to imagine!

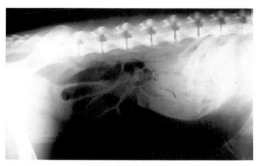

Intussusception: X-ray of the abdomen.

SIGNS
Most commonly seen in younger dogs with diarrhoea where vomiting may develop if the dog has a complete obstruction of the intestines.

CAUSE
Repeated straining to pass faeces results in one piece of small intestine invaginating, turning what is normally a soft tube into a hard sausage-shaped mass within the abdomen. The narrowing causes further straining, diarrhoea streaked with fresh blood, and abdominal pain.

TREATMENT
Once diagnosed, the dog will need operating on immediately. It may then be possible to reduce the invagination but, in many cases, a length of intestine will have to be removed by enterectomy. It is essential to treat the diarrhoea and control the diet after operating, as there is a tendency for reoccurrence if diarrhoea persists.

JAUNDICE

The yellowness of the tissues due to accumulation of bilirubin and other pigments is often accompanied by dark urine and pale faeces.

SIGNS
Jaundice as a yellow skin colour is described under icterus *(see page 193)*. There are other causes of jaundice, and any yellow coloration appearing in the whites of the eyes or elsewhere in the body should be a cause for veterinary attention.

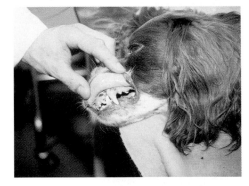

Jaundice showing in the gums of an English Springer Spaniel.

A Whippet with jaundice showing yellow-coloured skin on the flanks.

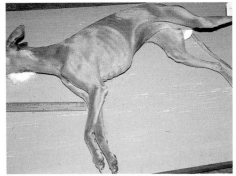

CAUSE
Traditionally, the word is used for a severe disease in dogs. 'Rat jaundice' was seen in terriers and others working near water courses, or in kennel dogs after licking up any urine left

by rats running through a yard. *Leptospira* bacteria, passed in the urine, survive in damp places for some time.

TREATMENT/PREVENTION
With the widespread use of Leptospira vaccine and the insistence on the annual booster dose, the disease has become uncommon, and the danger of this form of liver damage as a cause of the death of dogs has been greatly reduced.

JUVENILE BONE DISEASE

Growth problems in puppies may have a variety of causes. The term 'rickets' has now been replaced as it describes a very infrequent cause of bone deformity in puppies.

SIGNS
Affected puppies show lameness, with painful joints or swollen deformed legs.

CAUSES
Juvenile osteodystrophy, rickets and metaphyseal osteopathy *(see Barlows disease page 133)* are examples of bone disease in growing puppies where the development of bone is abnormal. Rickets due to a Vitamin D deficiency is hardly ever seen, but a similar condition can be produced by over-supplementation with calcium tablets, or by feeding a cereal diet where the phosphorus in the plant-derived food cannot be absorbed. Juvenile osteodystrophy occurs when there is a deficiency of calcium in the diet, such as when an all-meat diet is used. The growth plates (metaphyses) are the sites of bone growth, and they are the most easily damaged area of the young dog's bones.

TREATMENT/PREVENTION
The calcium to phosphorus ratio in the food is all-important: it should be between 1.2 and 1.4 to 1 to prevent these diseases. Over-feeding should be avoided as it is likely that most juvenile skeletal conditions are worsened by rapid bone growth. Proprietary foods are usually safe in this respect, but problems develop when a home-made diet is used for feeding young dogs for the sake of economy or some other reason.

KENNEL COUGH

An infectious disease of dogs, often associated with recent confinement in boarding kennels.

SIGNS

The harsh, persisting cough, more correctly called tracheo-bronchitis, was commonly seen in the summer months when dogs had been in kennels. It is now found in dogs at other times of the year, often unrelated to boarding kennels, and it has been suggested it should be renamed 'infectious bronchitis'. The cough is easily recognised, typically harsh and dry, and often occurs in bouts followed by retching. It may sound as if the dog has something stuck in its throat. Sudden changes in breathing, as produced by exercise, barking and temperature change, will bring on the cough. Affected dogs seem otherwise bright, eat normally and appear in good health, but occasionally the infection spreads into the lungs and the dog becomes much more ill with a high temperature.

CAUSE

There are several viruses involved, and the bacterium *Bordetella bronchiseptica* is often found in the trachea. The incubation period of five to seven days means that some dogs will not show signs of the cough until several days after they have left boarding kennels. The cough can spread on droplets to other dogs nearby, so dogs exercised in public parks may be affected by a similar cough, even though they have never been boarded out.

TREATMENT

Treatment involves using those antibiotics known to penetrate the sticky mucus that clings to the trachea lining at its base, and a course for at least 10 days is required. At the same time, cough suppressants such as codeine and butorphonol may be needed to give peace to the dog as well as the owners. Exercise should be restricted to short walks on the lead, or a harness may be preferred to keep pressure from the sensitive trachea. Excitement should be avoided, and the sleeping area should be kept warm at night. Annual booster vaccines containing a 'Pi' component give protection against some of the viruses involved – two to four weeks before kenneling is the best time to boost. The intranasal vaccine 'Intrac' is widely used before dogs go into kennels, and although it does not give 100 per cent protection, it does limit the spread of disease and shortens the length of illness in those dogs unlucky enough to start coughing.

KERATITIS

Inflammation of the cornea. The front surface of the eye may be deep, affecting the whole thickness, or it may be superficial when an ulcer may develop.

SIGNS
Keratitis is an inflammation of the 'window' surface of the eye – the cornea. It is of especial importance to recognise, as an ulcer of the cornea can develop in hours and, if untreated, can result in the eye bursting, with subsequent blindness – even if healing takes place. The affected eye is often painful, with the dog blinking and showing a tear flow. The cornea may become cloudy and full of blood vessels and, in some cases, dark pigment is laid down in the cornea.

CAUSE
Keratitis and ulceration are often the result of cat scratches, foreign bodies in the eye, and infections. It can also result from the dog rubbing an itching ear on a rough surface and, in an attempt to relieve the irritation, it damages the eye. A dry eye is an itchy eye, and dryness can lead to keratitis *(see keratitis conjunctiva sicca KCS, below)*.

TREATMENT
It may be necessary to apply fluorescein dye to test the cornea for ulceration. Where there is no ulceration, the veterinary surgeon will prescribe appropriate eye medication. Cortisone, in drops or ointment, will work to stop a dog rubbing its eye and perpetuating the situation. There are surgical operations to produce a flap of conjunctiva to cover an ulcer, and the procedure may be of great value in healing the ulcer.

KERATITIS CONJUNCTIVA SICCA (KCS)

The condition affecting both the cornea and the conjunctiva surrounding the eye is one produced by a lack of moisture, and the near absence of tears to lubricate.

SIGNS
When there is failure of the tear secretion, the eye loses its special 'sparkle,' and the sticky tear secretion accumulates to

produce a grey film on the eye surface that easily becomes infected.

CAUSE
The condition known as sicca or 'dry eye' develops if the surface of the front of the eye, that is normally moist, lacks the lubrication provided by the watery tears and a more greasy material produced by meibomian glands in the eyelids. Test strips can be used to measure tear secretion flow in the eye. The dryness causes an irritation and inflammation of both the cornea and the conjunctiva, known as kerato-conjunctivitis. The term 'sicca' refers to the dry state of the front of the eyeball.

TREATMENT
Some chemicals, such as sulphonamides, can be the cause of sicca. There is also a breed tendency to develop 'dry eyes'. Treatment with Hypromellose, used as artificial tears, is most commonly used. A substance to dissolve mucus may be added to the drops. Cyclosporin ointment, although expensive, does produce a cure in at least a proportion of dogs.

KIDNEYS

The paired organs situated in the abdomen, under the lumbar spine just behind the ribs, have many important functions, as well as that of filtering waste products from the body. The fluid balance of the body, the acid-base balance and several vital hormones are controlled by the kidneys. *(See Nephritis page 216).*

LABIAL DERMATITIS

A skin condition seen in dogs producing an excessive amount of saliva that then flows over the lower lips and soaks the skin. A dry form of lip dermatitis is seen in German Shepherd Dogs and other breeds where a crusting of the lip edges is found with a secondary bacterial infection.

SIGNS
Not always obvious as it occurs mostly in dogs with hair around the mouth; often the smell from the skin is the first reason that attention is drawn to the mouth region. Labial dermatitis is a moist inflammation of the skin around the lips. With a foul-smelling odour from the mouth, it is seen most commonly in Cocker Spaniels, but also in other breeds with pendulous lips.

CAUSE
The problem is caused by bacteria multiplying on saliva-sodden skin.

TREATMENT
Treatment involves clipping and cleaning the skin with antibacterial washes. Antibiotics that work on mouth bacteria may be given as well. Dental hygiene is also of importance in avoiding labial eczema, as often the over-production of saliva is due to a build-up of calculus on the teeth, and gum inflammation has resulted. Where medical treatments fail, surgical excision of the groove in the lips leads to improved ventilation of the skin surface, so the odour-producing bacteria can no longer grow.

LARYNGITIS

The voice or note of a dog's bark is produced by the larynx vibrating as air is expelled from the lungs. High notes are produced by smaller dogs with little larynxes, and deep barks are more typical of the larger breeds. Laryngitis is an inflammation of this organ.

SIGNS
Inflammation of the larynx may be first noticed by a change in the dog's bark. Sometimes a dog will almost lose its bark (as

has been seen in dogs kept in boarding kennels where there has been uncontrolled barking). Laryngo-tracheitis may be a complication of kennel cough infection *(see page 198)*.

CAUSE
An inflammation of the larynx.

TREATMENT
Inflammation of the larynx may require the use of antibiotics and anti-inflammatory drugs. The back of the throat can be soothed with demulcents such as honey, and the dog should be prevented from barking.

NOTE
In the older dog, paralysis of one or both sides of the larynx can occur particularly in the larger breeds. The condition produces an obstruction of the airway causing noise and difficulty in breathing. Affected dogs may be unable to walk far and may collapse when exercised. The problem can be treated by surgery on the larynx to widen the airway.

LEPTOSPIROSIS

***Leptospira* cause a bacterial infection which can be fatal, but vaccination with annual 'boosters' provides valuable protection against the disease.**

SIGNS
The form of the disease most often seen is jaundice and, after a few days, illness with a high temperature. The eyes, the mucous membranes, and then the skin develop the characteristic yellow colour.

CAUSE
Two forms of the disease are spread by infected urine: canicola fever was a common cause of kidney disease passing from dog to dog but, fortunately, it is now rare. Jaundice was usually associated with infection from rat urine traces in stagnant pools, ditches, and canals and was most often found in gundogs, working terriers and other dogs that became exposed to infection in these situations.

TREATMENT
Both diseases can be treated by penicillin injections if detected early enough, and the vaccines in use give strong protection, provided a repeat dose is given every 12 months. *(See jaundice page 196)*.

LEUKAEMIA

A progressive malignant disease of the blood-formimg

tissues of the body, often characterised by the production of excessive numbers of leukocytes, deformed in size and shape.

SIGNS
Vague/unusual signs of ill health.

CAUSE
Leukaemia is a condition where the bone marrow produces abnormally high numbers of certain white blood cells. These spill into the blood in circulation, and can spread to other organs. The production of other essential blood cells from the marrow is reduced so problems such as anaemia, secondary infections and bleeding can develop. In 'acute' leukaemia, large numbers of abnormal white cells of unusual shape and size are produced, and the normal marrow cells are soon suppressed. These leukaemias progress rapidly causing severe signs of illness and death. The outlook for these dogs is extremely poor and treatment is rarely beneficial. In 'chronic' leukaemias, the white cells produced in excessive numbers appear normal, but they are unable to function normally in the body.

TREATMENT
Chronic leukaemias progress quite slowly, and can be successfully controlled for long periods of time using simple drug treatments. Diagnosis involves clinical examination, laboratory tests on blood, and possibly a bone-marrow biopsy. Early diagnosis gives the best chance of successful treatment, so routine blood tests are recommended in any dog showing vague or unusual signs of illness.

LICE

SIGNS
The common lice of dogs are most likely to be found in out-door dogs with thick coats. Some dogs infested with lice hardly scratch at all, while others develop an almost frenzied itch and scratch non-stop. Lice eggs can be seen as white spots stuck to the hair. The ear fringes and elbows are favourite places for lice to inhabit.

CAUSE
The most severe itching is caused by the surface-feeding lice; there are also sucking lice that can produce anaemia when they feed on the dog's blood.

TREATMENT
Lice can be removed by bathing the dog in an insecticide. It is

essential to repeat the bath after 14 days. The life cycle of the louse is 21 days, and the eggs are more resistant to chemicals.

LIPOMA

A fatty tumour which is benign; composed of mature fat cells surrounded by a thin capsule.

SIGNS
These benign tumours usually occur under the skin on the body of the dog and consist of masses of fat cells. They appear to be most common in older bitches, and in breeds such as Labradors that have a tendency to store fat as layers under the skin.
CAUSE
The cause is unknown, but they do tend to occur in dogs that are already overweight and carry subcutaneous fat. Lipomas often appear at points of minor injury such as on the chests.
TREATMENT
Lipomas can be successfully removed by surgery.

LIVER

The liver is a very important internal organ involved in the dog's metabolism. Any liver disease can be serious but, fortunately, the cells of this large organ have great powers of recovery. The liver is normally protected by the ribs on the right side of the abdomen, but if it is greatly enlarged due to a tumour or other disease change, it will occupy a larger space and can then be seen behind the ribs as a bulge. The liver can be affected by infectious disease, toxins, tumours, etc. *(See hepatitis page 185, jaundice page 196).*

NOTE
A hepatoma is a fairly benign tumour of the liver if only affecting one lobe, but there are other tumours that lead to liver failure and death.

LUNGS

The lungs are a pair of organs surrounding the heart within the chest cavity. They are protected by the rib cage. The small 'pleural space' exists between the lung surface and the chest wall. A stethoscope is used to listen to the lung noises, and the appearance of the lungs can be assessed on an X-ray picture of the chest. The major airways of the lungs can be examined by an endoscope. The lungs may be affected by many disease conditions including pneumonia,

bronchitis, parasitic infections, and secondary tumours. Pleurisy exists if the lung surface becomes inflamed. *(See Pneumonia page 236).*

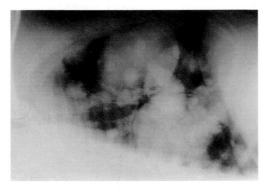

Lung X-ray of secondary tumours.

LUNGWORMS

A parasitic infection of the respiratory tract, more likely to affect the trachea than the substance of the lungs. It also refers to those worms that migrate through the lungs in the course of becoming adult in the dog's intestines.

SIGNS
Greyhounds are the breed most often affected with this worm, which causes chronic coughing.

CAUSE
Worms do not remain for long in the lungs but coughing may be caused by migrating roundworm larvae. The heart worm *Angiostrongylus vasorum* occurs in the pulmonary artery and more rarely in the right ventricle, so it can be grouped with lung worms, as their eggs are arrested in the pulmonary capillaries where they develop and hatch. The severe effect of heart worms is on cardiac function. Heartworms are rare in the UK. Infection is acquired when a dog eats a snail that contains infective larvae of *Angiostrongylus vasorum*, and the larvae pass through the alveoli before entering the heart chambers. *Oslerus osleri* is another type of parasite found as a nodule at the base of the trachea.

TREATMENT
There are a number of anthelminthic treatments to remove these sorts of worms. The veterinary surgeon will advise on the most appropriate drug to use.

LYMPHOMA/LYMPHOSARCOMA

Any neoplastic condition of the lymphoid tissue should be treated with respect. Fortunately lymphomas are often treatable, especially the sort known as pseudo Hodgkin's disease.

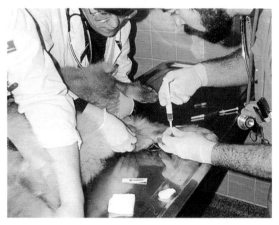

Chemotherapy injection being given as part of the treatment for lymphosarcoma.

SIGNS
Lymphomas produce varying signs of illness depending on the type and extent of the disease and any complicating factors.

CAUSE
Lymphoma is one of the most common tumours seen in the dog. It is a malignant disease affecting the lymphoid tissue and can affect many sites in the body including lymph nodes, the spleen, liver, stomach, intestines, chest, nervous system and skin. A common form seen in the dog produces swelling of many of the lymph nodes all over the body. Lymphosarcoma is the term used for the most aggressive form of the disease.

TREATMENT
The condition is diagnosed by careful veterinary examination. Other techniques including biopsy of the lymph nodes may be used. The outlook depends on where the disease is and how it affects the body functions. This condition can often be successfully controlled using a chemotherapy regime to produce a minimum of side-effects. Most dogs on treatment live a normal life for quite a long time, but those receiving treatment require careful monitoring of their condition.

MALABSORPTION

Any condition where food passes through the intestinal tract without being fully digested, and the nutrients absorbed, may be described as malabsorption.

SIGNS
In general, dogs suffering from malabsorption have repeated attacks of diarrhoea, lose weight and look thin. Young animals may fail to grow properly as inadequate amounts of protein and other essentials are not absorbed from digested food.

CAUSES
Malabsorption is a condition in which nutrients are not absorbed normally from the digested food across the wall of the small intestine. A huge variety of diseases affecting the intestine can lead to malabsorption, including food sensitivity, inflammatory bowel diseases, small intestinal bacterial overgrowth (SIBO), parasitic infections, and tumours usually affecting the wall of the intestine. A particular form of food sensitivity to gluten is seen in young dogs, especially Irish Setters. SIBO is most common in young adults of the larger breeds, while tumours are more often seen in middle-aged and older dogs.

TREATMENT
Diagnosis is based on veterinary examination, and further investigation using blood tests, faeces tests and exploratory procedures may be helpful in obtaining a definite diagnosis. The hydrogen breath-test is now used to look for abnormal fermentation of carbohydrate, which may occur in malabsorption. Treatment will depend on the underlying cause but, in all cases, a good-quality, low-fat diet will help the dog to improve its condition.

MALIGNANT TUMOURS

A proportion of the growths or tumours found in the dog are malignant (or cancerous). Malignant tumours have the ability to spread to form secondary growths elsewhere in the body. The cancer cells are carried by the blood or lymph fluid to other parts of the body where they grow new tumours or 'metastases'. The most common sites for

secondary tumours are the lymph nodes, the lungs and the liver. The condition of a metastasing tumour is rather like a growing plant that starts shedding its seeds to grow elsewhere.

The most common tumours that are known to be malignant are sarcomas such as osteosarcoma, carcinomas such as mammary carcinoma, and melanomas (known sometimes as malignant black warts). There are many other malignant tumours seen in the dog, such as mast cell tumours, fibrosarcomas and haemangiosarcomas.

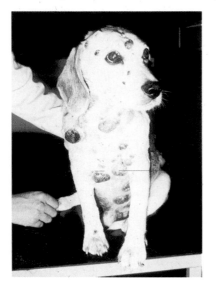

Mast cell tumours seen on a Dalmatian.

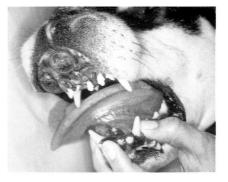

Mouth tumour: A fibrosarcoma of the upper jaw spreading on to the lips.

SIGNS

Malignant tumours usually grow in size quickly, but some will grow more slowly. Often there is no well-defined border or 'capsule' to the growth and the tumour cells can spread from

Fibrosarcoma of the skull bone.

the edge of the mass to invade the surrounding body tissue. Early diagnosis gives the best chance of successful treatment, so any unusual growths, sore patches or bleeding from body orifices should be assessed as soon as possible.

CAUSE
The causes are largely unknown.

TREATMENT
The veterinary surgeon will use his experience to examine any lump pointed out, but it will be necessary, in many cases, to take a biopsy for laboratory examination before deciding on further treatment, based on what sort of cells are causing the lump. A full examination may include chest X-rays to look for secondary tumours.

A number of treatments are available. Surgical excision is commonly used to remove tumours, but at some sites only a 'debulking' of a tumour is possible. There are then the possibilities of chemotherapy (injections or tablets) and radiotherapy to control the growth of tumour cells. Freezing by cryotherapy can be used for some tumours on the skin surface, and this produces good healing without the need for stitches. In some cases treatment is not possible, nor beneficial.

Surgery on an eye tumour where the eye and part of the cheekbone were removed.

MASTITIS

A condition affecting the lactating bitch where the mammary glands are affected.

SIGNS
The mammary gland is inflamed, and the condition becomes serious if the body temperature rises and the gland becomes hot and painful. If the abscess localises in the gland it may burst, leaving a large cavity.

CAUSE
Mastitis is usually caused by a bacterial infection that enters through the teat. It is usually seen in the bitch feeding puppies when infection enters one of the mammary glands.

TREATMENT/PREVENTION
Inspection of the bitch after whelping and checking for any swollen glands or blind teats will all help to avoid this disease developing. Antibiotics, and hormones to promote the milk let-down from the gland, will reduce the risk of serious consequences if mastitis has developed. If the puppy feeds from a gland with infected milk, it may become ill, so the puppies are sometimes removed and hand-fed to avoid this.

MANGE

Mange describes an infestation with parasitic mites which produces skin disease. The skin diseases due to burrowing parasites used to be very common, but the use of effective washes almost eradicated sarcoptic mange from dogs. However, in recent years, more cases are being found again, as there has been restriction on the continuing use of some of the most powerful washes against mites.

DEMODEX

SIGNS
The small, legless parasite burrows under the skin and lives mainly in hair follicles. It often causes no more than hairless patches of slightly thickened skin on the feet or the head. A more severe form of the mange causes widespread areas of hair loss, scales and crusting *(see demodectic mange page 156)*. Secondary bacterial infection can cause a generalised pustular form of mange, with inflammation and scratching. The presence of mites may lower the dog's immunity, and skin bacteria can cause widespread and deep skin infection. Demodex causes a variable amount of scratching but if secondary infections are present, more scratching is seen.

TREATMENT:
A number of treatments are available *(see demodectic mange page 156).*

SARCOPTES

SIGNS
This produces a different sort of mange. As a surface or sub-surface feeder, the mite causes much more itching, and skin crusting with thickening and redness. If left untreated there is hair loss and eventual black pigmentation of the bare areas. Young animals seem most susceptible and can become hairless, scratching almost non-stop. Multiple skin scrapings may have to be taken before the mites are found.

TREATMENT
Treatment with anti-parasitic washes produces relief in a few days once the sarcoptes mites are killed. Repeated baths are necessary to prevent re-infection *(see sarcoptic mange, page 252).* Both sorts of mange can be spread by direct contact, but sarcoptic mange is the most contagious and all in-contact animals should be treated. The mite can also cause a skin irritation in humans that have been in close contact, often on the bare arms.

OTODECTES

SIGNS
This mange mite does not burrow and only affects the inside of the ear. It usually causes intense scratching and head shaking. This may occur after a cat with mites has been in the vicinity, and mites have gained entry to the dog's ear tube. Research suggests that mites are more active and more eggs are laid in the winter months than at other times of the year.

TREATMENT
Specific mite remedies are included in many of the ear-drops sold for treatment. A check should be made that the preparation is one that does get rid of the mite, and in-contact cats must be treated as well.

MEGAOESOPHAGUS

The weakness and lack of muscle to propel food down the oesophagus leads to a dilated tube in the chest that will become even more distended when food is swallowed. Food soaked in barium will show up on X-ray of the dog, as it never reaches the stomach immediately.

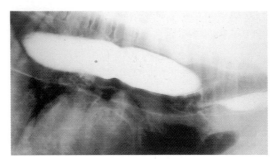

Megaoesophagus: X-ray of the chest.

SIGNS

Regurgitation of food soon after feeding.

CAUSE

This is a rare condition where the oesophagus becomes dilated, causing regurgitation or 'sickness' of food that has not reached the stomach. It may be a congenital condition that becomes noticeable as soon as a puppy is weaned on to solid food. The puppy is always hungry but soon after feeding, the food is returned within minutes after lying in the dilated tube of the oesophagus. Congenital megaoesophagus is usually due to an abnormal vascular ring causing a restriction in the oesophagus with a 'ballooning' in front. The condition can also develop after injury to the oesophagus such as swallowing a large foreign body.

TREATMENT

Diagnosis will involve an X-ray examination to follow the path of swallowed food. There is always the risk of secondary pneumonia if food is aspirated into the airway. Affected dogs should always be fed soft or sloppy foods from a raised surface. This allows gravity to help the food flow down to the stomach where it will then be retained for digestion. In puppies, the problem can be corrected with surgery. Where the condition is a result of disease affecting nerve and muscle function, medication can be successful.

MELANOMA

A form of cancer where black pigment is deposited in the newly-grown tissue.

SIGNS

Melanomas are benign or malignant tumours of pigmented cells, which most often occur in the skin, mouth and eye.

Melanoma (a cluster of black tumours).

Malignant melanomas are usually very aggressive and spread rapidly to form secondary tumours at other sites.

CAUSE
The causes are largely unknown.

TREATMENT
Biopsy specimens are necessary to distinguish benign from malignant types. The consequences of malignant tumours are fatal but the benign types respond well to surgery.

MITES

The main parasitic insects that affect the dog are the three sorts of mange mites: the harvest mite *Trombicula autumnalis* and the surface free-living 'fur mites' *Cheyletiella (see Cheyletiellosis page 146)*. The mange mites are described under Mange *(see page 210)*.

MITRAL VALVE DYSPLASIA

A deformity of the valve inside the heart that causes blood to regurgitate at each beat.

SIGNS
Shortness of breath and tiring after exercise in the younger dog.

CAUSE
This is a congenital heart defect in which the heart valve between the upper and lower chambers of the left side of the heart has a developmental abnormality. Valve 'murmurs' are expected in the older dog. When the edge of a valve is either thickened or too thin, a noise is made as the blood regurgitates through the poorly fitting valve edge and this is heard as a noise or 'murmur'. Heart failure may develop in young dogs. The condition is seen most commonly in puppies including German Shepherds Dogs, Bull Terriers and Great Danes. The Cavalier King Charles Spaniel breed, in particular, has a

hereditary condition of chronic valvular degeneration, where the valve edges become weak at a relatively young age, and mitral valve noise should be inspected for. *(See Endocardiosis page 165).*

TREATMENT
The murmur will be first heard on the left side of the chest by the veterinary surgeon, and ECG, X-ray and doppler ultrasound blood flows can be used as well for diagnosis. The sooner the condition is recognised, the longer the dog will live with treatment. Regular exercise and avoidance of adiposity will be needed, as well as medication with diuretics, followed by drugs that strengthen the heart beat and allow the blood to be ejected away from the heart (vasodilators). In cases of continued coughing, bronchodilators and non-specific cough suppressants such as codeine will be tried.

MULTIFOCAL RETINAL DYSPLASIA (MRD)

One of several diseases of the dog's retina where the the eye suffers permanently from a developmental abnormality.

SIGNS
Retinal dysplasia is a congenital condition where the retina at the back of the eye fails to develop normally before birth. This eye disorder can only be seen with an ophthalmoscope when the retina is searched for 'folds': grey streaks across the bright colour of the retina may be the first sign picked out. Brown rosettes in the retina are due to melanin deposits in the degenerate retina. There is a specific breed incidence of MRD.

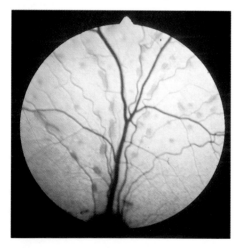

Marks on the retina due to folds resembling multifocal retinal dysplasia.

TREATMENT
There is no specific treatment. When a dog is identified with
this condition, it should not be bred from.

MYOPATHY

**Any disease of the muscles of the dog, but commonly it is
used to describe a degenerative condition where the muscle
fibres weaken and are less able to perform their work. The
Golden Retriever breed was thought to have a hereditary
myopathy with stiffness of gait and other changes in the
muscles.**

SIGNS
The word indicates a disease affecting muscle tissue. Different
types exist including hereditary, inflammatory, and forms due
to hormone imbalance. One type is in the heart muscle and is
known as cardiomyopathy, seen mainly in the giant breeds.
Usually middle-aged dogs are affected, but cases have been
seen in puppies as young as six months. The weakness of the
heart muscle reduces its ability to pump the blood efficiently.
The pulse rate increases, the breathing becomes rapid, even
when the dog is lying still. The heart rhythm is often abnormal.
(See heart disease, page 184).

TREATMENT
Cardiomyopathy can be treated with medication to dilate the
arterial blood vessels and help the circulation. Vitamin E in
high doses may have some beneficial properties.

N

NAIL DISORDERS

The nails should be kept short to prevent their ends from splitting, with painful exposure of the quick. Dogs tend to wear down their nails naturally, especially when walked on a hard surface on a lead. The front legs take less wear in this situation of propelling themselves when held back on a lead or choke-chain; usually the back leg nails need clipping less frequently. Although nails are used for digging, it may not be possible for the dog to wear its nails down this way. Regular inspection is necessary. Dew claws have been known to grow in a full circle and the point of the nail entering the skin causes a nasty abscess. This should be watched for in the Terrier breeds in particular.

The painful condition paronychia is an infection of the nail bed which may start with a spike of grass running in between the base of the nail and the skin. Once established, the infection is difficult to treat, even with antibiotics, and removal of the nail may be needed before the condition will clear up.

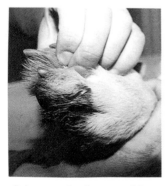

Injury to the foot resulting in the loss of a toenail.

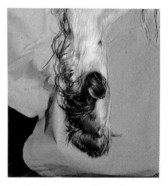

An ingrown dew claw.

?HRITIS

is an inflammatory condition of the kidney which the development of kidney failure.

SIGNS

Acute renal failure is the condition where the dog appears very ill, there is pain in the back region, and urine almost ceases to be produced. Chronic renal failure (CRF) is extremely common in the elderly dog; the changes take place over a longer period but, if recognised early enough, can be treated quite successfully.

TREATMENT

Dietary control of the protein breakdown and of waste products needing removal through the kidneys can be most useful. A protein source of high biological value – greater than 80 per cent – will be found in egg white and chicken flesh, although there are a number of very suitable canned diets available. A protein level of about 14 per cent is often aimed at. The phosphorus intake is even more important, as phosphates retained in the body do more damage than the urea from protein breakdown. This is the main reason for feeding a low-meat diet. Nursing care involves providing ample fluids, but preventing the dog vomiting is important. Several small meals, several small walks, and an avoidance of extremes of heat and cold, are advisable. There are a number of veterinary preparations and injections that can be used in the treatment of nephritis. In severe cases of advanced nephritis some form of intravenous therapy and/or peritoneal dialysis will be needed to save the dog's life.

NERVE INJURIES

The nerves are the main receivers of sensation and they conduct the impulses that cause muscles to contract. Neuropathy is a general term for any disturbance to the nerve function and pathological changes in the peripheral nervous system. Injuries to nerves can have long-lasting and serious consequences.

SIGNS

The worst form seen is the total paralysis of the hindquarters after an intervertebral disc has pressed into the spinal cord; th severity varies from the mild 'slipped disc' type of injury to most severe subdural haemorrhage that spreads up the and may cause death from respiratory failure.

CAUSE

Such paralysis may result from any injury to the when the nerve becomes 'trapped' or other Pressure on the spinal cord nerves may occ accident or an intervertebral disc injury.

TREATMENT
Massage and manipulation of a limp leg may be used but where there is any spinal injury suspected, the dog must be kept as still as possible to prevent further damage to the nerves. In all cases, a detailed veterinary examination of the extent of the injuries must be made.

NOCARDIOSIS

Skin infections with the disease caused by the soil organism *Nocardia asteroides* are notoriously difficult to clear up.
SIGNS
Lumps on the feet or sometimes elsewhere on the body, with non-healing ulcerated areas.

CAUSE
The infection from this soil organism normally enters the body through small skin wounds. Nocardiosis is occasionally found as an infection of the body cavity and organs. Granulomas with discharging sinuses can be biopsied to confirm the presence of *Nocardia*.

TREATMENT
Surgical excision, and long courses of appropriate antibiotics, are necessary to eliminate the infection.

NUTRITIONAL OSTEODYSTROPHY

A disease of the bones where there is a failure of normal development or abnormal metabolism of the bone in the adult dog, the result of some nutritional imbalance.
SIGNS
Young dogs with this type of illness have weak bones that fracture easily, or the bone softening may cause deformities. Affected puppies often have painful limbs and lameness but they may also suffer damage to the spine or other parts of the skeleton.

CAUSE
This is a condition where the bones fail to develop normally in the puppy, due to an imbalance of the calcium and phosphorus the diet. The cause is usually from feeding an all-meat diet which is high in phosphorus but low in calcium, is seen as a ing of the bones. This stimulates the parathyroid gland in to produce excess quantities of hormone to try to se levels in the blood

/PREVENTION
feeding a balanced diet to the younger dog
atio of calcium to phosphorus. *(See Feeding,
cising, page 31).*

OBESITY

Excessive accumulation of fat in the dog, or an increase in weight to an amount considered for that breed to be above normal for its age and height.

SIGNS
Excessive fat and increased bodyweight.

CAUSE
This is probably the greatest problem in dog ownership, with many dogs commonly becoming overweight, especially the low-activity breeds. Obese dogs are at greater risk of developing conditions such as diabetes, heart failure, or arthritis. Measures to reduce a dog's weight will definitely prolong life by reducing the risks of heart disease and arthritis. Fatty tumours known as lipomas are far more frequent in obese dogs such as Labrador Retrievers; and in other breeds the overweight, spayed bitch may get urine scalding of the vulva and the skin around it.

Obesity: One of the greatest problems in dog ownership.

TREATMENT
Management of obesity involves dieting with regular weighin̄ sessions, monitored by the veterinary nutritionist. An ener̄ restricted, low-fat, high-fibre diet in specified quantities s̄ be used. A number of proprietary diets are available. T̄ should be fed three or four very small meals a day. exercise encouraged and strict enforcement of nō titbits, and no scraps from the table. Obese probably in a pre-diabetic state, so a regular samples should be made for evidence of glu̇ the kidney into the urine.

OSTEO-ARTHRITIS

This is the most common form of degenerative joint disease found in the dog. The condition is also known as osteoarthrosis, and it is the most common form of arthritis seen in the middle-aged and older dog.

SIGNS
Limited movement and joint pain. Lameness may become progressively worse.

CAUSE
This is a degenerative joint disease that can occur without any obvious cause, or it may develop secondary to a condition that damages the joints, e.g. hip dysplasia, osteochondrosis and ligament rupture. Excessive exercise or obesity can worsen the disease by increasing the trauma to the joints. Changes develop in the cartilage, new bone is produced around a joint, and the joint lining membrane and joint capsule become thickened.

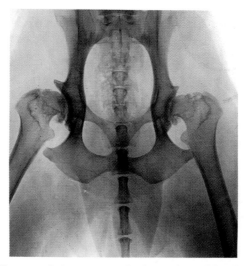

Osteo arthritis seen in the hips of an older dog.

¯MENT
dvances in the control of pain and joint inflammation
led a whole range of drugs that can arrest or delay
ˉgeneration of the joint. Rest, warmth and weight
ˉlp the joint repair, but movement should be
ˉp a joint stiffening up completely. Excessive
ˉvoided.

OSTEOCHONDROSIS

The disease of the growing dog characterised by abnormal thickness of the cartilage and a failure to convert the older cartilage layers into new bone.

SIGNS
Osteochondrosis is a disease affecting developing bones and joints at sites where cartilage is being converted into bone. This condition has become recognised as an important cause of lameness of the large breeds of dogs, especially during late puppyhood when the bones are growing rapidly.

CAUSE
The joint surfaces of the limb bones are covered with a plate of cartilage, and in osteochondrosis the growing cartilage does not convert normally to bone in its deepest layers. This produces cartilage so thick that it will crack when the dog stresses the joint. These fissures in the cartilage plate can lead to a flap detaching from the cartilage plate main surface. This eventually becomes loose and lies within the joint capsule. The damage produced by osteochondrosis leads to secondary changes in the joint. *(See osteo-arthritis, page 220).*

The joints most commonly affected are the shoulder, the elbow and, less often, the stifle and the hock joints. Signs of joint pain and lameness are usually seen in affected puppies between four and nine months of age.

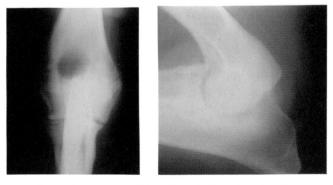

Osteochondrosis of the elbow joint, also showing secondary osteo-arthritis.

TREATMENT
The problem is diagnosed by a veterinary examination and X-rays to assess the joints by looking for specific changes of

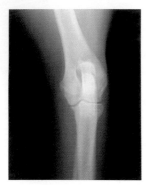

*Left elbow of a
Rottweiler showing
normal joint structure
(picture taken in the
cranio-caudal position).*

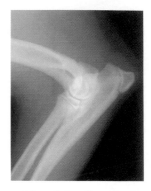

*The right elbow in the
the flexed position
showing minor changes
in the joint associated
with mild
osteochondrosis.*

osteochondrosis, or for the secondary osteoarthrosis changes in the joint. If X-rays are taken early in the disease there may be no signs of cartilage injury in the joint; any bone damage will show up later. Once the condition has been identified, there is a choice of either operating on the joint to remove any cartilage flap, or to rely on controlled exercise with non-steroidal anti-inflammatory drugs (NSAIDs) to limit the joint changes. The use of injections of a drug that is cartilage-protective may be tried on a weekly basis for one month. The development of osteochondrosis diseases is controlled by many influences. It is partially hereditary. Once present, it is made worse by diets that stimulate rapid growth. Most of all, excessive mineral supplementation should be avoided. Vigorous exercise at too early an age may cause more injury to the shoulder or elbow joints. Breeding with parents that have been X-rayed to show that they do not have OCD is the best advice possible in the present circumstances to avoid this condition.

OTITIS EXTERNA

Inflammation of the outer ear canal is very commonly seen in the dog. It may affect one or both ears.

SIGNS
The dog scratches the ear or an adjacent skin surface, or rubs the head on the ground, and sometimes violent head-shaking may ensue. The ear can be very painful, and the head may tilt

to one side. An offensive odour may develop, and fluid purulent discharges may be seen. Inspection of the ear may not reveal the grass seed lying on the ear drum nor wax blocking the horizontal canal, so an otoscope is necessary to see down the full length of the ear.

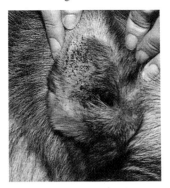

Otitis, showing a dry, brown discharge.

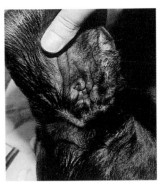

Otitis showing ulcers in the ear.

CAUSES
The condition has a variety of causes including bacterial, fungal and yeast infections, the ear mites *Otodectes*, and foreign bodies such as grass seeds. Allergic conditions such as atopy and food hypersensitivity may be responsible for the skin irritation in and around the ear and for general itchiness. Excessive moisture in an ear seems to be an important cause of otitis. Wax deposits build up and hair may drop into the ear lying near the ear drum, causing the first ear infection.

TREATMENT
Cleaning the ear with a very mild detergent solution will help break down any wax. As a household remedy, vegetable oil may be poured into the ear as a safer first aid application. Any foreign body in the ear must be removed by a veterinary surgeon. Once wax has been removed, many ear preparations can be used to soothe the skin lining the ear canal. The ear-drops supplied by veterinary practices often contain a steroid as well as an anti-parasitic component. Antibiotics and anti-yeast preparations may be included, depending on the type of infection present. In severe cases, surgical operations to ventilate the ear canal may be advised. The three types of operation are: lateral wall resection, vertical canal ablation, and – the most drastic – total ear canal ablation. It is best to discuss these options with the veterinary surgeon.

OTITIS MEDIA

An inflammation of the middle ear.

SIGNS
A painful ear that may cause loss of balance, head tilt, and circling to the affected side.

CAUSE
The inflammation of the middle ear often develops after an untreated otitis externa spreads, or a foreign body has penetrated in deeply.

TREATMENT
Otitis media usually needs surgical and medical treatment for successful resolution.

OVULATION

This is the time that the follicles in the ovary mature and eggs are released. Calculating the day that a bitch on heat releases eggs from her ovaries is important in planning matings, since there are only two opportunities each year for breeding. During the stage of pro-oestrus, the eggs develop within the ovaries and the bitch is receptive but will not allow mating. Traditionally, the second day after the pink discharge of pro-oestrus has finished is considered the best day for a first mating. Fortunately, the eggs, when released, survive in the oviducts for quite a long time, remaining fertile. The spermatozoa introduced during mating are also capable of fertilising released eggs several days after a single mating. The external signs that a bitch is ready for mating are: a softening of the vulva that has been quite firmly swollen during the first ten days of the heat, and, once the true heat (oestrus) starts, only a clear moist discharge is present. *(See Breeding and Health, page 44)*.

PALATE – CLEFT

During the growth of the unborn puppy, there may be some growth failure in the palatal area of the mouth, and the split is one of the first places that any defect may be found very soon after birth.

SIGNS
A congenital disease of puppies where the left and right halves of the roof of the mouth fail to join together before birth. Such fusion defects are seen in a more severe form as a 'hare lip' where the split continues up into the nostrils. All puppies' mouths should be examined within 12 hours of birth. Mild fusion defects may not always be spotted initially, but will become more noticeable in those puppies that fail to suck vigorously and may have milk coming back down their noses.

CAUSE
The cause is unknown but is most likely to be due to recessive genes.

TREATMENT
Although corrective surgery is possible, most breeders agree that euthanasia is indicated in the very young puppy with this fault.

PANCREATIC INSUFFICIENCY /EXOCRINE PANCREATIC INSUFFICIENCY (EPI)

The pancreas has a function of secreting digestive enzymes out of the gland, as well as being the gland involved in insulin formation. An insufficiency of the exocrine (digestive) output leads to a disorder in dogs.

SIGNS
Affected animals become undernourished and thin, and tire easily, and often have enormous appetites. Large quantities of pale grey or greasy, yellow faeces are produced, and the fermentation of the sugars and protein residue by bacteria in the large intestine causes diarrhoea and gassy distension of the abdomen.

CAUSE

This condition, often known as EPI, is one where the pancreas gland fails to produce an adequate amount of digestive enzymes. Normally these enzymes are secreted into the small intestine to produce the digestion of carbohydrate, fat and protein from the diet. In EPI, the lack of digestive enzymes means that food cannot be broken down and absorbed normally. The condition is most often seen in German Shepherd Dogs, and is also recorded in Collies and other breeds. EPI usually occurs in younger dogs between six months and five years due to a shrinkage of the pancreas cells. The cause of this is unknown. The pancreas cells that produce insulin are not affected by the shrinkage. Small intestinal bacterial overgrowth (SIBO) often complicates the disease.

TREATMENT

Once diagnosed by the use of the TLI blood test, the diet has to be changed to an easily digestible, low-fat, low-fibre diet. Supplements of glucose powder and coconut oil may be given to increase the available energy. Pancreatic extract can be given as powder or capsules mixed with the food immediately before feeding. As the extract is destroyed by the acid in the stomach juices, drugs such as cimetidine can be given half an hour before feeding the enzyme supplement, to ensure, as far as possible, that it gets to the small intestine where it is most needed. The cost of long-term treatment of EPI is high and should be taken into consideration in such cases.

PANCREATITIS

Inflammation of the pancreas gland is quite rare but it is a condition that causes a lot of pain and may prove fatal.

SIGNS

Dogs with acute pancreatitis become suddenly ill, with a high temperature, showing extreme depression, abdominal pain and repeated vomiting.

CAUSES

The pancreas is an internal gland close to the small intestine which may become diseased following acute injury to the abdomen. This injury could be the result of a road accident or arise from unwise surgical manipulation during an operation. Diets that are very high in fat, some drugs, and toxins such as alcohol are thought to cause a spontaneous pancreatitis. Dog owners should reduce the risk factors of obesity, never feeding a large quantity of fat nor having unnecessary glucocorticoid injections.

TREATMENT
Acute pancreatitis is a veterinary emergency that needs skilled attention as soon as possible to counteract shock and correct electrolyte levels. No food should be given, and water and electrolyte should only be given by mouth. Some affected dogs will develop jaundice after four days or so. This can happen after leakage of pancreatic enzymes causing fat necrosis and obstruction of the bile duct from the liver. Some dogs may subsequently develop diabetes. Fortunately, the majority of dogs respond to treatment in 48 hours, but some dogs with acute pancreatitis will need more specific therapy or surgical exploration of the abdomen. A low-fat diet is recommended for all dogs that have had pancreatitis and then apparently recovered.

PANOSTEITIS

Panosteitis is not well-known as a bone disease in fast-growing dogs of five months up to one year, but it has been seen in dogs up to six years of age. Male dogs are more often affected than females.

SIGNS
Lameness due to painful leg bones; the pain may be so severe that the dog cries out when the bone is touched.

CAUSE
The pain comes from inside the bone where the marrow is undergoing some change: on X-ray, hollow areas and thickening of the bone cortex may be seen. The cause of panosteitis is uncertain, although it may be an auto-immune disease.

TREATMENT
The disease usually improves spontaneously with time, but injections of a corticosteroid may help the dog. Long-term treatment with anti-inflammatory drugs may be needed.

PARALYSIS

The complete loss of movement in the affected part is especially devastating to dogs if the legs are affected, as normally dogs are used to a lot of free exercise. The milder form of limb weakness is known as paresis *(see page 230)*, and is more readily treatable.

SIGNS
Paralysis can be recognised by the dog being unable to walk, or support its limbs when lifted up, and having no sensation when

the toes are pinched. If paraplegia has been caused by a spinal cord problem, where the hind end is paralysed, the dog is unable to control the bladder or the bowel movement.

CAUSE
The causes of paralysis may be from injury to the spine or from damage or disease affecting the nervous system. Conditions of the spinal cord may be the result of a road accident or a protrusion of the intervertebral disc. The site and extent of the spinal cord problems influences the part of the body that suffers paralysis.

TREATMENT
Some cases have a hopeless outlook, while others may benefit from surgical or medical treatments. Careful nursing is important.The veterinary surgeon will probably want to test all the nerve reflexes and X-ray the spine before coming to a firm diagnosis. The likelihood of recovery will then depend on the amount of damage to the nerves. If there is the risk of neck injury or a back injury, such as a 'slipped disc', then great care must be taken if attempting to move the paralysed dog.

PARAPHIMOSIS

A swelling of the penis may make the dog unable to retract its penis, and the swollen organ hangs down out of the prepuce.

SIGNS
The inability to retract the penis into the prepuce.

CAUSE
Over-excitability of the male, and a small or narrow opening of the prepuce.

TREATMENT
Traditionally, treated by applying ice-packs or immersing the lower half of a small dog in cold water.

PARAPLEGIA

Paralysis of both hind legs and, in some cases, the posterior part of the body behind the neck vertebrae.

SIGNS
Paralysis of the rear half of the body with loss of muscle control, and sometimes sensation of pain in the back legs.

CAUSE
Paraplegia is often the result of an injury to the lumbar spine, as after a road accident or protrusion of an intervertebral disc, damaging the spinal cord.

Paraplegia.

TREATMENT
The treatment of the paraplegic will depend on the cause. Surgical operations may help. Nursing care is always important.

PARASITES

The variety of parasites affecting the dog are less common because there is a greater understanding of how they are spread, and because more effective drugs are being used to control them. *(See Fleas page 173, Hookworms page 189, Lungworms page 205, Mange page 210, Roundworms page 249, Tapeworms page 261).*

PARATHYROID GLAND

This very important gland, located in the neck, controls calcium and phosphorus levels in the blood by producing parathormone (PTH). If blood calcium levels are low, and blood phosphorus levels are high, PTH will try to correct the levels by removing calcium from bone and reduce its excretion by the kidneys – at the same time increasing the excretion of phosphorus. When a puppy is fed on a very unbalanced diet, the PTH will increase and the condition of nutritional osteodystrophy *(page 218)* will weaken the developing skeleton. The use of a balanced diet with a nutritional formula with a calcium/phosphorus ratio of between 1.2 and 1.4 to 1 is advised to avoid or correct this condition.

A similar problem can develop in dogs with severe kidney disease where the kidney is unable to excrete the phosphorus and by drawing on calcium reserves in the bone, the condition of 'rubber jaw' or renal hyperparathyroidism develops. Occasionally a tumour of the parathyroid gland can produce excessive quantities of PTH, leading to problems in body function caused by the high blood calcium levels.

PARESIS

The term implies an incomplete paralysis. Walking may be only slightly affected, but the dog may have greater difficulty rising after rest.

SIGNS
This is seen as a weakness in the muscles and reduced control of their movement, as compared to the complete loss of movement that occurs in paralysis

CAUSE
Paresis results from conditions of the nervous system and muscles similar to those causing paralysis. Pressure on the spinal cord may produce paresis of the limbs with a swaying gait and difficulty in rising. Spinal cord pressure may result from invertebral disc disease *(see page 194)* or spondylosis *(see page 257)*.

TREATMENT
Nursing the dog requires a close watch on bowel and bladder actions, and care that pressure sores do not develop on the legs or body.

PAROTID SALIVARY GLAND

This gland, situated below the ear, produces saliva which is discharged into the mouth inside the cheek. The saliva produced by the parotid glands is used to moisten and lubricate food before it is swallowed. Chewing stimulates saliva flow. Some of the complete pellet foods may never be chewed, and there is therefore an increased risk of air swallowing and gastric tympany *(see bloat page 135)*. The saliva produced by the gland is mucoid enough to be used for dry eye lubrication when a complex operation, known as a parotid duct transplant, is used to move the salivary duct from the cheek up into the corner of the eye. The operation is rarely used now, as better medical treatments have become available for dry eye *(see Keratitis conjunctiva sicca KCS page 199)*.

PARVO VIRUS

Canine Parvo Virus, (CPV) is one of the newer virus diseases that killed many puppies and dogs when it first appeared in the late 1970s. Protective vaccination has made this a quite rare disease, but it may still be seen from time to time in litters of puppies with severe diarrhoea or unvaccinated adults.

SIGNS
Persistent vomiting and diarrhoea. These cause rapid loss of fluids which can lead to shock and death in 48 hours. There is a typical smell to 'parvo puppies', with frequently passed, sour-smelling, liquid faeces. Pinkish colour to the liquid faeces is another sign.

CAUSE
The virus produces severe gastro-enteritis with persistent vomiting and diarrhoea. CPV2 is the virus that causes the worst disease. It can live away from the dog for up to one year, and is resistant to destruction by many of the common disinfectants. CPV1 virus produces only mild diarrhoea.

TREATMENT/PREVENTION
Unvaccinated dogs with sudden diarrhoea and vomiting should receive immediate veterinary attention. A rapid (Elisa) test can be used by the veterinary practice to confirm the presence of CPV. Intravenous fluid therapy, sedatives and good nursing all help recovery. Oral fluid electrolytes have been of great help in aiding recovery. On recovery, low-fat diets, including boiled rice, egg white in water and boiled chicken meat, aid absorption of nutrients. Dairy products are best avoided, but low-fat cottage cheese can be the first food given after 48 hours of oral fluid therapy.

The disease can be prevented by an effective vaccine, which should be given to all puppies at 6 and 12 weeks of age, followed by a regular booster every 12 months.

PASTEURELLA INFECTION

A specific bacterial infection of animals, *Pasteurella* tends to prefer moist sites of the body to multiply in.

SIGNS
An infected discharge from the nose or from the dog's prepuce.

CAUSE
A bacterial organism that is associated with respiratory tract infections e.g. the nose or the lungs. It is also associated with abscesses, and is found in swabs taken from discharge from the prepuce of male dogs.

TREATMENT
Pasteurella is sensitive to antibiotic treatment, but with the preputial infection there is a tendency for it to return – possibly because of mouth bacteria reinfecting the site after licking.

PATELLA LUXATION

Dislocation of the kneecap is found from time to time in young dogs.

SIGNS
A hind leg lameness that may develop quite suddenly. It may then correct itself if the patella returns into place.

CAUSE
This condition, in which the kneecap or patella dislocates, is not uncommon in smaller breeds such as Yorkshire Terriers, Shih Tzu, and Jack Russell Terriers. It is usually seen in young dogs due to an abnormal development of the stifle joint. This is usually a hereditary fault, although any severe injury to the knee-joint ligaments will have a similar effect.

TREATMENT
A surgical operation to correct the luxation, by either deepening the groove in the femur, strengthening the joint capsule, or by reinforcing weak ligaments, is successful. Some dogs go through life with patella luxations and do not seem to be subject to any crippling joint disease.

PELVIC FRACTURE

The bones that make up the pelvis are relatively weak in strength, and they may be fractured after road accidents when the vehicle hits the dog's hind parts.

SIGNS
Severe pain in the hindquarters, retention of faeces and urinary retention after an accident.

CAUSE
Fractures of one or more pelvic bones is usually a result of a road traffic injury to the hindquarters. This can be a severe injury, and there is always the risk of complications affecting the bladder, the nerves and the soft tissues. On recovery in the bitch, the width of the birth passage becomes narrow.

TREATMENT
Analgesic pain killers, X-ray, and possible replacement of the fracture bones, will form the basis of veterinary treatment, but the outlook for full recovery is always unsure at first. Rest in a

hospital cage, absorbent bedding to prevent pressure sores, and nursing to observe the output of urine and faeces, are all important.

PENIS INJURIES

The penis can be injured by trauma, producing swelling and bleeding. Blood from the tip of the penis has to be distinguished from blood coming down the opening of the urethra originating in the urinary tract. Prostate disorders *(see page 241)* and excessive licking at the penis tip may be an indication for castration, but a full examination is necessary to find out the nature of an injury.

PERICARDIAL DISEASE

The pericardial sac is a space around the heart between an inner membrane surrounding the heart and an outer membrane. This membrane produces a small amount of fluid which moistens the sac.

SIGNS
Collapse, muffled heart sounds and distended veins.

CAUSES
Pericardial diseases are quite uncommon in the dog and account for only one per cent of all heart disease. Most cases of pericardial disease produce an excessive accumulation of fluid in the sac. The pressure of this fluid can compress the heart chambers, which can lead to heart failure. Tumours such as haemangio sarcomas are attributed as a cause, but the cause of the fluid effusion in the sac is not always known. Bleeding from tumours in or around the heart may fill the sac. After road accidents haemorrhage into the sac may occur, with rapid collapse and death. In some cases 'Idiopathic Pericardial Haemorrhage' is seen. Sudden bleeding is most often found in the large breeds.

TREATMENT
Once a diagnosis has been confirmed, surgical drainage of fluid may be attempted.

PERINEAL RUPTURE (HERNIA)

The furthermost rear protruding part of the abdominal cavity may produce a bulge under the tail if the muscles and ligaments become weak.

SIGNS
Perineal rupture produces a swelling on one or both sides of the anus.

CAUSE
The condition is due to a breakdown of the support muscles. At first, the swelling is often thought to be from distended anal sacs. However, an increasingly larger swelling on one side of the rectum may be due to a rupture of the pelvic support muscles, so the fat – and even the bladder – hang outside the abdomen in the swelling beside the rectum. If the bladder becomes trapped when it inverts, no urine will be passed. Rupture from repeated straining, as seen in older male dogs with large prostates, may be the cause of the condition.

TREATMENT
Laxatives and faecal softening materials will help at first, but surgical repair and possible castration may be the long-term cure of the disorder.

PERIODONTAL DISEASE

The area around each tooth, known as the periodontum, may become infected or show other inflammatory changes.

SIGNS
Periodontal disease is very common in dogs and affects the gums at their junction with the teeth. At first, exposure of the tooth roots will not cause obvious pain, but it will lead to loosening of the teeth and teeth dropping out.

CAUSE
Dental calculus or plaque will cause gum pressure and hasten the disease. Bacteria are usually present.

TREATMENT/PREVENTION
Preventive care and suitable diet will prevent the worst of the disease. Established periodontal disease in dogs requires the cleaning and polishing of the teeth at the veterinary surgery, and regular tooth brushing or chewable materials in the diet, to prevent its return. Antibiotics may be used for mouth infections.

PERTHE'S DISEASE

A disease of the hip joint, also known as Legg-Calve Perthe's Disease.

SIGNS
A back leg that is almost permanently carried, seen in young dogs of the smaller breeds such as Jack Russell and other terriers.

CAUSE
A failure of the blood supply to the bone in the head of the femur leads to death of the bone. It is also known as coxa plana from the flattening of the femur head seen on X-ray. This can lead to collapse of the bone and subsequent osteoarthritis in the joint. It is probably genetic, caused by an autosomal recessive inherited disease, as not all puppies in a litter are affected.

TREATMENT
Some dogs improve with kennel rest, but surgical excision of the head of the femur may be resorted to where there is obvious pain.

PHANTOM PREGNANCY

A 'normal' stage in the female's reproductive cycle, since many bitches will show mammary gland enlargement or behaviour changes seven or eight weeks after the end of a regular heat. *(See Breeding and Health, page 44, and False Pregnancy, page 171).*

PHARYNGITIS

Inflammation of the part of the throat, known as the pharynx.

SIGNS
The dog may refuses food or show gulping movement when taking in food.

CAUSE
Pharyngitis is an inflammation of the back of the throat, which may be due to bacterial or viral infections. Often the tonsils are enlarged at the same time.

TREATMENT
The food should be moistened or soaked with warm water. Antibiotics may be required as well.

PITUITARY GLAND

The pituitary gland is a very important endocrine gland, situated at the base of the brain. The gland produces a number of different hormones that control essential body functions. A wide variety of diseases, such as diabetes insipidus, uterine inertia and Cushing's disease may be the result of pituitary gland problems.

PNEUMONIA

A traditional term used to describe inflammation of the solid parts of the lung. It is often accompanied by inflammation of the airways and the pleura that cover the lung surface (pleurisy).

SIGNS
Rapid, shallow breathing, coughing, purple lips and tongue, and reluctance to lie fully stretched out, may be signs of acute respiratory failure. A high temperature, poor appetite and a discharge from the nose are other signs to look for.

CAUSES
Pneumonia is an inflammatory condition of the lungs, often caused by viral and bacterial infections. It may be seen in dogs with severe kennel cough, after periods of prolonged unconsciousness, or after food or fluids are inhaled by accident. Pneumonia may also be due to an allergic response to inhaled substances.

TREATMENT
Immediate veterinary attention is required with antibiotics, and supportive measures, such as oxygen and drugs to aid breathing, are also essential.

NOTE
Pleurisy is the inflammation of the lung surface. When inflamed, the pleural lining between the lung substance and the outer thoracic wall may cause a harsh 'dry' sound on breathing.

PNEUMOTHORAX

The presence of free air in the chest cavity.

SIGNS
The lungs collapse, breathing becomes rapid and shallow, and the dog becomes more and more distressed.

CAUSE
The condition is usually caused by an accident producing chest damage that allows air to leak from the lungs. This can be easily detected on chest X-ray, where there is an unusual quantity of air in the chest seen outside the lungs.

TREATMENT
Mild cases can be treated with complete kennel rest, but more severe cases require drainage of the air from around the lungs, where it would not normally be expected to be present.

POISONING

Fortunately a rare condition – many accidental cases are from dogs swallowing tablets and household remedies that may not always be thought of as dangerous for dogs. When in doubt, consult a veterinary surgeon. If the poison has been recently swallowed, an emetic such as several large crystals of washing-soda (sodium carbonate) put down the throat may be sufficient to make the dog vomit any swallowed substance before much of it has been absorbed. In the USA 1-2 teaspoonfuls of hydrogen peroxide liquid may be used as an emetic. Only a few examples will be given, but reference books list many more poisons.

ALPHACHLORALOSE

As a poison used for killing rats and birds, it was first used as an anaesthetic agent for laboratory animals.

SIGNS

Dogs that have swallowed bait are drowsy, salivate a lot, then suffer from muscle twitching and convulsions.

TREATMENT

There is no specific antidote, but the dog should be rested in a warm, quiet bed and the veterinary surgeon can administer other drugs as necessary, depending on the severity of the signs.

BLUE GREEN ALGAE

Poisoning from stagnant pond water is due to *cyanobacteria,* a poisonous substance produced by those algae which bloom on stagnant water in warmer weather. Poisoning may occur suddenly, after a dog wades in and drinks some of the affected water.

SIGNS

Signs of poisoning can develop in 15 to 20 minutes with vomiting, diarrhoea, muscle tremors and hind leg weakness. Convulsions and death may follow due to toxins that affect the nervous system. Dogs that survive may have severe liver damage and subsequently die of shock after several days.

TREATMENT

First aid treatment aims to remove the water drunk from the stomach with an emetic – provided there are no fits – then treat the dog for shock with warmth. The use of intravenous fluids and corticosteroids should be available at the veterinary surgery as soon as the dog can be transported. Oxygen and manual lung ventilation may be needed. Once a pond has been identified as having blue green algae present, dogs must be kept away until the water temperature drops, and it is too cold for algae growth.

ETHYLENE GLYCOL

A poisonous substance found in car anti-freeze that can cause severe damage to the kidneys if accidentally licked or swallowed.

SIGNS
At first the dog may show lack of co-ordination and rapid breathing, but then the illness progresses to a kidney failure and collapse.

TREATMENT
General supportive nursing, and the use of a specific antidote by the veterinary surgeon.

LEAD

A poisonous substance found in car batteries and some white paints.

SIGNS
It rarely affects dogs, but it can cause brain damage and even blindness.

TREATMENT
Supportive nursing, and the use of an antidote by the veterinary surgeon.

ORGANOPHOSPHATE POISONING

Organophosphates are commonly used as insecticides and can be found in many preparations to kill parasites such as fleas.

SIGNS
Overdose produces signs of vomiting, diarrhoea, constricted pupils, salivation, muscle twitching, seizures and collapse.

TREATMENT
First aid treatment requires the use of atropine injections as a specific antidote, and supportive care.

WARFARIN *and other anticoagulants*

These substances were used as rat baits and were a common cause of poisoning and death of dogs by internal bleeding.

SIGNS
The signs of bleeding from the teeth roots, swollen joints, bruising of the skin, pale mucous membranes, and collapse, are characteristic for the condition.

TREATMENT
The number of incidents of accidental poisonings has fallen as baits of oatmeal are no longer in use and there is greater care in where poisons are placed. The specific antidote of Vitamin K_1 by injection should be given, and then repeated several times for up to a week after the poison has been eaten.

PROGRESSIVE RETINAL ATROPHY (PRA)

The nerve layers at the back of the eye are particularly sensitive as they receive and process light stimuli. Any developmental change or damage to the eye of the unborn puppy may lead to atrophy of the light receptors. Generalised progressive retinal atrophy (GPRA) implies that most of the rods and cones of the retina are failing.

SIGNS
The first form was recognised as a hereditary disease of Irish Setters as a form of night-blindness. The disease can be recognised with an ophthalmoscope early in the puppy's life, and certificates of GPRA-'clear' eyes can be given to Irish Setters and Rough Collies at four months. The GPRA-clear certificate is given where no signs of eye disease are detected. Other breeds such as Toy and Miniature Poodles may not show signs of PRA until they are adult, and three years is the age for their certification.

CAUSE
This eye disease is due to a degeneration of the light receptors (rods and cones).

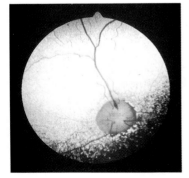

Retina of the eye showing progressive retinal atrophy in three-month-old Irish Setter puppy.

TREATMENT
There is no cure for GPRA, and control by breeding out is the best advice that can be given.

CENTRAL PROGRESSIVE RETINAL ATROPHY (CPRA)
This is another type of retinal atrophy. It is a retinal pigment dystrophy of epithelium, first recognised in Briards, then in some other breeds such as Collies, Retrievers and Spaniels.

SIGNS
Unlike the first form of retinal atrophy, this takes the form of a daytime blindness. The disease is mainly seen in the UK in the various breeds of working dog, and both eyes will be affected.

CAUSE
The centre of the retina, where the cones as light receptors are most closely packed, becomes damaged so the sight fails in the brightest light conditions. Dogs develop blindness only slowly from two to three years of age onwards, but they may lose a considerable amount of vision by eight years of age.

TREATMENT
There is no known treatment, but a mixed protein diet should be fed.

PROLAPSE

Any displacement of a body organ may be called a prolapse. The direction may be upwards with an intervertebral disc, outwards with an eyeball, backwards with a rectum, or downwards with a vaginal polyp.

SIGNS
A protrusion of an internal organ is known as a prolapse.

Pink swelling after prolapse of the third eyelid in a Bulldog puppy.

Prolapse of the vagina and of polyps growing from inside the vagina may occur, while the prolapse of the rectum is less often seen. After an injury to the head, the eyeball may prolapse, especially in flat-faced breeds such as the Pekinese.

CAUSE
Usually an inherent muscle weakness, but sometimes injury will produce a prolapse.

TREATMENT
Emergency treatment is to apply a moistened pad to the prolapsed organ to prevent tissue dying and further injury, and to seek veterinary help as soon as possible.

PROSTATE DISORDERS

The prostate is a gland located around the neck of the bladder. It surrounds the urethra that drains the bladder and lies below the rectum.

SIGNS
An enlarged prostate in the older male dog may be seen to cause straining as if constipated, but as the enlarged prostate presses into the floor of the rectum, the dog then produces flattened or ribbon-like faeces. A prostate abscess can develop from a case of prostatitis and will be more difficult to treat. Malignant tumours of the prostate are very rare – they almost always spread rapidly with secondary tumours. The bladder is not often affected. Unlike the human condition, prostate disease in the dog is less likely to cause restriction of bladder emptying and urinary incontinence.

CAUSE
Hormone imbalance in the older male dog is the most common cause.

TREATMENT
Once the condition of a large prostate is identified, often involving an internal examination of the pelvis with a gloved finger, hormone injections such as delmadinone (Tardak), or even castration, may be advised.

PSEUDO PREGNANCY

See False Pregnancy page 171

PYLORIC STENOSIS

Much of the stomach has enormous ability to stretch and hold food or gas, but the exit through the pylorus into the intestines is very muscular and not easily dilated.

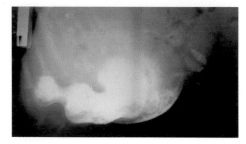

Pyloric stenosis: X-ray of the stomach.

SIGNS
Stenosis is a narrowing of the exit from the stomach to the intestine which may cause vomiting, often several hours after a meal has been eaten normally.

CAUSES
The pylorus or stomach exit may be blocked by tumour tissue, or constricted by the thickening of the stomach lining or muscle. In some puppies, the muscle ring is thickened and over-tight at the pylorus as a congenital condition. Affected puppies vomit with a projectile expulsion after feeding when they start on solid food.

TREATMENT
In the case of puppies, surgical correction is possible, and techniques have been developed to treat other types of this condition.

PYODERMA

Skin diseases have a variety of names, but this traditional term is often used to describe an infection where pus forms in the skin layers.

SIGNS
Superficial pyoderma affects the skin, which may look red, have 'rashes' and small pus-containing spots. The amount of irritation is greater in some infected skins than others. A special form of infection is juvenile pyoderma, seen in puppies at between weaning and four months of age, especially in short-coated breeds such as Labradors. The eyelids become swollen and sticky, and the muzzle swells up together with swollen lymph glands ('Head gland disease'). Unless prompt treatment is given there will be permanent scarring of the head and loss of hair on the face for life. It is possible that *Demodex* mites reduce the puppies' skin immunity *(see demodectic mange page 156)*. Deep pyoderma is rare, but the infection spreads into the deepest skin layers, as seen in muzzle folliculitis on the face and anal furunculosis.

CAUSE
Bacterial infection of the skin, usually caused by *Staphylococcus intermedius*. Dogs with lowered resistance may have infection with *Malasezzia* as well as the *Staph*.

TREATMENT
Intensive and prolonged courses of an appropriate antibiotic may be accompanied by skin-cleansing agents.

PYOMETRA

A purulent fluid that accumulates in the uterus may be retained within by a closed cervix, or the discharge may appear at the vulva when it is known as an open pyometra. Pyometra is an infection within the uterus, usually seen in bitches up to eight weeks after the end of heat.

SIGNS
Bitches will show increasing thirst, a high temperature, poor appetite, then vomiting caused by the toxins in the uterus being absorbed into the bloodstream.

CAUSE
Due to hormone levels, fluid in the uterus may accumulate some weeks after the end of oestrus in the bitch *(see false pregnancy page 171)*. If infection enters the uterus from the bloodstream or from the vagina by an open cervix, then infection or 'pus in the uterus' will cause a sudden illness with vomiting and collapse. A vaginal discharge may not be seen for several days if the cervix remains closed.

TREATMENT
Medical treatments can be used, but in the majority of cases an ovariohysterectomy operation should be performed as soon as the diagnosis is certain. The recovery rate is very good, provided the operation is performed promptly.

PYREXIA

Feverish conditions are measured by an increase in the dog's body temperature.

SIGNS
Pyrexia or fever is a rise in body temperature above the normal range. In the dog, the normal range is 100.9 to 100.7 degrees Fahrenheit (38.3 to 39.7 Centigrade). Any temperature 1.5 degrees Fahrenheit (0.5 Centigrade) above normal taken on more than one occasion, can be considered cause for concern.

CAUSE
Fever is a common response to infection with bacteria or viruses – many invading organisms cannot multiply so rapidly when the body temperature is raised. A persistent raised body temperature for three weeks or more, linked with weight loss and tiredness, may indicate a pyrexia of unknown origin (PUO).

TREATMENT
The dog with PUO would require a careful investigation. Conditions such as chronic internal infections, abscesses, endocarditis, panosteitis, tumours and 'immune-mediated diseases' such as rheumatoid arthritis and polyarthritis can cause persistent fever. Dogs with heat-stroke may have temperatures well above 106 degrees Fahrenheit (41.1 Centigrade), and they will need total body cooling with iced-water, cold-water stomach wash-outs, and intravenous cooled 5 per cent Dextrose solution.

QUARANTINE

Quarantine implies a period of isolation of an animal and, in general use, it is applied to the present six months compulsory segregation and separation of dogs imported from countries outside the island of Great Britain. The long incubation period of rabies after infection by the virus requires a longer period of isolation than with most other infectious diseases.

In July 1994 it became possible to import dogs from registered premises outside the UK under strict supervision to registered breeding establishments. Vaccination, permanent identification and blood tests to check the imported animal's level of immunity are requirements of the UK Ministry of Agriculture, Fisheries and Food. A review of quarantine arrangements is planned for 1997, and it is anticipated that there will then be a further weakening of the defences used to reduce the risk of imported diseases.

QUADRAPLEGIA

See Tetraplegia page 263

RABIES

A rhabdovirus infection that spreads through the nervous system. It is invariably fatal, and anyone who has had direct experience of the infection in humans will know of the horrific death that may be experienced after an unexpected animal bite.

SIGNS
Dogs with rabies will generally show signs of abnormal behaviour when they bite another animal or a person – but the saliva may contain rabies virus for up to 14 days before nervous signs develop. It is customary to confine dogs for 14 days after any unexpected dog bite of a person, to see if the dog then shows hyper-excitability and 'furious' rabies develops. Dumb rabies is probably the more usual form, causing a progressive paralysis, drooling of saliva and an inability to swallow, before death ensues.

CAUSE
Rabies is a widely recognised fatal disease caused by a virus that affects the dog's nervous system, and it may be transferred to man. Rabies is almost unknown in the UK due to effective quarantine regulations, but there are still reservoirs of infection in wildlife elsewhere in the world. In the USA the skunk, racoon and bat are infected hosts, and ground squirrels or smaller wildlife should be suspected whenever an outbreak of rabies in dogs is reported. The fox rabies strain, present in some parts of Europe, does not appear to be very dangerous to dogs, although it is necessary to keep up vaccinations so that any bitten dog can put up a rapid immune response.

TREATMENT
Once the virus enters the dog's nervous system, the antibodies are unable to protect the infected animal and there are no anti-viral drugs that can effectively stop the disease affecting the brain. Vaccination against rabies is very effective using a single dose vaccine with boosters at recommended intervals. Some form of identification of each dog vaccinated is necessary by the use of a distinctive collar and/or a microchip. Rabies vaccination is not routinely necessary for dogs in the UK, but it is required before dogs are exported to certain countries. In the control of a rabies outbreak a minimum of 75 per cent of

dogs must be vaccinated to stop a major spread of this
dangerous disease.

RESPIRATORY DISTRESS

**The respiratory tract carries air from the nose to the lungs,
and it is important that a clear airway is maintained.
Oxygen must be able to reach the lungs to supply the rest of
the body and waste gases have to be removed. If these vital
functions are not maintained, respiratory distress will
develop.**

SIGNS
The dog appears anxious, and breathes rapidly with the mouth
wide open. In all cases, the colour of the gums or eye
membranes should be examined to see if lack of oxygen has
produced a bluish-purple colour.

CAUSES
Any obstruction of the airways will cause respiratory distress.
Obstruction at the larynx can be caused by a ball being wedged
at the back of the throat, or by the condition of laryngeal
paralysis. Breeds with compact skulls, such as Bulldogs and
Pugs, often suffer obstruction from a long, soft palate and a
small larynx. The trachea can be partially obstructed by
tracheal collapse and, occasionally, dogs will inhale foreign
bodies that will lodge at the base of the trachea or in a main
bronchus, causing obstruction. Tumours and thickenings of
inflammatory change or discharges can also block the airways.
Spasm and narrowing of the airways and swelling of the larynx
can occur with allergic diseases. Pneumonia, pleurisy and fluid
or bleeding in the lungs will cause severe distress.

TREATMENT
Opening the mouth and drawing the tongue forward may
provide a freer flow of air to the lungs. Tight collars must be
removed, and any fluids obstructing the nostrils or the back of
the mouth should be swabbed away with cloth tissues or
whatever is immediately available. An oxygen supply, given by
a loose face-mask, is ideal – but in extreme distress in the semi-
conscious patient, mouth-to-nose resuscitation can be
attempted.

RETINAL DYSPLASIA

**Retinal dysplasia is an abnormal development of the layers
of the retina. Total retinal dysplasia can be a cause of
blindness in the young puppy when the retina detaches.**
(See Multifocal retinal dysplasia page 214)

RHEUMATOID ARTHRITIS

Rheumatoid arthritis is an inflammatory, erosive joint disease. It is much less common in the dog than the degenerative forms of arthritis – inflammatory joint disease is responsible for only 5 per cent of arthritis in dogs. The inflammation leads to cartilage destruction.

SIGNS
The joints may be affected one after another, or a single joint may be swollen and painful.

CAUSE
The cause is thought to be an abnormal immune response, and often other parts of the body will be affected as well.

TREATMENT
High doses of corticosteroids are needed to suppress the immune response and improve the dog's daily life.

RHINITIS

Rhinitis is inflammation of the lining of the nasal chamber.

SIGNS
The typical signs are sneezing, snuffling, difficult noisy breathing, and discharge from the nostrils.

CAUSES
Viruses, bacteria or foreign bodies in the nose may be the cause. Aspergillosis is a fungal rhinitis that is difficult to treat.

TREATMENT
Dogs that snuffle or have a persisting nasal discharge will need detailed veterinary examination to look for a cause before treatment can be given.

RINGWORM

Fungal infections of the skin are caused by dermatophytic fungi. Ringworm is one example where the outer layers of skin and the hair fibres are invaded by these parasitic fungi.

SIGNS
The appearance of affected skin is variable, and the dog rarely has the typical circular ring seen in humans. Small patches of hair loss and scaliness may be suspected. They may be redder at the edges, where active inflammation in response to the spread of the fungus occurs. Infection of the nail bed is also

*Ringworm
seen on the
nose of a
West
Hightland
White Terrier.*

possible, as well as deep skin infection. The skin signs may easily be confused with small patches of demodectic mange.

CAUSE
Ringworm is a fungal infection of the skin in no way associated with 'worms'. The disease can spread from dog to dog. The fungus lives in the base of the hair in the follicle and can be difficult to reach with ointments and liquids.

TREATMENT
In all cases, samples should be taken for laboratory examination as well as a preliminary screening with the ultraviolet 'Wood's' lamp to look for those sorts of ringworm that will fluoresce. Treatment with anti-fungal skin washes may be supplemented by antibiotic tablets against the fungus. Long courses of treatment are needed to eliminate all the ringworm spores from the slow-growing skin layers and hair roots.

ROUNDWORM

SIGNS
The signs of poor general health and diarrhoea are usually indicative of worm infestations.

CAUSE
The most common parasitic worm in puppies and dogs up to a year of age are *Toxocara* and *Toxascaris*. The other round-worms *(Nematodes)* seen in the dog are hookworms *(see page 189)* whipworm *(see page 277)* and tracheal worms.

Puppies with roundworms start to pass lots of worm eggs when about seven weeks of age, so this is the most dangerous time for the environment to become contaminated with eggs. If young children play with puppies and then lick their fingers, they may easily catch zoonotic toxocariasis. Adult dogs pass roundworms, and about 12 per cent will have eggs in their faeces. The worms in adults are rarely seen, but they may be seen emerging from the rectum of a bitch nursing puppies that then has diarrhoea, or worms may also come up in the vomit if the worm moves forward from the intestine into the stomach, by accident.

TREATMENT
Control of worms is by frequent dosing of young puppies. This should be from as early as two weeks of age, with the dose repeated every two to three weeks until the puppy is three months old. To prevent puppies carrying worms, the pregnant bitch can be wormed from the 42nd day of pregnancy with a safe wormer licensed for use during pregnancy, such as fenbendazole. The worming can then be given daily until the second day after all the puppies are born. Routine worming of adults, twice a year, against round and tapeworms is a good preventative measure. When there are young children in a household, more frequent worm dosing may be advisable to reduce the risk of roundworm larvae migrating to the child and any possible damage to the eyes .

SALMONELLA INFECTION

The organism *Salmonella* is found in intestinal infections, but the most serious aspect is the zoonotic one as infections may pass to the persons handling the dogs.

SIGNS
Persistent diarrhoea and raised temperature.

CAUSE
This bacterial infection of the dog's intestine causing enteritis is of importance because of its infectious nature to other dog and humans. It is probably the second most common form of bacterial food poisoning in people. Strict hygiene should always be practised when handling any dogs with diarrhoea symptoms, in order to avoid food contamination.

TREATMENT
Culture of the dog's faeces in the laboratory is the only certain way of diagnosing the infection. However, any dog that has persistent diarrhoea with a raised temperature, and signs of general illness, should be treated with caution and examined by the veterinary surgeon. Antibiotics may be given but it is often better not to use drugs that may cause resistance to develop.

SARCOMAS

Defined as tumours of the connective tissues, they are often highly malignant.

SIGNS
Sarcomas are a group of malignant tumours that occur at many different sites of the body.

CAUSE
The cause of tumours are still unknown.

TREATMENT
Lymphosarcoma or lymphoma is the most common type seen in the dog and can respond to chemotherapy. Osteosarcomas are a highly malignant tumour of bone with a very poor outlook in affected dogs. Fibrosarcomas, affecting fibrous tissues, are quite common in the dog and can sometimes be controlled by surgery and other treatment methods. A tumour of blood vessels is the haemangiosarcoma, often found affecting the

spleen, and has grave consequences in most dogs. Other sarcomas are less common tumours of dogs.

SARCOPTIC MANGE

A serious problem in dog kennels when the parasitic mite spreads from dog to dog by direct skin contacts.

SIGNS
A severe irritation and damage to the skin. The early signs of the disease are seen on the edges of the ears, the elbows, the hocks and the brisket, where their irritation provokes scratching and biting with loss of surface skin.

Sarcoptic mange seen in a puppy.

CAUSE
Sarcoptic mange is an infection where the parasite mite *Sarcoptes scabei* burrows beneath the skin surface. The mange mite burrows just below the skin surface and mites cannot always be found, even after repeated skin tests. The disease is spread by one infected dog rubbing against another. Humans handling dogs with infected skin may also develop itchy places on the inside of their arms or elsewhere on their bodies – but this generally clears when the dog is treated. The human disease of scabies is caused by a different sort of mite.

TREATMENT
The disease is confirmed by examining skin samples to demonstrate the presence of the mites. Repeated samples may be necessary before mites are found. Treatment by anti-parasitic skin applications should be repeated weekly so as to catch burrowing mites that come up to the surface. Not all medicated baths are effective, and painting with an organo-phosphorus wash may be needed to penetrate the skin. All in-contact animals should be treated whether they show signs or not, as it can be difficult to get rid of the disease in a kennel once dogs become partially-treated carriers of the mange.

Foxes may also be a reservoir of infection; vulpine mites can infect dogs but the disease is usually self-limiting.

SCLERITIS

The white of the eye is known as the sclera, and any inflammation is shown as red or pink blood vessels on the surface.

SIGNS
The lids will have to be opened and the head rotated to inspect the sclera. Usually it will be seen as a sore eye with blood vessels running across the white where it joins to the cornea of the front of the eye. A discharge is not expected unless infection subsequently develops.

CAUSE
A blow to the eye will cause a scleral haemorrhage. Any other injury or pressure increase as in glaucoma will cause the surface or deep blood vessels of the sclera to increase in size or number causing a pink or red colour.

TREATMENT
Haemorrhages will go away, and so little treatment is needed. If the scleritis is associated with glaucoma (see page 180), or uveitis (see page 272) then treatment will be needed.

SEBORRHOEA

Implies an abnormal secretion of the sebaceous glands, but this skin condition is a complex one as it may vary in appearance from anything with a greasy, ill-smelling skin to a dry, scaly skin with dandruff-type crusts.

SIGNS
Dry or greasy skin which is caused by the outermost skin layers failing to grow properly, and an itchy, dry, scaly skin results. Some dogs then progress to an oily skin and a waxy ear condition – this is most frequently seen in Cocker and Springer Spaniels. There may be hair loss in round patches often with scaling at the skin edge. A deep bacterial infection of the skin may then develop in many dogs affected with seborrhoea *(see pyoderma page 242)*.

CAUSE
This condition may be the result of a hereditary disorder found in specific breeds.

TREATMENT
Treatment with skin washes, anti-scaling shampoos and GLA

supplements may have to be continued over a long period before an improvement is seen in the skin.

SHOCK

A failure of the blood circulation to supply all the tissues produces the condition known as 'shock'.

SIGNS
The signs of shock include dullness, progression to collapse with a weak rapid pulse, pale mucous membranes, shallow breathing and cold extremities.

CAUSES
There are many different causes including blood or fluid loss, heart failure, massive allergic reactions, certain infections and toxaemias.

TREATMENT
Shock is a complicated process which may become fatal if not treated promptly. Where possible, steps to prevent the development of shock are important. The first aid treatment is to stop further blood loss, keeping the dog warm and calm until veterinary attention can be given. Intensive veterinary treatment is necessary to control shock using intravenous fluids and appropriate drugs.

SINUSITIS

The sinuses are air-filled spaces in the bones of the face which connect with the nasal cavity.

SIGNS
A persistent disharge from the nostrils, often accompanied by nose breathing with some difficulty.

CAUSE
An inflammation of the sinuses is usually caused by a spread of infection from the nose or blockage of the normal drainage of the sinuses. The watery discharge from the nose serves to keep the nose moist and glandular secretions are stimulated by nose licking. Occasionally, a thick white discharge will appear at the nostrils that may be associated with a bacterial or fungal infection of the maxillary sinus and the turbinate bones. The frontal sinuses lie adjacent to the eye, the maxillary sinus lies as a pouch off the main nasal chamber. This pouch becomes infected when there is a molar tooth abscess.

TREATMENT
Steam inhalations may be used to treat a mucoid discharge,

although specific drugs given by mouth will be needed if an organism is identified in a swab from the nose discharge. Tooth extraction is essential for a maxillary sinus abscess. The nose and sinuses may become infected with *Aspergillus*, when a mucoid discharge changes to a purulent one which frequently is associated with nose bleeding. Treatment may involve long courses of medication and surgical treatment to drain the sinuses and flush them regularly, using tubes.

SKIN TUMOURS

Tumours of the dog's skin are unfortunately seen more and more, and exposure to many of the carcinogens produced by mankind may cause these growths to appear in domestic pets.

SIGNS
Tumours of the skin are relatively common, especially in the older dog. The majority are benign but some, such as squamous cell carcinoma and fibrosarcoma, are malignant. Mast cell tumours are commonly seen in younger dogs and can behave in a benign or a malignant fashion.

CAUSES
Skin irritants, excessive sunlight, and unknown viruses may cause some skin tumours.

TREATMENT
Examination of biopsy material is essential to distinguish the nature of the tumour and the treatment most appropriate. Surgical excision is usually successful.

SOFT PALATE DISORDERS

Hard palate defects in the mouth are rare, but the soft tissue forming the rear of the palate may be the cause of restriction of the airway behind the tongue base.

SIGNS
Noisy breathing which may lead to choking respiration and even collapse, particularly if the dog is hot or over-excited.

CAUSE
Some breeds of dogs, especially those with compact skulls such as Boston Terriers, Bulldogs, and Chow Chows may have excessively long or fleshy soft palates that obstruct the airway.

TREATMENT
The shape of the mouth makes it difficult to examine the soft palate at the back of the mouth, unless the patient is first

anaesthetised. Sometimes corrective surgery may be needed to provide a better way for the dog to get air into its lungs. The soft palate can be shortened to remove the obstruction to breathing.

SPAYING

In the operation of ovario-hysterectomy both ovaries and the uterus are removed. This can be considered a positive contribution to a bitch's health when she is not intended to breed puppies. Spaying not only removes the risk of pyometra infection by the hysterectomy, but it is now well proved that removal of the ovaries before 15 months of age reduces the risk of tumours in the mammary glands to nil. The repeated stimulation of the mammary glands by hormones from the ovaries during the false pregnancy time, five to eight weeks after heat, may eventually lead to mammary tumours in middle to old age, eventually resulting in premature death of a bitch.

The preferred age for spaying is after the first heat when the bitch has matured with a full length vagina and well-developed vulva. This helps prevent some of the incontinence seen in bitches when bitches are spayed too young, and the bladder neck becomes drawn into the pelvis following spaying. As the sphincter muscle at the neck of the bladder is not very strong, urine leakage may occur when the bladder is not stretched over the pelvic brim to hang down in the abdomen. Urinary incontinence and a prediposition to put on weight are quoted most frequently as the reasons why bitches are not spayed. If a sensible diet is fed, and the bitch's weight immediately after spaying is closely maintained, then there is no need for a spayed bitch to be overweight.

SPINAL DISORDERS

From the skull to the tail, the spine is the only protection that the main nerve pathway from the brain to the rest of the body receives. Any disease or damage to the spine may have very serious consequences to the dog.

SIGNS
Pain, paralysis and weakness in muscles may all be due to disorders of the spine.

CAUSES
Protrusion of the intervertebral disc is the most common spinal disorder seen in middle-aged and older dogs, especially those

breeds with long backs and a lack of supporting muscle. The canine wobbler syndrome is another example of a spinal disorder in the neck of dogs, and some large breeds are especially prone to this condition. Cauda equina syndrome is a condition when pressure at the lumbo-sacral junction is applied to the nerves in the spine, and those that exit the spine.

TREATMENT
Specific veterinary treatment is needed once these conditions have been diagnosed. Usually X-rays are necessary to confirm the disorder's presence *(see spondylosis, below)*.

SPLEEN

This organ in the abdomen is part of the lymphoid system. In adult life, the spleen also has a function of storing blood. When the muscles of the spleen capsule are contracted by involuntary nerve control, red blood cells can be forced into the general circulation, as needed. Unfortunately, tumours of the lymphoid system often invade the spleen causing it to enlarge. Haemangiosarcoma of the spleen is quite common, but splenic tumours are not easily recognised, although the dog becomes anaemic. If the spleen ruptures there is internal bleeding, and collapse as blood is lost internally into the abdomen. The tumour can be surgically removed, but dogs rarely live more than six months after surgery due to the development of secondary tumours.

SPONDYLOSIS

The vertebrae of the spine form a series of solid bodies of bone. Any degeneration of the vertebral joint, or fusion of the bodies together as a result, is known as spondylosis. Ankylosing spondylosis is when several vertebral bodies have become bridged to act as one stiff bone in the back.

SIGNS
A disease of the vertebrae of the spine may be diagnosed from X-rays after a dog has been found to have lumbar back pain, or it may have been seen dragging its back legs (occurs especially in older German Shepherd Dogs).

CAUSE
The inflammation of the bone of the vertebrae, possibly from repeated injuries and back strain, causes pressure on the nerves adjacent to the lumbar spine that supply the hind legs with sensation and effect muscle contractions.

TREATMENT
Rest and anti-inflammatory agents may be required over a long period.

STAPHYLOCOCCUS INFECTION

Bacterial infection with one of the types of *Staphylococcus* is one of the commonest infections of the dog.

SIGNS
Skin infection with pustules, erytheme and scaling crusts. The infection may be found in other body organs.

Staphylococcus skin infection on the abdomen.

Staphylococcus skin infection on the head.

CAUSE
The bacterium most commonly found causing skin disease of the dog is *Staphylococcus intermedius*. Staphylococci are also found in respiratory infections as well as at other sites of the body.

TREATMENT
Bacterial dermatitis or 'pyoderma' can be difficult to treat unless prolonged courses of antibiotics are used, combined with skin washes of anti-bacterial shampoos. It is considered good practice to take swabs from infected sites for culture in the laboratory to find out which antibiotic is most appropriate to use in the dog, based on the sensitivity tests to a range of the available antibiotics.

STROKES

Defined as a cerebral vascular 'accident', they are thought of in humans as being a rupture or blockage of a blood vessel in the brain. This type of injury is rarely found in dogs on post-mortem examination after suffering fatal attacks.

SIGNS
A sudden paralysis of the hind legs or facial nerve palsy with

head tilt and poor co-ordination of the legs is fairly typical in the affected old dog. Signs of vestibular syndrome *(see page 273)* with loss of balance, head tilt and rapid eye movements and sometimes unequal size of the two pupils will appear very similar to a stroke. The dog may become totally unconscious and be breathing heavily. Often the dog is responsive to noises but apparently unable to move or walk.

CAUSE
A condition in the older dog, where there is a problem of the blood supply to the brain, is similar to the blood clot or spasm of the small blood vessel in the brain known in humans as a 'stroke'.

TREATMENT
The veterinary surgeon will wish to make a neurological examination to assess the case, so sedatives should not be used. Provided there is no vomiting, a small dose of soluble aspirin may be given by mouth as a first aid measure. Recovery may take several days, and the head tilting may remain for several months. Good nursing care will help the dog's recovery.

SYSTEMIC LUPUS (SLE)

This 'auto-immune' or 'immune-mediated' disease is one in which the body's own immune system turns against the dog, causing damage in a wide range of organs.

SIGNS
In SLE many systems of the body are affected. Some or all of the joints may be swollen, there may be anaemia due to destruction of red cells, the kidneys may be damaged, as well as more obvious skin changes. Platelets in the blood may be destroyed leading to blood-clotting problems. Skin changes are mainly seen on the head and ears with hair loss on the muzzle, redness and erosions of the skin. These are not easily recognised, and they may be confused with the scaling of the nose seen in sunlight sensitivity. The urine may be dark, due to breakdown of haemoglobin.

CAUSE
The cause of the abnormal immune reaction is not known, but it may be triggered by a viral infection.

TREATMENT
SLE is diagnosed by the presence of more than one of these typical signs plus the detection of specific antibodies in the blood. There can be no doubt that a severe disease is present. Treatment involves using high doses of corticosteroid or other drugs that suppress the immune response. Drug treatment will have to be continued on a long-term basis.

T

TACHYCARDIA

The term means an increased heart rate above the normal heart rate of between 70 and 140 beats a minute.

SIGNS
A rapid heart beat will be seen after severe exercise but in a healthy dog the rate should return to normal in five minutes. A heart rate that remains fast after rest may be the first indication of heart disease; a dog with early heart failure tries to compensate for the poor output of blood from the heart by speeding up to maintain the circulation. Small breeds have much faster heart rates than average that are almost impossible to count unless some electronic measuring device is available.

CAUSES
Causes of rapid heart rate are shock, some feverish conditions, hyperthyroid states, and any condition of extreme nervousness or anxiety.

TREATMENT
Once the cause has been identified, specific treatments for heart or thyroid disease can be given.

TAIL GLANDS

These are a group of glands found on the upper side or dorsum of the tail, near its root. They become more noticeable in the older, short-haired dog as a brownish or grey hairless patch. These are sebaceous glands that form part of the scenting or recognition system used by dogs, similar to the circumanal glands surrounding the outside of

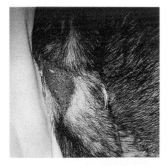

Stud tail alopecia.

the anus. The hairless skin area can sometimes be found in long-haired dogs such as Collies, at the base of the tail.

TREATMENT
If the area around the base of the tail becomes greasy, washing daily with a mild detergent shampoo helps to keep the patch clean.

TAPEWORMS

Tapeworms have a worldwide distribution, and each type has a specific intermediate host. The most common tapeworm is probably the short tapeworm *Dipylidium caninum*. It infests the intestine but very rarely causes signs of illness unless there is a very heavy infection.

SIGNS
Tapeworm infection may only be recognised by the presence of creamy-white segments stuck to the tail hairs. Segments can move slightly when first voided and develop an hour-glass shape. Later, once dry, they look like flattish rice grains.

TREATMENT/PREVENTION
Because the intermediate host of the Dipylidium tapeworm is the flea or the louse, control of tapeworms involves keeping the dog's coat free of external parasites. There are a number of effective wormers that eliminate tapeworms but an infection can recur as soon as a flea containing the worm larvae is swallowed. Routine worming against tapeworms should be repeated every three to six months depending on the risk factor.

The *Taenia* tapeworms which can infect dogs that eat raw rabbit (*T. serialis, pisiformis*) or sheep, cattle, and pig carcase meat (*T. ovis, hydatigena,* or *multiceps*) are now less common. *Echinococcus* tapeworms are a zoonosis that can have very serious consequences for infected humans. *Echinococcus* is now only found where dogs have access to sheep carcasses.

TEAT

The mammary glands of the dog each have a teat, although they are not always even in number on the abdomen. Most bitches have five glands and teats on each side of the lower abdomen, but occasionally they are not all arranged in pairs. In the bitch feeding puppies, milk passes through the teat sinuses, several of which open into the end of each teat. Puppies soon develop a preference for one teat to feed from; sebaceous glands on the teat have a characteristic odour that allows each puppy to recognise its mother, and its preferred feeding place.

TENESMUS

Straining during urination or defaecation may be painful, producing little result.

SIGNS
Tenesmus describes excessive straining, as if to defecate, with no result.
CAUSE
This can be the result of constipation or an obstruction in the rectum. Colitis, whipworm or an enlarged prostate at the entrance to the pelvic canal may all cause similar signs.
TREATMENT
A fresh faeces sample taken before treatment will be helpful, as medication may have to be given at once to help the dog. There are a number of antispasmodics, and sometimes antibiotics will be given by the veterinary surgeon as well.

TESTES

Normally a pair of these organs of reproduction lie in the scrotum, although soon after birth they are still located inside the puppy's abdomen. If one or both testes fail to descend the dog is known as a cryptorchid *(see crypt-orchidism page 152)*. Up to nine months of age, it is possible for the testes to move in and out of the scrotum, so a firm diagnosis of cryptorchidism should not be made at too early an age. The testes are not only the source of spermotazoa, they also act as an endocrine gland producing the hormone testosterone. This helps to develop and maintain the male characteristics such as the shape of the head and neck, coat consistency and the erectile tissue of the penis. For these reasons removal of the testes (castration) is normally delayed until after puberty (indicated by leg-lifting when urinating), so the dog will have some male characteristics for the rest of his life.

TETANUS

A highly fatal disease caused by neurotoxins from a soil *Clostridium* bacteria.

SIGNS
The first signs of tetanus developing are a high temperature and loss of appetite; affected dogs first go stiff as they try to walk and within a few days, they are unable to drink and the mouth

can be almost impossible to open due to muscle spasm. Eventually the stiffness spreads to other muscles of the body and paralysis of the respiratory muscles causes death.

CAUSE
Tetanus is a serious disease caused by the effects of a toxin produced by the bacterium *Clostridium tetani*. This organism is found in soil and horse faeces and can infect deep-seated wounds by contamination. Fortunately, dogs seem to have a high level of immunity to this bacterium. In humans the disease is known as 'lockjaw', but it is extremely rare in dogs so routine vaccination is not used.

TREATMENT/PREVENTION
Any contaminated wound in the dog should be cleaned, and antibiotics such as penicillin given soon after the injury to reduce the risk of tetanus. Treatment of a dog with tetanus involves intensive nursing care, the use of muscle relalaxants and appropriate antibiotics. Vaccination is not commonly advised.

TETRAPLEGIA

A term used to describe paralysis of all four limbs.

SIGNS
Tetraplegia describes paralysis of both the front and the back legs, also known as quadriplegia.

CAUSES
Tetraplegia is an unusual condition in the dog as it is usually caused by disease or damage affecting the brain, spinal cord or neck. If these signs are seen after a head injury, as with a road accident, the injury to the neck may be so severe that the animal will not recover. An intervertebral disc protrusion (slipped disc) may also be followed by haemorrhage around the spine and tetraplegia develops.

TREATMENT
Urinary incontinence and faecal retention may accompany tetraplegia and will require special nursing care. Sometimes the dog will improve with a gradual return of the use of its legs, but in many cases there is no hope of recovery.

THROMBOSIS

Clotting of the blood in the arteries and veins is normally prevented by the natural flowing movement and certain anticoagulant processes. A thrombus may form whenever there is slowing of the flow of the blood or the vessel wall is

damaged. **If a part of the thrombus breaks away, this becomes known as an embolus.**

SIGNS
Swelling of sudden onset, or unusual disorder in the nervous system may be the first signs.

CAUSE
Thrombosis is a serious condition in which there is abnormal blood clotting in the circulation. If a part of the clot breaks off it may cause an embolism, lodging in the lungs, brain, or kidneys and cause more damage.

TREATMENT
The veterinary surgeon will advise on appropriate measures.

THYROID DISEASE

The thyroid gland, located in the neck, is an important gland involved in the production of a hormone that controls metabolism in the body.

HYPOTHYROIDISM
A condition where the thyroid gland malfunctions, resulting in reduced output.

SIGNS
The signs shown may include poor hair growth, a cool feel to the skin, tiredness, muscle weakness, and a poor appetite in spite of increased weight gain. Loss of muscle on the head, and oedema, produce what has been described as a 'tragic' expression.

CAUSE
The condition of hypothyroidism occurs when insufficient hormone is produced by an under-active gland. This condition is quite common in the dog, particularly in young to middle-aged large breeds such as Dobermanns, Golden Retrievers and Irish Setters. Blood tests are used to confirm the condition.

TREATMENT
Treatment involves replacement therapy with daily doses of thyroid hormone. The tablets should be given for at least six weeks before an improvement is expected. Medication may have to be continued for life.

HYPERTHYROIDISM
The over-active thyroid condition of hyperthyroidism is rare in the dog, but more common in elderly cats.

SIGNS
Affected animals are usually hyperactive, restless, and continuously hungry, with poor coat and skin condition. A swelling of the thyroid glands in the neck can be felt just below the larynx.

CAUSE
The cause may be a tumour of the thyroid gland. In the dog these are mainly malignant carcinomas which invade local tissues and form secondary tumours.

TREATMENT
Surgical excision of part or all of the thyroid gland is possible.

TICKS

These parasites are less dangerous in the UK than overseas where ticks transmit fatal diseases. The most common ticks found on dogs in the UK are the sheep tick and the

A tick seen on a dog's coat.

hedgehog tick. Ticks may be the cause of Borrelia infections when dogs are bitten and develop Lyme disease.

SIGNS
At first only a small grey dot is visible when a tick attaches itself to the dog's skin, but by feeding on the dog's blood the tick engorges its body and could be mistaken for a greyish wart. On close examination the tick's legs can be seen close to the dog's skin, the head and biting mouth parts are buried below the skin. Once the tick has fed fully, it drops off the dog and the female lays several thousand tick eggs on the ground. Tick infestations can produce itching and scratching in the dog.

TREATMENT
The temptation to pluck the tick from the dog should be resisted, as the mouth parts can remain in the dog's skin and produce festering sores. The tick should be dabbed with a cotton-bud soaked in anti-parasitic ear drops or, failing this, the tick's body can be soaked in olive-oil to clog up its breathing holes. After an interval the tick can be coaxed off by a gentle lifting action applied at its neck.

LYME DISEASE

Recent evidence suggests that certain ticks in the UK can transmit Lyme Disease (Borreliosis) in dogs and humans. This disease is much more frequently seen in the USA.

SIGNS

Lyme disease produces fever, poor appetite and repeated episodes of arthritis in several joints. The disease can be treated by an appropriate antibiotic, but ticks should be removed as soon as possible.

TREATMENT/PREVENTION

Dogs in tick areas may be regularly dipped in an anti-parasitic wash; or a pyrethroid 'spot on'-type application, repeated monthly, is usually effective.

TONGUE ULCERATION

The tongue is covered with a thick mucous membrane and protective papillae that contain the taste buds. Any defect in the tongue surface is likely to be seen as an ulcer.

SIGNS

Dogs with tongue ulcers salivate excessively and may have difficulty eating their food.

CAUSES

Small areas of raw tongue may be found after a corrosive substance has been licked by the dog. Ulcers are seen in advanced kidney failure. The state, once known as Stuttgart disease, was one of foul breath and tongue ulceration due to the waste products being excreted in the saliva. Tongue ulcers are sometimes associated with disease of an adjacent tooth.

TREATMENT

Mouth washes may help, but the underlying problem causing the ulceration should be investigated.

TONSILLITIS

Tonsillitis is an inflammation of the tonsils at the back of the throat, often seen with pharyngitis *(see page 235)* which leads to tonsil enlargement.

SIGNS

The affected tonsils are painful, so the dog will show difficulty in swallowing and a loss of appetite. Some dogs may gag and retch.

CAUSE

Tonsillitis may be due to bacteria or a virus infection causing swelling of the local lymph nodes as well as of the tonsils.

TREATMENT
Nursing care involves offering warm liquids to drink, and a warm cloth around the neck. The dog will need veterinary attention and often antibiotics will be given.

TOXAEMIA

Toxaemia is a state of poisoning in the body caused by toxic substances.

SIGNS
Depression of appetite, signs of shock, and dehydration may develop.

CAUSE
Toxins can be produced by bacteria. This is seen with some abscesses that cause illness of the whole dog, not just at the infected site. Alternatively, toxins can accumulate in the body in certain disease states such as kidney or liver failure. Such toxins can affect the function of vital organs including the brain and heart with a potentially fatal result.

TREATMENT
Treatment with antibiotics may not always be sufficient. An abscess may have to be drained surgically to remove dead and poisonous substances from the abscess cavity. Toxaemias can produce a state of shock with collapse of the circulation. This requires intensive treatment with intravenous fluids and drugs. In cases where the kidneys are normal, intravenous fluids are used so that toxins can be washed out of the body. Unfortunately, in many toxic conditions, food and water intake is depressed and fluid losses occur by vomiting and diarrhoea, so the condition will worsen as dehydration develops.

TRACHEA

The trachea is the semi-rigid tube which carries air to the lungs from the back of the throat. Rings of soft cartilage support the trachea, but these can be damaged with any severe pressure such as that exerted by a metal choke-chain. The trachea can collapse and obstruct air movements. In older dogs, especially miniature and toy breeds, the condition of tracheal collapse with the soft cartilage collapsing and flattening causes noisy breathing and a honking cough.

The parasitic worm *Oslerus (Filaroides) osleri* will produce nodules at the base of the trachea causing inflammation and a chronic, dry cough. The problem

occurs in Greyhounds in a kennel situation, but is rarely seen otherwise. A bitch may infect her pups as she washes them. Diagnosis is by using an endoscope to examine the bifurcation of the trachea, or by finding eggs in the sputum. Treatment with a suitable wormer is effective.

TRACHEITIS

Inflammation of the trachea can occur after dust inhalation or infection with bacteria such as *Bordetella (see kennel cough page 198).*

TUMOURS

The word tumour is often used as an equivalent to cancer. Tumours are also called neoplasms, which means that they are composed of new and actively growing cells.

SIGNS
Any swelling may be a tumour. Tumours are commonly seen in dogs and may be divided into benign and malignant types. Malignant tumours can spread into adjacent structures or they may release cells to form secondary tumours into other filtering organs; these are known as metastatic tumours. Benign tumours do not behave in this way. *(See sarcomas page 251, melanoma page 212, carcinoma page 141, benign tumours page 133).*

U

ULCERS

A defect of the surface or an excavation of the coat of an organ or tissue, often resulting from some dead tissue sloughing off as part of an inflammatory process.

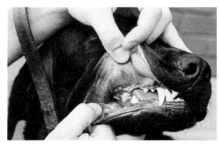

Ulcer on the gum of a black Labrador.

Ulcer on the lip.

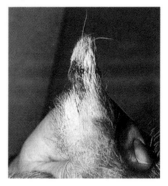

Ulcer on the tip of the tail.

SIGNS

Any fault in the surface of an organ can be described as an ulcer. It may be the stomach ulcer that bleeds or the scratch on the surface of the eye that turns into a corneal ulcer. Pressure sores on the elbows cause decubital ulcers that are difficult to heal; padding around the elbow will be needed in the large breeds of dogs to help this type of ulcer to heal. Ulcers inside the mouth on the gums can be painful and difficult to heal. Calculus (tartar) on the teeth may be the cause of the ulceration where the gum touches the harsh surface.

CAUSE

An ulcer is caused by inflammation breaking the surface of

269

mucous membrane or skin. Ulcers may be caused by injury, infections or by chemical irritants. Any failure of the blood supply to the surface may lead to ulceration.

TREATMENT
The first step in the treatment of ulcers must be to remove any irritant or foreign body. As most ulcers easily become infected, anti-bacterial treatment is important. Protection of the ulcerated surface by dressings or surgical skin-flaps will speed the healing process. Stomach ulcers require medication to suppress excess acidity.

UMBILICAL HERNIA

The umbilicus represents the point of the body where the blood supply was received from the mother before birth took place. The dog should have no swellings in the mid-line and the umbilicus is not even depressed as in humans.

SIGNS
A swelling in the mid-line.

CAUSE
This is often found in young puppies, where a protrusion of fat through the umbilicus causes the skin of the abdomen to bulge.

TREATMENT
Many of these hernias will seal themselves up but the larger ones will need surgical repair to close the weak spot in the abdominal muscle wall.

URINARY TRACT DISEASES

The system that connects the kidneys to the outside of the body is known as the urinary tract. The kidneys lead into the ureters that drain urine to the bladder for storage. The urine is then emptied through the urethra to the outside. Both in male and female dogs a number of important disorders can develop in this system, leading to disease or discomfort. Problems of the kidney are dealt with under nephritis *(page 216)*. The bladder is dealt with under cystitis *(page 153)*, and the older male dog is dealt with under prostate disorders *(page 241)*.

There are a number of other conditions of the urinary tract such as incontinence, where urine is passed without voluntary control. Incontinence may be congenital in origin, due to ectopic ureters that fail to connect the kidney to the bladder but open further down the urinary tract. Another condition,, known as urinary calculi or 'stones', may cause bladder irritation or an obstruction to the

urinary tract at various levels – in the kidney, at the renal pelvis, in the ureters or, most commonly, in the urethra at the ischial arch or at the base of the os penis *(see calculi page 139)*.

UROLITHIASIS

Often known as stones or 'gravel' in the urine *(see calculi page 139)*.

URTICARIA

The skin reaction with fluid blobs produced by oozing from the blood vessels may be due to exposure to irritant chemicals, or often it is an immunological response .

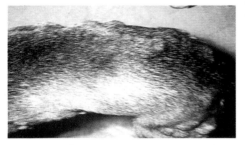

Urticaria.

SIGNS
One of the skin diseases of allergic origin, it is more commonly known as 'nettle rash' from the appearance of multiple swollen blemishes, fluid-filled blisters and weals. Redness of the skin is also seen, usually occurring in the short-coated breeds of dogs. In Boxers and Dobermanns, the urticarial weals seem larger because the short hairs stand up as tufts enhancing the size of each swelling.

CAUSE
Urticaria is usually caused by a reaction to insect bites or stings, sometimes to plants touched by the dog, and even veterinary injections have been known to produce this sort of response.

TREATMENT
Where possible, avoid further contact or exposure. Corticosteroids and antihistamines will help to control the signs – the itchiness will pass off and the lumps will go in 24 hours or so.

UTERUS

An abdominal organ in females that carries the puppies up to the moment of birth, it has an important function in reproduction to produce the live puppies. Any disease of the uterus such as endometritis will cause infertility, as fertilised eggs from the ovaries will not be able to become attached to the uterus to develop further. Similarly, if the uterus muscle is weak from repeated breeding or from an overlarge litter, then uterine inertia may delay birth so that puppies, when they are eventually expelled, are stillborn.

Breeding from young healthy bitches, and avoiding too frequent breeding, are the best ways to avoid some of these problems. Calcium supplements in pregnancy are now discouraged, but an injection of calcium at the time of birth may help the muscles of the uterus to contract better when expelling puppies. The injectable hormone oxytocin is also used for the same purpose, but even greater care is necessary when using this hormone, as it acts directly on the muscle and can be dangerous if a puppy is firmly stuck in the pelvic canal. The operation for removing the uterus is known as a hysterectomy.

UVEITIS

Uveitis is an inflammation of the structures within the eye including the iris.

SIGNS
The condition is usually very painful, making the dog flinch if touched and avoid bright lights. The pupil constricts and appears darker, and there is often a poor pupillary light reflex and a redness of the sclera.

CAUSE
It may be caused by ocular trauma, virus infections, or a foreign body such as a thorn piercing the cornea at the front of the eye. Uveitis may develop in the small terrier breeds secondary to a lens luxation. Many cases of uveitis are thought to be immune-mediated reactions, where the underlying trigger is unknown. Anterior uveitis leads to glaucoma, or adhesions within the eye, causing permanent damage and loss of sight.

TREATMENT
If the eye is painful, or where the eyeball swells, urgent veterinary treatment is needed. This will involve removing any cause, such as a foreign body or bacteria, then controlling the inflammation with corticosteroids, NSAIDs, and eye-drops to dilate the pupil. To relieve any pain, the dog should be placed in the dark, and systemic analgesics may have to be given.

VAGINITIS

The condition of inflammation of the vagina of the bitch is sometimes confused when the word is used for a vaginal sheath inflammation. The testis has a structure known as the tunica vaginalis. For example, the ring is known as the annulus vaginalis where the testis cord leaves the abdomen.

SIGNS
A discharge that can be seen at the vulva is usually the first sign of vaginitis. The inflammation of the vagina is also accompanied by an irritation that may cause the bitch to lick excessively. The discharge produced in vaginitis is usually cream or yellowish in colour. Other conditions produce a darker discharge: if it is from the uterus in metritis it is brownish-black, and in pyometra it will be a thick creamy-greenish to black-coloured fluid.

CAUSE
Vaginitis is an inflammation of the lining of the vagina in response to bacterial or viral infections. It is sometimes seen in bitches before puberty and usually clears up with the first oestrus. The discharge should not be confused with the normal pink secretions of pro-oestrus or the clear straw-coloured discharge of oestrus, as normally the vulva will be characteristically swollen when the bitch is on 'heat'.

TREATMENT
Mild vaginitis will resolve itself, but any persistent or unusual discharge needs veterinary investigation and specific medication.

VESTIBULAR SYNDROME

A balance condition seen in older dogs is characterised by its sudden onset. It originates in the inner ear.

SIGNS
The signs of head tilt and loss of balance can be attributed to a disturbance of the inner ear. Damage or disease affecting the vestibular system produces signs of head tilting, staggering or stumbling, walking in a tight circle and rapid eye-ball movements (nystagmus). The condition can develop quite suddenly, and is often described as a 'stroke' by the owner. Severely affected dogs may collapse but remain alert.

CAUSE

In the dog vestibular syndrome develops from infections in the ear or throat that spread to the inner ear's vestibular (balance) system. Toxic substances and inflammatory brain disease can produce the condition, although in other cases seen, in older dogs, there seems to be no obvious reason. Any brain injury, such as after an accident, may affect the vestibular system.

TREATMENT

A full veterinary examination is needed and any ear or circulatory disorders dealt with as soon as possible. With appropriate care some dogs recover in 48 hours, although the head tilting will remain for some time. Sometimes the neck may be so badly twisted that the dog has difficulty in eating from a dish on the floor, but can manage if food is given by hand.

VITILIGO

Vitiligo is a rare condition in the dog causing loss of dark skin pigment (melanin). The condition is seen in certain breeds of dogs, with small patches of skin of different colour on the muzzle, lips and footpads. The paler patches are not raised as with skin tumours and skin nodules. Vitiligo may be associated with poor reproductive ability.

Vitiligo: De-pigmentation of a black Labrador's nose.

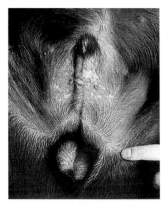

Vitiligo: Scrotum and small prepuce.

SIGNS

Loss of pigment from the skin at various sites of the body. This may produce a comic appearance in a dog that has previously been all one dark colour. The bare patches are cool to touch, do not itch, and the bare areas often enlarge slowly with an even darker hyperpigmented border to them.

CAUSE
This is probably due to an auto-immune condition that destroys pigment-forming cells. A condition of increased skin pigment-ation is seen in the tumour of the male dog, known as a Sertoli cell tumour that affects the testes. A form of skin-pigment loss of unknown cause that affects the nose and muzzle is sometimes called 'Dudley nose' by breeders. Vitiligo has been shown to be hereditary in one of the Belgian terrier breeds.

TREATMENT
There is no specific treatment, but excessive exposure to sunlight should be avoided. Irritation from parasites should be dealt with, as it is known that the horse with microfilaria worms develops vitiligo as areas of depigmentation surrounded by hyperpigmentation of the scrotum.

VOMITING

Vomiting is a reflex action triggered by nerve impulses causing the expulsion of the stomach contents.

CAUSE
Vomiting may be seen after a dog has been out to eat grass, or it may be more severe vomiting such as in kidney failure or abdominal cancer, where little food is eaten but the dog tries to be sick repeatedly through the day. Vomiting may occur just before or soon after diarrhoea, and this needs reporting to the veterinary surgeon. Repeated vomiting will need investigation involving blood tests, X-rays and endoscope examination. *Helicobacter* are bacteria that can live in the stomach-wall and cause problems in humans and cats, but their significance in dogs has yet to be established. Blood in the vomit is not always as serious as it would first seem, especially if it only occurs the once, as healing takes place quickly.

TREATMENT
Short-term vomiting can be treated by withdrawing food, preventing grass eating and then allowing the dog to drink very small quantities of iced water, until small amounts of food can again be offered after 12 to 24 hours. Fluid therapy may be needed, and there are medications to suppress vomiting, reduce acid production and protect the stomach lining.

WARTS

The oldest skin lesion to be described, appears as small excrescences on the skin surface.

SIGNS
Any small skin blemish may be described as a 'wart'. Typical warts are small benign cauliflower-shape growths, which have a stalk attaching themselves to the skin. They are usually seen in older dogs, especially on the head, feet and eyelids. They occur most commonly in dogs that have been regularly clipped, such as Poodles and some terriers. The warts may bleed if injured, or cause irritation, as when found near the eye.

Warts in the mouth.

CAUSE
Papilloma virus will cause one type of wart, but most warts develop after long-term exposure to irritants.

TREATMENT
Warts can be treated by surgical removal. The wart is best sent for biopsy to ensure it is benign. Another sort of wart is seen in younger dogs that is caused by a papilloma virus – multiple warts may be found in the mouth and on the lips as 'canine oral papillomatosis'. These occur especially in dogs that have been kept in kennels. They will disappear in three to four months by 'self-cure', but some may require treatment if large or bleeding. This wart is best treated by cryosurgery, using liquid nitrogen. Skin tumours may be malignant, so it is important to have any skin growth checked in the early stage by the veterinary surgeon, who may advise a biopsy or other appropriate course of action.

WATER DEPRIVATION

Any condition in the dog that has been unable to drink or retain fluid can become life-threatening.

SIGNS
Water deprivation will lead to dehydration, weight loss and collapse of the circulation. The dog will have sunken eyes, mucous membranes that are dry and sticky, and skin that stands up in a fold if lifted up.

CAUSE
In hot weather, dogs confined in cars risk the coagulation of their blood due to water deprivation after a thickening of the blood in the circulation, even though it is called 'heat-stroke'. A dog allowed ample fluid can keep cool by evaporating moisture from the tongue surface and the respiratory tract, but once there is no opportunity to drink, matters can quickly deteriorate.

Dogs suffering from diabetes insipidus are unable to concentrate their urine and can become rapidly dehydrated in times of reduced fluid intake. This form of diabetes may be a hormone failure of the pituitary gland or a failure of the kidney to respond to fluid loss. A test called the 'water deprivation test' may be carried out by the veterinary surgeon. A Dachshund may drink 6 litres a day with diabetes insipidus, and even when there is no water to drink, it will keep on producing watery dilute urine as shown in this test.

TREATMENT
Fluids to drink must always be available, and any specific disease needs veterinary treatment.

WHELPING

Birth as a normal physiological process should, ideally, take place with the minimum of human interference. There are some breeds where difficult births can be anticipated, and then close supervision and the possibility of a caesarean birth should be considered. The preparations for birth, adequate nutrition, exercise and a quiet place for the bitch to whelp will all help to ensure a 'normal' whelping. *(See The Birth of Puppies and Aftercare, page 58).*

WHIPWORM

The whipworm *Trichuris vulpis* is one of the less common roundworms of the dog; it is more associated with dogs in kennels.

SIGNS

The worm embeds its head in the lining of the large intestine and can cause infections seen as poor body condition and recurrent bloody mucoid diarrhoea. In this situation, routine faeces samples should be screened, as the worm has a very distinctive egg that can be recognised under the microscope.

TREATMENT

Fortunately, it is easily treated with the standard anthelminthic preparations. Control of the parasite in some kennels is difficult as the egg can persist for years, especially in grass paddocks. Concrete exercise runs should be regularly scrubbed and hosed to avoid eggs accumulating.

WORMS

See Roundworm (nematodes) page 249, Tapeworm (cestodes) page 261.

WOUNDS

Most injuries to the body result in wounds, the most obvious being surface wounds with blood loss following damage to the skin. There are also more life-threatening internal wounds, such as those following a road accident where the lung has collapsed or the spleen has ruptured. Any accident involving a dog should not be lightly dismissed.

Wounds are classified by the type of injury, e.g. incised, contused, abraded, lacerated. Compound fractures, where a piece of broken bone projects through the skin, are obvious, nasty wounds. However, scalds from hot fat falling on the dog's back may be overlooked until a piece of flesh drops off the dog, leaving an oozing wound underneath – often several days after the first injury.

TREATMENT

First aid management varies with the type of wound. The most important thing is to calm the dog, control blood loss, immobilise the wound area and prevent the dog from damaging the wound further. A pressure bandage may be applied, but at the veterinary surgery bleeding will be stopped, pain and shock treated as necessary and injuries investigated. Open wounds require cleaning and repair and the use of appropriate dressings, bandages or casts to protect and support the area and assist healing. Wounds in which large areas of skin are lost are often impossible to repair surgically and are allowed to heal by natural processes using suitable dressings.

X-RAYS

Most veterinary clinics are equipped with X-ray machines that permit quite detailed examination of patients, and with the greater use of automatic developers, X-ray photos can be processed within a few minutes, to help in diagnosis. The major restriction on the use of X-ray equipment is the ionising radiation produced by all machines. This can be a health hazard to persons working in the vicinity, and those members of staff helping most frequently may accumulate a hazardous dose. Safety regulations insist that animals are not held for X-ray, so that staff can keep well away from the main X-ray beam.

Most animals requiring an X-ray are sedated or given a general anaesthetic before an X-ray is taken. The stillness of the patient is assured to position the body correctly. In some situations such as chest injuries only the lightest sedation can be used; or it may have to be dispensed with, relying on propping with sandbags near affected parts, and, as a shocked dog is not wanting to move, by attaching cords to fasten the legs of the patient to restrict unexpected movements. X-ray examination is frequently used to check the skeleton for diseases such as hip dysplasia, osteo-chondrosis, osteosarcoma, panosteitis or damage from fractures or dislocations. The soft tissue inside the chest and abdomen can be X-rayed and contrast-media such as barium can be used as well to outline some of the internal organs of the body.

YEASTS

The small organisms that inhabit the surface of a dog's skin include a yeast *Malasezzia*. This organism will multiply in some dogs and cause persistent otitis with a blackish-brown, waxy ear discharge. High numbers of *Malasezzia* may be found in dogs with generalised skin inflammation, scaling of the skin, crusts and, in some dogs, hair loss and scratching. Underlying skin disease such as atopy may favour the multiplication of *Malasezzia* on the skin, but it may normally be found in moist places such as under the tail or in any skin folds. *Candida albicans* is another yeast that may be found in the body cavities. Specific treatments are available for yeast infections.

ZINC

Zinc is a trace element essential for skin health, and for the function of the immune system that protects the body. Zinc may be deficient in the dog's diet, especially if levels of calcium and phytates 'tie up' available zinc. Most proprietary dog foods are adequately supplemented with zinc. Some breeds of dogs, particularly Arctic breeds, may have an inherited tendency to be unable to absorb zinc efficiently from their diet. In skin diseases, where excess scale forms on the nose and feet, it may be beneficial to give a zinc and additional essential fatty acid (GLA) supplement on a daily basis.

ZOONOSES

Zoonoses are those diseases of animals that can be transmitted to humans. Important zoonoses which can be carried by dogs include Ringworm, Salmonellosis, Toxocariasis and Echinococcus disease. Appropriate control measures should always be followed to reduce the risk of such diseases being transmitted to humans.

INDEX

A

Abdominal pain 96
Abdominal
    enlargement 96
Abscess 83, 121
Accidents 87
Addison's disease 121
Adult nutrition 36
Ageing dogs
(see geriatric dogs) 178
Aggression 122
Allergies 123
Alopecia 124
Anaemia 125
Anal adenoma 125
Anal sacs disease 126
Anoestrus 127
Appetite 21
Arthritis 127
Artifical insemination 128
Ascites 128
Atopy 129
Aural haematoma 83, 130
Aural resection 131
Auto immune disease 131

B

Bacterial skin dieases 132
Balanitis 132
Bandaging 90
Barlow's disease 133
Bathing 41
Benign tumours 133
Bilious vomit 134
Birth 54

Bladder obstruction 83
Bloat 81, 135
Blood clotting disorders
(see haemophilia) 183
Blood loss 81, 97
Body temperature 22
Bone tumours 136
Breathing difficulties 98
Breech birth 65
Bronchitis 137
Burns and scalds 138

C

Caesarean section 64, 139
Calculi 139
Campylobacter 140
Cancer
(see Carcinoma 141,
Malignant tumours 207)
Carcinoma 141
Cardiac failure 142
Cardiogenic shock
and heart failure 142
Caries and
    dental disease 143
Castration 144
Cataract 144
Chemosis 145
Cherry eye 146
Cheyletiellosis 146
Choking 81, 98
Chronic degenerative
radiculomyelopathy
    (CDRM) 147
Cirrhosis 148
Coat and skin 22